C. Lawler

WOMEN [illegible] EAST AN[illegible]

Women in every land and in every era of history have been known as the guardians of religion. Despite today's shift from ancient values, it is still the women who have the responsibility to bring religion into the home and inspire higher values.

Here we have a collection of women saints including the famous singer Mira Bai, known for her poetic songs to Krishna, and the Christian mystic Julian of Norwich who perceived God as Mother.

The women in this collection are shown not just as women who were highly spiritual, but as human beings who had to struggle and face many difficulties to find peace with God.

WOMEN SAINTS EAST AND WEST

Editorial Advisers

SWAMI GHANANANDA

SIR JOHN STEWART-WALLACE, C.B.

Vedanta Press

HOLLYWOOD, CALIFORNIA

International Standard Book Number: 0-87481-036-1
Library of Congress Catalog Card Number: 79-65731
Vedanta Press, Hollywood, California 90068

First U.S. edition 1979
3 4 5 6 7 8 9
Printed in the United States of America

Readers interested in obtaining further information on the subject matter of this book are invited to correspond with The Secretary, Vedanta Society of Southern California, 1946 Vedanta Pl., Hollywood, CA 90068.

PREFACE TO THE ENGLISH EDITION

THIS volume is published in honour of the sacred memory of Śrī Sāradā Devī, the Holy Mother, the consort and first disciple of Śrī Rāmakṛishṇa, on the occasion of her first birth centenary. She was born on December 22, 1853, and the centenary was celebrated between December, 1953, and December, 1954, by all the centres of the Ramakrishna Order in the East and the West. The Ramakrishna Vedanta Centre of London formed a centenary committee which celebrated the event during 1954 by holding a public meeting in January and an inter-religious conference of women in June. The publication of this volume thus forms a fitting conclusion to the centenary celebrations.

The volume brings together essays on great saints and mystics among women of different religions and countries, prepared at our invitation by earnest and devoted writers. In spite of prolonged efforts we did not succeed in obtaining essays on Chinese and Japanese women saints of the major religions of the Far East. It was one of our aims, and the writers were accordingly requested, to describe as far as possible the struggles and difficulties, the spiritual disciplines and realizations, of the women saints portrayed, so that the reader might feel drawn to the divine ideal which they attained, and glimpse their fervour of soul.

The life of the Holy Mother, who like Rāmakṛishṇa taught that all religions are paths to God, is the inspiration behind this volume. A sketch of her life, work and teachings has been given in the penultimate chapter of the section dealing with women saints of Hinduism.

The Note on Pronunciation on pages xvii and xviii explains the diacritical marks used over Oriental words. Diacritical marks have been omitted from the titles of chapters, and as a rule from names of well-known institutions and names of living authors. They have been used in the names of places in their Indian form. The Western reader may ignore the marks if he wishes, and read the words as if there were no such marks.

We offer our sincere and heartfelt thanks to all the writers of essays appearing here, who have done the work as a labour of love, and to all others who have helped us in one way or another to publish this volume. The execution of this piece of dedicated work was to us a source of spiritual joy.

We offer our warm thanks to Mrs. Vijaya Lakshmi Pandit for having kindly written the Foreword in the midst of her various official duties and responsibilities, to Mr. Kenneth Walker for having promptly sent his Introduction, and to our Editorial Advisers for their constant help and advice in the preparation of this volume.

Ramakrishna Vedanta Centre
London

December, 1955

FOREWORD

AS the lamps of Dīvāli brighten the darkness of the Indian sky, so the lives of the women saints of East and West illuminate a world too often shadowed by disillusionment and doubt. Their message has taken its place as a part of the earth's spiritual heritage, reminding us of the greatest common bond between all peoples: the belief in God and the yearning to worship Him.

It is particularly appropriate that on this, the birth centenary of the Holy Mother, the examples of women saints alone should have been selected to commemorate the occasion. Woman in every land and in every era of history has been the guardian of her family's faith. However far afield modern times may have taken us from ancient values, one ideal still endures—that of the anonymous woman, one of many millions, who in her own limited sphere daily achieves a harmony of relationships, nurturing her religious beliefs in the same simple, unostentatious manner in which she cherishes her husband and children. Religion, for a man and his children, is, more often than not, embodied in the calm guiding spirit of the woman of the house.

The Holy Mother was herself such a woman and so her life has a universal appeal. Born in a typical Indian village in lowly circumstances, married at an early age to the saintly Rāmakṛishṇa, she became the ideal Hindu wife, selflessly serving her husband and giving him her whole-hearted co-operation in his search for God. Despite her absorption in this lofty pursuit, the most humble and menial tasks of her home continued to receive her thoughtful attention. Side by side with her husband she strove for and achieved great mystical heights, yet she never neglected the constant demands material life made on her. As she served Śrī Rāmakṛishṇa, looking after his every comfort, so she cared for the devotees who flocked to him, tending them as though they had been her own children. Her life symbolizes the essence of Hindu womanhood, fulfilling its twin aspirations: dedication to duty, and through its performance the attainment of spiritual glory.

Like Sāradā Devī, these women saints of different countries and eras represent the full flowering of the feminine spirit in its efforts to worship the divine. Here woman is shown in all her gentle dignity, with all the tenderness of her being concentrated on her infinite capacity for devotion and service. This book tells of the search for godliness, but in recording the various saints' experiences of it, it pays tribute to human character at its highest level—character which is not a divine gift but a human achievement, attained through human effort, through prayer and meditation, self-discipline and suffering. Self-realization, the goal of all religions, is what the saints sought, and their lives illustrate that the path to Self-realization is, strangely, the one which leads away from the self. Only in forgetting ourselves, our own struggles and sorrows in those of others do we begin to approach a measure of Self-realization, and through it come nearer to God. These women did not teach through words. The radiance of their message is borne on the wings of their unwavering faith, bringing vision and understanding to their fellows for all time to come.

Ultimate realization is given to few, but the lesson of endeavour is within reach of all who care to learn it. Therein lies the value of what the saints teach us. The poet Kabīr has pointed this out:

> Behold: before me stand both my guru and the Lord
> of Creation;
> At whose feet shall I prostrate myself?
> At the feet of thy guru, O disciple,
> For was it not he who lighted thy way to the
> Lord?

May she who lighted the path for so many pilgrims during her lifetime continue to provide inspiration for all who seek the spirit's soaring horizons. May this volume, dedicated to her memory, serve the purpose of placing her precept and those of all the women represented in these pages, once more before the world.

VIJAYA LAKSHMI PANDIT

INTRODUCTION

I REALIZE from the start how poorly qualified I am to write an Introduction to a book on the subject of the women saints of the East and of the West. I am not a woman and I am almost as far from being a saint as I am from being a woman. I am no scholar and am completely unversed in the science of hagiology, yet, despite all these handicaps, I find one small redeeming trait in myself which perhaps justifies me in doing what I have been asked to do—write an Introduction to this book. It is my great veneration for the ancient culture of India, a culture in which, to my way of thinking, human thought and feeling have attained the highest level they have ever reached. So brilliant have India's past attainments been in the realms of religion and philosophy that I am convinced that she has a great contribution to make to present world thought and to the growth of world peace. Readers of this book will agree with me that the preservation of peace is much more than a political problem, for no harmony between nations can be maintained for long by means of external organizations alone. It can come only from a much better understanding between the individuals of the different national groups and from a deeper realization by all of the brotherhood of man. And this sense of brotherhood will be deepened when we appreciate more fully than we do at present the universality of the truths proclaimed by all the great world faiths. As Rāmakṛishṇa's greatest disciple Vivekānanda long ago wrote: "Each must assimilate the spirit of the others and yet preserve his own individuality, and grow according to his own law of growth. . . . The whole universe is a play of unity in variety and of variety in unity."

Consequently, whether equipped or not to write an Introduction to a book on women saints, I have accepted it as both my duty and my privilege to do so. No one can read the accounts given in this book of the lives and teachings of the great saints of both the East and the West without sensing the existence of a "play of unity in variety and of variety in unity". Although Śrī Sāradā Devī, the Holy Mother to whose memory this book is dedicated, did not directly expound the metaphysical doctrines of the Vedānta to her disciples, they formed the background of all her teachings. And being a practical woman—in the way that most women are practical—she demonstrated the unity of mankind and of man's religions in her own life. When she was weak and ill and about to die, a disciple came to see her, and in a low voice the Holy Mother managed to give her the personal guidance she was obviously needing. "If you want peace of mind," she said, "do not find fault with others. Learn rather to see your own faults. Learn to make the whole world your own; no one is a stranger, my child, the whole world is your own." In these few simple words she was warning her visitor against that superficial egoism which separates us one from another and was stressing to her the underlying unity of all mankind, a unity in which there is no room for such words as "yours" and "mine", and no place for strangers.

The means of attaining sainthood are the same in all the great religions, as Rāmakṛishṇa has clearly shown. To become a saint entails a long struggle to a higher level of being and to another state of consciousness, and the various steps along this difficult path are described with exactitude and precision in the world's sacred literature. It is true that in some religious books this science of saintship is so overlaid with dogmas and theological theories that it is difficult to discover it, but it is there nevertheless.

Reduced to its elements the philosophy of the Vedānta, which may be regarded as being the very essence of all religions, consists of three propositions. The first is that man's real nature is divine, the second that the aim of a man's life should be to discover the spark of the divine within him, and the third that the great fundamental religious truths are the same, even though their expression differs. With these three working hypotheses and entirely unencumbered by theological doctrines, catechisms and creeds, the devotee sets out on his spiritual journey in search of truth and of Self-realization. It is not surprising that many young people in the West, tired of religious quarrels and of the wiseacreing of theologians and religious instructors, are looking to the ancient knowledge of India for help, and are finding what they needed in the simple yet profound teaching of the Vedānta. And what makes this spiritual venture of theirs still more exciting and satisfactory is that, instead of finding as they had expected a gulf fixed between science and religion, they are discovering in the Vedas, ideas which seem to have anticipated by thousands of years some of the most modern discoveries of the physicists.

East and West have much to give each other and the closer the partnership we form in a stupendous effort to build a new and nobler world the better for us all. Although he wrote the words many years ago, Vivekānanda described the position in which we find ourselves at the present moment so aptly that I am compelled to quote him again. "It is not that we Indians ought to learn everything from the West, or that they have to learn everything from us, but each will have to supply and hand down to future generations what it possesses for that dream of ages, the harmony of nations, an ideal world." East and West both have their respective parts to play in this work of world construction and it is because I regard it of such paramount importance that we should get to understand each other better and better that I commend this little book on Eastern and Western saints to its many future readers.

KENNETH WALKER

CONTENTS

PART I

WOMEN SAINTS OF HINDUISM

Part II

WOMEN SAINTS OF BUDDHISM AND JAINISM

Part III

WOMEN SAINTS OF CHRISTIANITY

PART IV

WOMEN SAINTS OF JUDAISM AND ṢŪFĪSM

NOTE ON THE PRONUNCIATION OF TRANSLITERATED WORDS IN SANSKRIT AND OTHER ORIENTAL LANGUAGES

a sounds like *o* in *come*.

ā sounds like *a* in *far*.

i sounds like *i* in *kin*.

ī sounds like *ee* in *feel*.

u sounds like *u* in *full*.

ū sounds like *oo* in *cool*.

ṛi may be pronounced as *ri*.

e sounds like *e* in *bed*, only longer; e is always long in Sanskrit.

o sounds like *o* in *note*; o is always long in Sanskrit.

ṣ may be pronounced like s (e.g. Ṣūfī).

ch sounds like *ch* in *church*.

ṅ (guttural) may be pronounced like *n*.

ñ (palatal) is like French *gn* and may be pronounced like *n*.

ṇ (lingual) may be pronounced like *n*.

ṭ and ḍ are hard like *t* and *d* in English.

t and d are soft as in French *th* and *dh*.

ś (palatal sibilant) may be pronounced almost like *sh*.

sh (lingual sibilant) sounds like *sh* in *shine*.

Such of the remaining consonants as appear in the transliteration sound as in English:

kh, ch, chh, jh, ṭh, ḍh, th, dh, ph, bh, are the simple sounds *plus* an aspiration.

ṁ stands for : (*anuswāra*) and sounds like *ng* in *ring*.

ḥ stands for : (*visarga*) in Sanskrit.

w has been used for v after consonants.

ḷ stands for the letter of the Dravidian alphabet which sounds like *l* in *all*.

zh stands for the letter of the Dravidian alphabet explained below.

Sanskrit does not use zh. This occurs, for instance, in *pazham*, the Tamil equivalent of Sanskrit *phalam*, meaning "fruit". "Tamiḷnāḍ" has come into vogue and has been used in the book. Strictly speaking, it should be written "Tamizhnāḍ".

Diacritical marks over e, which is always long in Sanskrit, the basis of North Indian languages, have not been used in the essays dealing with women saints of North India, but in essays on women saints of South India, where the languages belong to the Dravidian group and distinguish between short e and long ē, such distinction has been retained in those essays (Chapters II, III, IV, V, XI and XII). In the other essays as well as in the Contents and the Index all the e's are from Sanskrit words and have been left unmarked, though long: an exception has been pointed out in a Note on the last page of the Index.

When a place-name is pronounced and written in two ways, e.g. "Vṛindāvan" and "Vṛindāvana", "Madurai" and "Madurā", both the forms have been used in this book. "Punidavati" in Tamil for "Punitavatī" in Sanskrit has been retained.

PART I

WOMEN SAINTS OF HINDUISM

CHAPTER I

SPIRITUAL TRADITION AMONG HINDU WOMEN

INTRODUCTORY

I

IN the words of Louis Jaccoliot, the French writer, India of the Vedas entertained a respect for women amounting to worship. He exclaimed: "What! Here is a civilization, which you cannot deny to be older than your own, which places the woman on a level with the man and gives her an equal place in the family and in society."

Manu the lawgiver, "whose laws are related to the digest of Justinian and the Mosaic laws of the Old Testament as a father to his child", accepted the teachings of the Vedas and gave equal rights to men and women by saying: "Before the creation of this phenomenal universe the first-born Lord of all creatures divided his own self into two halves, so that one half should be male and the other half female." In one of His aspects God is regarded even today as half man and half woman. This and other instances have always kept before the Hindu mind the idea of the fundamental equality of men and women. Indeed it was the corner-stone of the massive structure of Hindu religion and ethics which has stood the ravages of time. According to the ethical, moral and religious standard of the Hindus, no partiality was to be shown for either man or woman. It is eloquently expressed in the words: "The wife and husband being the equal halves of one substance are equal in every respect; therefore both should join and take equal parts in all work, religious and secular."[1] In Vedic times equal opportunities were afforded to men and women, boys and girls, for education and work. Girls like boys were given the *upanayana* or initiation into *Gāyatrī*, and *brahmacharya* (celibacy and study). No other scriptures of the world have ever given to woman such equality with man as the Vedas of the Hindus.

[1] *Ṛig-Veda*, 5. 61. 8. Cf. *Brihadāraṇyaka Upanishad*, 1. 4. 3.

II

Even in later Vedic times there were two classes of educated women: (i) *sadyodwāhās*, who studied till they married, and (ii) *brahmavādinīs*, who did not care to marry and studied throughout their lives. The list of great Vedic teachers whose memory was honoured at the time of Brahmayajña includes the names of three great women, Gārgī Vāchaknavī, Vaḍavā Prātītheyī and Sulabhā Maitreyī.[1]

Thus the highest education, including the study of the Vedas, was open to both men and women alike. Many women became Vedic scholars, and also great philosophers, keen debaters and brilliant teachers. Furthermore, Vedic sacrifices were usually to be offered jointly by a man and his wife.

In the early Vedic period the father usually taught the children. In the Brāhmaṇa-Upanishadic age girls' education was usually attended to at home by their fathers, brothers and uncles. Some, however, received instruction from outside teachers; and a few of them lived in boarding-houses called *chhātrīśālās*. Some women of this period continued the tradition of the earlier age by taking part in discussions in learned assemblies.

There were women scholars who specialized in the Mīmāṁsā school of Kāśakṛitsna, and philosophical studies became increasingly popular. Sulabhā, Gārgī and Vaḍavā were deeply interested in them. Some of these women gave up the pleasures and prospects of married life and took to a life of asceticism. There were nuns in Indian society even before Buddhism, though in small numbers. Slowly the spirit of asceticism became more and more appreciated, and normal married life and the life of the spirit came to be considered incompatible.

It was in such an atmosphere of equality that women acquired knowledge and spirituality in ancient India. That saints, sages and seers arose among both men and women was largely due to the high standards of Hindu married life. So deeply have the spiritual traditions of the country sunk into the minds of the people that marriage and family life have always been viewed as stages in the growth of the soul towards perfection, and not as means to self-gratification. Hinduism has consistently refused to accept the romantic view of marriage.

[1] Āśwalāyana Gṛihya-sūtras, 3. 4. 4.

The couple are spiritual partners, each of whom supplements the other, and both proceed towards a spiritual goal. Marriage is fulfilled in discipline and service, and not in pleasure.

All individuals, young and old, grew up in families and village communities in which all the activities of life, even the humblest, were given a spiritual direction. It is therefore not surprising that through the ages and in such a vast country men and women should have been produced in large numbers who were fit for the final stage of spiritual evolution—the life of renunciation—and became saints.

In the *Ṛig-Veda* we find names of so many women who realized the highest spiritual truths. They are recognized as seers of Truth, as spiritual teachers, divine speakers and revealers. In the *Ṛig-Veda* alone there are a large number of inspiring hymns called *sūktas* ascribed to as many as twenty-seven women seers or *ṛishis* or *brahma-vādinīs*. The one hundred and twenty-sixth hymn of the first book of the *Ṛig-Veda* was revealed by the Hindu woman, Romaśā, and the one hundred and seventy-ninth hymn of the same book by Lopāmudrā. It is remarkable that several of them rose to great heights of spiritual experience. One of the seers, called Vāch, who was the daughter of the sage Ambhṛiṇa, realized her oneness with the Absolute, and cried out in spiritual joy: "I am the sovereign queen. . . . He who eats does so through me; he who sees, breathes or hears does so through me. Creating all things, I blow forth like the wind. Beyond heaven, beyond the earth am I—so vast is my greatness."[1]

There were also other women revealers of the Vedic wisdom, such as Viśwavārā, Śaśwatī, Apālā, Ghoshā and Aditi, every one of whom lived the ideal life of spirituality, being untouched by the things of this world. They devoutly performed religious rites, sang holy hymns and discussed with great philosophers the subtle and difficult problems of life and death, of soul and God, and sometimes defeated the most advanced contemporary thinkers.

Even in early Vedic times spiritual tradition amongst Hindu women had been well established. We see the working of this tradition in the days of the virgin philosopher Gārgī who boldly challenged the great sage Yājñavalkya in open court in abstruse philosophical argument.[2]

[1] *Ṛig-Veda*, 10. 125. [2] *Brihadāraṇyaka Upanishad*, 3. 6.

That the eternal problem of how to attain peace and immortality agitated the minds not only of the unmarried women but also of the married is revealed by the dialogue[1] between Maitreyī and her husband Yājñavalkya, who wanted to settle her share of the property on her, and take leave of her before renouncing the world and embracing the monastic ideal. But Maitreyī asked him: "If, indeed, venerable sir, this entire earth filled with wealth were mine, would I become immortal through it?"

Yājñavalkya: "No, like the life of the rich even so would your life be. Of immortality, however, there is no hope through wealth."

Maitreyī: "Then what shall I do with that by which I cannot become immortal? Tell me, venerable sir, of that alone which you know to be the only means to immortality."

Yājñavalkya: "You have been truly dear to me even before. Now you have increased what is dear to me in you. If you wish, my dear, to know the means to immortality, I will explain them to you. While I explain them please meditate upon their meaning: Verily the husband is dear not for the sake of the husband, Maitreyī; but it is for the sake of the Self that he is dear. Verily the wife is dear not for the sake of the wife, Maitreyī; but it is for the sake of the Self that she is dear. Verily the sons are dear not for the sake of the sons, Maitreyī; but it is for the sake of the Self that they are dear. Verily wealth is dear not for the sake of wealth, Maitreyī; but it is for the sake of the Self that it is dear. . . . The Self, my dear, should be realized—by being first heard of from teachers and scriptures, then reflected on through reasoning, and lastly meditated upon. When the Self, my dear, is known by being heard of, reflected on and meditated upon, all this that is other than the Self is known, for there is nothing other than the Self."

When philosophical discussions took place, women often acted as arbiters, and won the appreciation of one and all for their profound learning and strict impartiality. In later times, when Śrī Saṅkarāchārya was discussing the Vedānta philosophy with Maṇḍana Miśra, the great exponent of the school of ritualism, it was the latter's wife, Bhāratī, a learned Hindu lady well versed in all the Hindu scriptures, who acted as umpire. Though her dear husband was Śaṅkarāchārya's

[1] *Brihadāraṇyaka Upanishad*, 2. 4. 3.

opponent in the debate which lasted seven days, she declared Śaṅkarāchārya the winner! That Śaṅkarāchārya held her in great respect is clear from his appending the name "Bhāratī" to his monastic name after the momentous discussion.

In the post-Vedic period some women teachers were called *upādhyāyā* or *upādhyāyī* or *āchāryā*, to distinguish them from the wives of teachers, who were known as *upādhyāyānī* or *āchāryānī*.

III

Coming down to the times when the Purāṇas and Epics were written, we find great saints, ascetics and *yogis* among women. The *Rāmāyaṇa* speaks of the woman ascetic Sramaṇī and of Śabarī. The latter was a disciple of a great sage called Mātaṅga, and of high spiritual attainments. She was engaged in hard penances and used to wear the bark of trees and matted locks. In the *Mahābhārata* we read the account of Sulabhā, a wandering nun and great *yoginī* (a woman *yogi*). She went to the court of King Janaka and exhibited great powers and wisdom which she had acquired by the practice of *yoga*. Another woman ascetic, known as Śivā, was learned in the Vedas and attained spiritual perfection. The daughter of Sāṇḍilya also embraced a life of celibacy and became a perfected soul. Sometimes, too, married women became ascetics. The wife of Prabhāsa became a *brahma-vādinī* and embraced the life of the wandering nun and practised *yoga*.

Even today there are many *yoginis* living in India, who are highly advanced souls. Many of them became spiritual teachers of men and women. Śrī Rāmakṛishṇa had such a *yogini* as one of his *gurus*. He had also several women disciples who lived the life of nuns and who themselves became teachers.

The nuns and women ascetics of Jainism and Buddhism form the subject of chapters of a subsequent section.

The *Smṛiti-Purāṇa* period (500 B.C.–A.D. 600) of Indian history may be called the dark age in which educational opportunities for girls were lacking. Early marriage became a custom and marriage of girls became obligatory. Sufficient facilities were not afforded for their full mental and spiritual development. Early during this period the *upanayana* of girls became something formal and was not followed by study of the Vedas. It was even advocated that the *upanayana* might be performed in the case of girls without their reciting the Vedic *mantras*. Social leaders gradually felt that as it had become a mere formality, it might be abolished. Yājñavalkya, therefore, does not permit *upanayana* for girls, nor do the later Smṛiti writers.

Though there were a few nuns amongst the Hindus, they were not prominent in the Hindu religious life. A *vānaprasthin* (recluse) could retire to the forest along with his wife to devote his life exclusively to spiritual disciplines, but such cases were few. Hinduism later withdrew this permission for the wife to retire, and declared that monastic life was not permissible to women in the Iron Age. This withdrawal of permission became all the more strict when corruption crept into the Buddhist order of monks and of nuns.

IV

In the period A.D. 600–1800 the religion of the Epics and Purāṇas became popular. Classical Sanskrit, in which the Purāṇas and Smṛitis were written, ceased to be intelligible to the people in general by about the eleventh century A.D. Women were completely denied Vedic privileges. It was in this period that the cult of *bhakti* arose, and women became its ardent followers. All Hindu women saints were followers of one school or another of the cult of *bhakti*. Such saints were born in all the provinces of India. *Vrata* (fasting with or without vigil), worship, recital of sacred hymns, hearing readings of sacred books, and other spiritual disciplines, were practised by them. Several of the prominent women saints of this period have been included in this volume.

It may seem strange that there was no order of nuns in such a vast country as India which produced so many women saints and women devotees of deep spirituality. The absence of such an order was due to various causes. First, the country was passing through a period of national decline and social disintegration, brought about by internal forces of disruption in the Hindu fold and by handicaps arising from Muslim rule. Secondly, there was not one single personality in Hinduism who could appeal to the masses and to the intelligentsia, though Śrī Śaṅkarāchārya dominated the intellectual and spiritual section of society by his profound learning and exalted spirituality. Thirdly, the women saints of the period were followers of one or other of a variety of cults—of Śiva, or of Śaktī (the Divine Mother), or of Vishṇu or any of His Incarnations such as Rāma and Kṛishṇa, Ganeśa or Sūrya—and so there was a definite lack of cohesive power needed for the establishment of an order of nuns. Fourthly, woman's position in family and society was one of complete economic dependence on man, and she had not the freedom to act, which is the first condition of growth, mental or spiritual. Fifthly, the spiritual women of the different provinces had no opportunities of contact, nor a common language for purposes of intercourse. Thus, largely for these reasons, after the extinction of the order of Buddhist nuns, there was not a strong enough urge among the women of India to establish an order of Hindu nuns, which could demand and receive recognition by the leaders of Hinduism in those times. Emphasis was laid only on individual spiritual attainments and not on the institution of any formal order.

V

Modern India, which may be said to have been born in the first quarter of the nineteenth century, has witnessed a great national renaissance. Hindu culture and religion, which had been slumbering for a time, received a quickening impulse with the introduction of modern thought and the imparting of modern education. The awakening that followed benefited both men and women. The spiritual tradition among the women, which had been kept alive as a glowing ember during the centuries, was soon to be kindled into flame in the succeeding generations. The inspiration came from renascent Hinduism. Its pioneers attempted to revive Sanskrit learning and ancient Indian wisdom. All this helped woman to recover her lost status. She soon began to acquire a certain degree of social freedom, and receive equality of opportunity in education, and in civic and social life.

All the religious movements that came in the wake of renascent Hinduism contributed their share in helping woman to rise. Not a little was achieved by the Rāmakṛishṇa Movement under the dynamic inspiration and enlightened guidance of Swāmī Vivekānanda and his fellow monks, as well as by the nation-wide work of Mahātma Gāndhi. Today women in India breathe an atmosphere of greater social equality and greater mental and spiritual freedom. Big strides have been taken by them in their onward march, notably in Bengal, Mahārāshṭra, Keraḷa, Tamiḷ nāḍ and other provinces of India.

The lives and teachings of Rāmakṛishṇa and Sāradā Devī, and of Vivekānanda and other disciples of Rāmakṛishṇa, have helped to produce not only noble-minded and all-renouncing men, but also self-sacrificing and spiritual-minded women. So far-flung has been their inspiration that it has drawn to the service of India even a few women of the West, such as Sister Niveditā (Miss Margaret Noble) and Sister Christine, who lived as nuns and conducted work for Indian women. The call of renunciation and service has already received response from hundreds of women and girls in the different provinces of India, who have dedicated themselves to the ideal of Self-realization and all-round service throughout the country, and it is not unreasonable to expect the more earnest among them to form themselves into an order of nuns similar to the one established with the permission of the Buddha nearly two thousand five hundred years ago. An informal beginning in this direction without the help of any organization had been already made by Śrī Sāradā Devī, the Holy Mother, and her associates, who were all women disciples of Rāmakṛishṇa. The women of the last two generations have received a powerful spiritual impetus from the lives of these women saints. May their inspiration mould and guide generations of women yet unborn!

CHAPTER II

AVVAIYAR

AVVAIYĀR is one of the greatest literary figures in ancient India. She was one of the many distinguished women saints whose names have lived through the ages up to modern times.

Many do not know that Tamil is perhaps the oldest living language in the world. The beginning of Tamil dates back more than 4,000 years. We have old Tamil literature which has been assigned to 500 B.C. and even 1000 B.C. That literature is as profound, varied and interesting as the most highly developed modern literature of any country. It can therefore be inferred that the language must have been in existence many centuries previously. It is said that the then land of the Tamils extended beyond the present borders of South India. A whole subcontinent which existed then has gone under the sea, according to the references in the most ancient Tamil literature available today. This is supported by recent geological observations that, many thousands of years back, India was connected by land with Africa and the land extended far south of the present Cape Comorin. Many languages have existed in various parts of the world and flourished in their own times, but disappeared after many centuries. There were the Sumerian, the Assyrian and other civilizations which each developed a rich language, but decayed later. Sanskrit, itself one of the most ancient and mother of many of the modern languages, while it possesses some of the highest literature in the world, is not now a spoken language except among the pandits. The case of Tamil is peculiar: born many thousands of years back and possessing one of the richest literatures from ancient times, Tamil has continued in use till today. In that ancient literature we see a civilization and culture rich in ideas and expounding the highest view of life.

Many personalities occur in this ancient literature, and one of the most famous of these is Avvaiyār. There seem to have been two Avvaiyārs, one a contemporary of the great Tiruvaḷḷuvar, the author of the famous *Tirukkuraḷ*—one of the greatest ethical books of all times—dating a few centuries before

Christ, and another belonging to the seventh century A.D. The earlier Avvaiyār, who is the subject of this essay, seems to have been the more outstanding personality, the later one having taken the name of her distinguished predecessor. It is natural that the life of this great saint coming from many centuries back is shrouded amid legends; but it is not difficult to see through the legends and find the real Avvaiyār, a great woman, full of wisdom, great in her human sympathy and a friend of all people from mighty kings to the humblest men and women.

It is said that she became an orphan while yet a child and was found and brought up by a man, himself a poet. At the age of sixteen, when she became famous for her beauty, many kings vied with one another to secure her hand in marriage; but she was deeply devoted to religion and literary pursuits and wanted to serve the people. With that end in view she refused to become bound in marriage. The pressure of her foster-parents was great: they could not resist the handsome offers emanating from such high personages, and they at last decided to give her in marriage to a neighbouring prince. Faced with this pressure, Avvaiyār wept and prayed before her chosen deity, Vighnēśwara,[1] to save her from this predicament. She said: "Oh! my lord, these people are only after my youth and my beauty; but I want to dedicate myself to the Goddess of learning and to the spread of learning. Please take away my youth and my beauty so that I can have peace and follow my chosen way of life." It is said that God heard her request and she immediately became an old woman with a common appearance. This relieved her from further proposals of marriage and she then went round the Tamil world of those days, preaching words of wisdom to everyone she met. This may be a legend; but the truth is not far to seek. It is a truism to say that one can reach the highest knowledge only by undivided consecration to that cause. The joys of youth and beauty have to be discarded when one seeks the highest. This is what Avvaiyār seems to have done, and in the course of a few years it became a legend.

[1] Sanskrit *e*, which is always long, is not usually marked as such, but if left unmarked in chapters containing Dravidian words, it is liable to be mistaken for the short *e* of Dravidian languages which, unlike Sanskrit, use both short *e* and long *e* (*ē*). For this reason Sanskrit *e* in this chapter and chapters III, IV, V, XI and XII had to be marked long. It has not been marked long in other chapters.

She went round imparting her wisdom to whomsoever she met, from the humblest to the highest. During her wanderings she met a certain couple: the wife was a termagant and the husband was ill-treated by her in the worst possible manner. He found Avvaiyār in a starving condition and, taking pity on her, invited her to his house; but he dared not suggest to his wife to feed Avvaiyār. In order to persuade his wife he caressed her, combed her hair, spoke sweet things to her, and at last mentioned that he had brought a poor, starving old woman to the house to be fed. The wife flew into a rage and belaboured him. Avvaiyār observed it and walked away; when the man came apologizing, she sympathized with him and said: "Married life is a joy and pleasure only when you get an affectionate and suitable wife; but when that is not possible it is hell, and the proper thing is to give up the household and take to *sannyāsa*".[1]

Similarly on another occasion during her perambulations she met a rustic doing agricultural work. His wife—this time they were an affectionate couple—was persuading him to leave his occupation and become a servant under a neighbouring chieftain. They consulted Avvaiyār and she advised them as follows: "The tree on the bank of a river and a life of dependence on a king—both these have an insecure existence and will crash some time. There is no more dignified profession than tilling the land. No other profession is as independent and dignified as agriculture."

She was highly respected by the many kings who were ruling in various parts of the Tamil land of those days. They vied with one another in inviting her to their courts. When there was danger of war on one or two occasions, she acted as a successful mediator between them. She pointed out to them that it was the ambition of the kings that created wars; but the people who suffered were the common men and women on both sides. She explained the evils of war and persuaded them to lead peaceful lives.

Though very much sought after by kings for her wisdom, she avoided them and liked to lead a simple life amongst the poor and unsophisticated people, who flocked to her wherever she went. She lived in their humble dwellings, ate their simple food, wore their plain clothes and guided them in their sorrows and worries. She was so loved by everyone that she was called

[1] The life of a monk, usually a wandering one.

the Universal Grandmother. She lived to a ripe old age, a blessing to all the people in the many years that she lived.

Avvaiyār wrote many ethical works. Some of them are studied even today by children in schools. The most famous of them are *Ātti Chūḍi, Konrai Vēntan, Ulaka Nīti, Mūturai, Nalvazhi, Nanneri, Nīti-neri-viḷakkam, Nīti Veṇbā* and *Ara-nerichāram.* Some of these are pithy sayings consisting of a few words, and the others are quartets in the usual *veṇbā* form. All of them are words of wisdom addressed to the young or to grown-ups. A few examples of these are given below:

1. Speak not to provoke. —*Ātti Chūḍi*
2. Love to give gifts. —*Ātti Chūḍi*
3. Ponder ere you act. —*Ātti Chūḍi*
4. Boast not your parts. —*Ātti Chūḍi*
5. Though it is really rice that sprouts out of the husk, yet if the husk be gone paddy will not grow; likewise even unto men of great energy, nothing will be possible except with suitable instruments. —*Mūturai*
6. Big is the frond of the palm but scentless; sweet scented is the tiny magizha[1] flower. Judge not men therefore from size merely. The vast ocean has water not fit for a bath; the tiny spring by its side has good drinking water. —*Mūturai*
7. Harsh words do not conquer soft ones; the arrow that strikes down elephants harms not a piece of cotton; the rock that is not split with the long iron crowbar, splits when the roots of a tender shrub enter it. —*Nalvazhi*
8. However virtuous one may be, the low always speak of one's faults; even as in a fruitful garden, full of flowers and haunted by the bees, the crow seeks only the margossa fruit. —*Nanneri*
9. The irrigation tank needs bunds. The sea has need of none. So too of those who seek esteem; the low need to protect themselves; not so the very wise. —*Nanneri*
10. Youth is a bubble on water; abundant riches are the long rolling waves of the ocean, and the body lasts no longer than letters traced on water. Why then, my friends, do you not worship in the Court of the Lord? —*Nīti-neri-viḷakkam*

[1] A small flower with sweet scent.

11. The justice of the king[1] consists in not being content with the information of spies but endeavouring to ascertain the truth in person, concealed and unattended in certain places; and in hesitating to act before mature deliberation, knowing that justice may fail by hasty action based on mere discovery of facts. —*Nīti-neri-viḷakkam*

12. True ministers fail not to approach the king and rouse him to the call of reason, assailing his ears with their good counsels undeterred by fear of his anger. The lusty elephant is guided by its driver and even so is the king by his ministers. —*Nīti-neri-viḷakkam*

13. With the mother's death, one loses delicacy of taste in food; with the father's death, education suffers; with a brother's death, the might of one's arm is gone; alas! when a wife dies everything goes with her! —*Nīti Veṇbā*

14. The gem that adorns an assembly is a man of learning; that which adorns the sky is the sun; . . . that which adorns the house is the son. —*Nīti Veṇbā*

15. At the time of marriage of a girl, the father desires learning; the mother desires wealth; the kinsmen look to caste; and the girl herself looks to the beauty of the bridegroom. —*Nīti Veṇbā*

16. The very noble are as the lofty palmyra in giving. They take very little and give much. Next below are those who, like the arecanut and plantain, yield much less than they take. —*Nīti Veṇbā*

17. Cool are the rays of the moon; cooler still is sandal paste; coolest are the pleasant words of the gracious who have love, learning and patience. —*Nīti Veṇbā*

18. O King of cool mountains! A man's accumulations stay behind in the house. His weeping kinsmen leave him at the crematorium. Fire consumes his body. If well thought of, only his virtues keep him company. —*Aranerichāram*

19. The days that are gone may be counted on the little fingers; the days before us none can compute. Great is the harm of letting the days pass without doing good. —*Aranerichāram*

[1] This refers to the old practice of Tamil kings who used to disguise themselves and go amongst the people to know for themselves the real state of affairs.

20. It is not possible to calm down the waves before bathing. Even so it is no use waiting to do good after one has grown rich, for riches may not then stand one in good stead. A man should do good then and there according to his means. To him alone riches prove useful. —*Aranerichāram*

21. There is no virtue higher than philanthropy; no companion better than one's own wisdom; no conduct worthier than living with self-respect. These are the ways to be trodden by those who want to be free from blame. —*Aranerichāram*

22. Too much eating results in the revolt of the senses, in the increase of desires and in ultimate ruin. To eat just enough to keep alive and to get the best out of this life is the duty of every wise man. —*Aranerichāram*

CHAPTER III

KARAIKKAL AMMAIYAR

SAINT KĀRAIKKĀL AMMAIYĀR is one of the three women saints included in the list of the sixty-three canonized Śaiva saints of Tamiḻnāḍ furnished by Saint Sundara, one of the four Āchāryas of Śaivism. Saint Mangaiyarkaraśiyār, the queen of a Pāṇḍyan king and Saint Iśai Jñāniyār, the mother of Saint Sundara, are the other two Śaiva women saints. Saint Kāraikkāl Ammaiyār is so called because Kāraikkāl[1] was her birthplace. No precise information is available about the century in which she lived; but there is evidence that she lived much earlier than Saint Tirujñāna Sambanda, another of the four Śaiva Āchāryas whose age is definitely known to be the earlier half of the seventh century A.D. The date of Kāraikkāl Ammaiyār must have been somewhere between A.D. 400 and A.D. 600.

The primary source of our information about the life of this saint is *Tirutonḍar Purāṇa*—popularly known as *Peria Purāṇa*—by Sēkkizhār,[2] the Prime Minister of the Choḷa Emperor Kulottuṅga II (A.D. 1133–1146). Her own poetical works give us an insight into her convictions, aspirations and spiritual attainments.

An account of the life of the saint will now be given, following fairly closely the narration in *Peria Purāṇa*.

Kāraikkāl had been a busy and prosperous seaport for several centuries, carrying on a large import and export trade. Its rich merchant community adhered to the principles of honesty and righteousness in all its activities. One Dānadatta was the headman of this community during the time of Ammaiyār. She was born as his daughter, of extraordinary beauty, and she was named Punidavati, meaning "she who is pure".

Even in her early childhood, Punidavati lisped the holy names of Lord Śiva with love and delight. In one of her hymns sung in later life she exclaims thus:

Oh Thou Lord of the celestials with Thy shining blue throat! From the time that I learnt to speak, I approached Thy Holy Feet

[1] This seaport on the Coromandel coast was one of the French possessions in India. It is an enclave in the Tanjore District of Madras State.

[2] See the first footnote under Chapter II, page 10.

with ever-increasing love. When wilt Thou be pleased to remove my suffering?

Needless to say, the only daughter of the chief of the merchants was brought up in the best possible surroundings. Her natural beauty grew with age. But it was noticed that all her play as a little girl was associated with the worship of Śiva. Her love and regard for the devotees of the Lord and her eagerness to serve them also developed likewise.

In due course she attained the age of maturity—the time when a Hindu girl is not allowed to move out of her house, and when talk of marriage begins. At that time there lived at Nāgapattiṇam, another big seaport, one Nidhipati, a rich merchant. He had a son, Paramadatta, and he sent elders to Kāraikkāl to seek the hand of Punidavati for his son. This proposal of marriage was accepted by Dānadatta. The marriage was celebrated at the bride's place with great pomp. As Punidavati was his only daughter, Dānadatta persuaded his son-in-law to live at Kāraikkāl itself, and provided him with a palatial residence. He also gave him plenty of wealth to carry on trade independently.

The married life of Punidavati thus commenced under apparently good auspices. She loved her husband and served him to keep him happy, as all dutiful wives of cultured families do. But her deep-rooted and incessant love for Lord Śiva, which manifested itself even in her early childhood, also grew with age. So, whenever devotees of Śiva called at her house, she would feed them well, with deep devotion, and offer them gold and good clothing as presents; and in this way her love for God grew more and more intense. Her husband did not have any such inclination, though he did not prevent her from doing these devotional acts.

One day when Paramadatta was at his place of business a small band of visitors called on him and presented him with two delicious mangoes. After concluding his business talk with the visitors, he sent the fruit to his wife through a servant. Punidavati received them and kept them safe. Then there called on her an aged devotee of Śiva. He looked very hungry and famished. The lady felt that she should feed him at once. She gave him water to wash his feet, and spread a leaf for serving food. But at that time only the rice had been cooked, and no vegetable dishes were ready. So Punidavati served first the boiled rice, and then one of the two nice mangoes which her husband had sent to her for safe custody. The aged visitor was fully satisfied with the food served to him, and the love and respect with which it was served. He left the house after thanking and blessing the lady.

Then, at noon, Paramadatta came home for his meal. After a bath he sat for his food. His dutiful wife first served him rice and a number of delicate dishes, and then placed on the leaf the remaining mango. Finding the fruit extraordinarily sweet, he asked her to give him the second mango as well. The lady felt stunned and confused for a moment; but in obedience to the command of her husband, she moved, more or less involuntarily, to the place where she had first kept the two fruits. Then she concentrated all her mind on Lord Śiva, and prayed that a mango might be sent to her. And lo! an exceptionally delicious mango came to her hand. She quietly served it to her husband with pleasure. But after tasting it and finding it to be exceedingly delicious, Paramadatta said that this fruit could not be the one he had sent, and then bluntly asked her whence she got it.

Punidavati found herself in a terrible dilemma, and her body shivered: on the one hand, she felt that it was improper as a devotee to divulge to others the divine grace shown to her; on the other, she felt that, as a dutiful wife, she had to obey the command of her husband and give him the information he had asked for. She finally decided that her higher duty was to report to her husband what had really occurred. Then, after lifting up her heart to God in worship, she narrated to him what had really happened. Paramadatta felt astounded on hearing this, and promptly ordered that if the fruit had really been given by Lord Śiva, she should obtain another such fruit from Him. Punidavati had no option left but to beseech the Lord for another fruit, as otherwise her husband might think that she had spoken an untruth. She moved a little from the presence of her husband and prayed. She got another splendid mango, and gave it to her husband, to his great wonder. But as he took it in his hand it disappeared.

Paramadatta got confused and frightened. He soon concluded that his wife was not an ordinary woman, but some goddess in human form, and decided to leave her. He ceased to treat her as his wife, though he continued to live with her in the same house, and bided his time for departure from Kāraikkāl.

In ancient Tamilagam several merchants used to cross the seas in sailing-ships laden with merchandise for purposes of trade. Paramadatta also built some merchant vessels, and sailed with goods to far-off lands. He made ample profits and returned to his homeland, Tamiḷnāḍ, but not to Kāraikkāl or Nāgapattiṇam. He reached Madurai, the famous capital of the Pāṇḍyan kingdom, and settled there, carrying on his business without revealing his identity as the husband of Punidavati. Not only that, he married a maiden of Madurai—all without the knowledge of his first wife and her relatives. In due course his second wife gave birth to a beautiful girl. Paramadatta, who never failed to pay his daily homage to Punidavati as a goddess, gave this very name to his daughter. Unaware of all these developments, Punidavati was just carrying on her household duties as best a model Hindu wife could do in the absence of her husband.

In due course news reached her relatives about Paramadatta's second marriage at Madurai. After verification, they took her in a beautifully decorated palanquin to the fairly distant city of Madurai, and sent word to her husband about her arrival. On hearing this he felt nervous at first, and then took with him his second wife and their little daughter, and prostrated himself at the feet of his bewildered wife. His new wife also made her obeisance. He said: "By thy grace I am living here, and this little child has duly been given thy name." Punidavati, with a tremor of fright, moved aside. The relatives asked him why he had done the unusual act of prostrating before his own wife. Paramadatta said firmly and clearly: "The lady Punidavati is not just a human being, but a great and gracious god. I left her only on realizing this truth, and I have also named my child after her. Therefore I prostrated myself before her in worship. You may all do likewise."

The relations stood wondering at this behaviour. On hearing her husband's words, Punidavati fixed her mind on Lord Śiva and prayed with deep and transforming emotion thus: "My Supreme Lord! This is the man's attitude towards me. So I pray to Thee that the flesh of my body, which has been sustaining beauty for his sake, may now be removed from my physical frame, and I may be granted the form of the ghosts which dance round Thee with devotion." As she stood, with a sense of transforming emotion the Lord's grace descended upon her; and lo! all the beauty of her body, through which her soul's beauty had been shining, was shed, and she took the form of a worshipful ghost of skin and bone, a form loathsome to the mortal eye. The angels showered on her celestial flowers, and the strange music of the spheres filled the earth. The hosts of heaven danced with joy. But the assembled relatives, who became frightened at this transformation, left her after offering their salutations.

Kāraikkāl Ammaiyār now began a new life. She broke forth in song and praised Lord Śiva, feeling supremely blessed in her new ghost-body. In this mood she composed one hundred and one verses in Tamil, known as *Arpuda Tiruvantādi*[1] and another garland of twenty verses, known as *Tiru Iraṭṭai Maṇi-mālai.*

The casting away of her bodily flesh was thoroughly symbolic of the severance of all connection with her earthly life. One supreme passion got possession of her now, and that was to have a sight of Lord Śiva seated in glory on Mount Kailāsa on this planet. She turned her footsteps northwards, and pressed on with her pilgrimage to Mount Kailāsa. People who happened to meet her on the way were scared at the sight of her and fled. She said to herself: "What does it matter to me what form I present to the people from the eight corners of the world who are ignorant of the Truth, if only the Supreme Lord of all knows me as one of His devotees!"

Some inexplicable feeling came over her that she should not ascend the Holy Mount on her feet, but with her head downwards! Some scholars have interpreted this to mean only that she had taken to a mode of life and thought which was just the opposite of what we see in this world. Others take it that this may also be literally true, as all things are possible to devotees who have surrendered their all to God, and whose body, mind and soul have been possessed by Him. Whatever the truth of this phenomenon might be, Ammaiyār reached the Abode of the Lord on the summit of Mount Kailāsa.

The eyes of Umā, the gracious consort of Śiva, fell on the

[1] This literally means "miraculous verse in the *antādi* form", a form of verse in which the last word of each stanza wholly or in part begins the following stanza.

ghostly form of the Kāraikkāl saint coming up with head downwards. She observed to her Lord: "How wonderful is this Love for Thee, which is manifested through this skeleton body!" The Lord replied: "Umā! Realize that She who is approaching us is My Mother. Her present worshipful frame was obtained from Me in response to her earnest prayer." When Ammaiyār stood in the immediate presence of the Lord, He greeted her with the word "Mother!" Choked with emotion, she addressed Him as Father and fell at His feet. Lord Śiva then asked her what her wishes were. Her reply is conveyed in a soul-stirring verse of the poet Sēkkizhār:

> She asked first for never-fading blissful love for Him, and then prayed thus: 'Grant unto me freedom from birth. But if it is Thy wish that I should be born again, grant me the boon that I should always be conscious of Thee. One more boon I ask of Thee, O Lord of Dharma: it is that when Thou performest Thy cosmic dance, I may witness it standing near Thy Feet.'

Lord Śiva thereupon told her that she might witness in bliss His Eternal Dance at Tiruvālaṅgāḍu,[1] and sing His praise. Ammaiyār felt supremely happy and blessed. She returned from Mount Kailāsa to Tamiḷnāḍ in South India, and proceeded straight to Tiruvālaṅgāḍu into which she moved with her head downwards. She remains there for ever, witnessing the never-ceasing cosmic dance[2] of the Lord Śiva as Naṭarāja. After reaching this sacred shrine and witnessing the dance, the saint composed two garlands of eleven hymns each, in praise of the weird aspect of the Lord's dance at Tiruvālaṅgāḍu.

It will be obvious from the above account that the husband of the Ammaiyār was not as advanced as his wife in education, culture or spiritual enlightenment. The biographer naïvely hints at this when he compares the husband to a fine and youthful bull, and the wife to a delicate peacock which can display or hold back the beauty of its feathers. Still, she honoured and served him as an obedient and dutiful wife. It is

[1] This shrine is situated at a distance of two miles from the railway station of the same name, some thirty-seven miles west of Madras, on the way to Arkonam.

[2] This Eternal Dance takes place in the atoms and in the souls. Its five objects are Creation, Preservation and Growth, Dissolution, Concealment and Revelation. The first three relate to the material universe, and the remaining two to the universe of souls.

clear also that she was a well-educated lady who could compose fine verses of deep devotion and insight, which have been considered worthy of inclusion in the Śaiva scriptures in Tamil. She has since been venerated by Saint Sambanda and other saints up to this day. We can still find her image in all the Śaiva temples where the images of the sixty-three Nāyanmārs are kept.

As specimens, a few verses from the saint's *Arpuda Tiruvantādi* are translated below:

1. Even if my Lord who dances with fire in hand and a garland of bones does not remove my sufferings, does not show compassion, and does not even show the path I should follow, my heart will never give up its love for Him.
2. Some may say that God is high up in the heavens; others may say that He is seated as the Lord of the celestials. But I will say that He who is the Lord of *jñāna* (wisdom) and whose shining throat is black with the poison He has swallowed, is the dweller in my heart.
3. I alone have reaped the fruits of *tapas* (austerities); my heart alone is a good one; I alone have firmly resolved to sever the bonds of birth (and death); because I alone have become the servant of the three-eyed Lord whose covering is the elephant skin and who wears the sacred ashes.
4. It is only the Lord's grace that rules all the worlds. It is the same grace that removes the bondage of births for souls. As my rule of life is to see the Supreme Reality through the eyes of His grace, all things are ever within my reach.
5. Of only one thing have I been thinking; only one thing am I determined to do; only one thing I have treasured in my heart; and that single thing is to become the servant of the Lord who bears the Ganges and the crescent moon on His braided head, and carries the sparkling fire in one hand.
6. Shall I call Him Hara, or Brahmā, or the one beyond them? I know not His nature. . . .
7. It is He who knows. It is He who teaches. It is He who knows as Knowledge. He is the Supreme Reality to be known. He is the shining light, and earth and ether as well.
8. They who are incapable of understanding His real nature make fun of Him. They see only His fine form besmeared with ashes and bedecked with a garland of bones like a ghost.
9. Let those wrangle who have only book-knowledge, but no

capacity to see through the scriptures and catch sight of the Truth embedded in them. The nature of the blue-throated Lord is for Him to appear before His seekers in the very form and with the appurtenances that they assign to Him in their devotion.

10. Father! This is my one ardent and never-fading desire; wilt Thou not reveal that to me one day? That is the region where, during the night of *saṁhāra* (dissolution of all things), Thou dancest with fire.

11. When Thy feet move, the nether worlds give way. When Thy head is lifted, the dome of the heavens cracks. When Thy crossed hands with bracelets move, the very cardinal points shiver. The platform of the universe cannot well bear the vigour of Thy dance.

12. We have conquered death and avoided hell. We have uprooted the bonds of good and evil *karma*—all this has been achieved by uniting ourselves with the sacred Feet of the Lord who has burnt to ashes the fortresses of the Tripurāsuras with the fire of His eye.

CHAPTER IV

ANDAL

O Saintess, basil-born, God-married nun,
Bodied Piety, Devotion incarnate!

ABOUT fifty miles south-west of the historic city of Madurai in South India, rich with spiritual and cultural traditions of hoary antiquity, there lies the fair town of Śrīvilliputtūr, evergreen in the memory of Śrī Vaishṇava devotees. Śrīvilliputtūr, which means the new town of Villi, owes its existence to the piety of two valorous hunter-chieftains, the brothers Villi and Kantan, who in obedience to divine mandate transformed the nearby dreadful jungles and dense forests infested with wild beasts and poisonous reptiles, into the celebrated homes of two of the greatest of Śrī Vaishṇava saints and their devoted followers. Such a transformation in the material realm was not only a necessary prelude to, but also a true symbol of, the glorious metamorphosis in the spiritual realm that was to be brought about in this world by Āṇḍāḷ, the eternal Divine Queen of *prēma*[1] (selfless pure devotion to God), and the subject of our sketch.

The supreme devotees of God, who are in a state of perpetual soul-communion and union with God, are patterns of divine love. In Śrī Vaishṇavism they are called *Āzhwārs*. The Tamil term *Āzhwār* signifies "he who dives deep into the ocean of countless auspicious attributes of God", and the corresponding feminine term is *Āṇḍāḷ*—"she who dives deep into the ocean of love divine". That this generic term *Āṇḍāḷ*, unlike the term *Āzhwār* which is applied only to eleven saints, has become the distinctive appellation of a single saint, itself speaks volumes of the spiritual eminence of that Divine Maiden, shining as a star of bridal mysticism.

As is the case with so many of the great saints, the entrance of Āṇḍāḷ into the arena of the world and her exit hence are shrouded in mystery: none the less she was an historical personage, who lived in the middle of the seventh century A.D. She claimed Periāzhwār of Śrīvilliputtūr as her earthly father, very much as in the case of Sītā, whom Janaka was privileged to

[1] See the first footnote under Chapter II, page 10.

call his own daughter. Tradition says that the saint Periāzhwār was engaged one day in digging and turning the soil in his garden of *tulasī* plants (sacred to Vishṇu), when suddenly his attention was arrested by the mysterious appearance of a fair young girl, bigger than a baby, lying under a plant. The childless Periāzhwār looked upon the girl as a daughter divinely bestowed upon him and named her Godā ('she who was born of Mother Earth'). Like the miser coming in sight of his treasure trove, the saint appreciated her worth, brought her up in the lap of extreme affection, made her undergo the customary purification rites current among the Śrī Vaishṇavas of the period, and in time performed the duty of imparting the spiritual instructions suited to her age and capacity.

Vishṇuchitta ('he whose consciousness was ever centred in Vishṇu'), as Periāzhwār was called in his early days, was a born mystic. With his instinctive devotion to the Supreme Being in the attitude of a sworn vassal to his liege-lord, he effaced himself in doing deeds of loving service to Him without the least taint of egoism and with the sole desire of pleasing Him only. His special interest lay in cultivating flower gardens and making garlands of choice flowers with which he would adorn the local Deity both morning and evening. In his eyes the Deity in the temple was the concrete manifestation of divine grace, the voluntary self-limitation of the Infinite Being out of love for the devotees with a view to making them feel and enjoy the rare bliss of divine communion on earth. Illiterate as he was, suddenly in response to the call of God to establish the truths of religion, he found himself miraculously endowed with a profound knowledge of Sanskrit and skill in dialectics. Once he was blessed with the vision of God of entrancing beauty before his physical eyes, and such was the flood of parental affection that it awakened in his heart that instantly he composed hymns in Tamil attributing to the Lord perpetual life. After this his devotion took a new turn and assumed the form of a deep and abiding motherly solicitude for the divine child Kṛishṇa, as in the case of Yaśodā of Vṛindāvana. For the rest of his life he lived, mentally and spiritually, in the land of Vṛindāvana with the cowherds and milkmaids, and delighted in the spiritual experience of *Kṛishṇa-Līlā*, the divine sport of Kṛishṇa.

It is no wonder that such a blessed parentage and spiritual heritage should have quickened the unfoldment of Āṇḍāḷ's inherent spiritual genius even at a tender age. Āṇḍāḷ was born with *prēma,* like the *tulasī* with its sweet aroma, and was brought up in an atmosphere surcharged with the fervid love of Kṛishṇa. Her pure feminine nature, sensitive to the most delicate shades of conjugal love, easily responded to the *gopī* ideal of a spiritual marriage with Kṛishṇa. Even from her childhood she began to look upon herself as the destined bride of the Divine Enchanter of Vṛindāvana, and revelled in ceaseless contemplation of the charms of His love and glory. One day, to test her own fitness to be His bride of beauty, she surreptitiously decked herself with the garlands intended by her father for the local Deity, gazed at her own reflection, and then replaced them. Since then, day after day, she played the same game in the strictest privacy, and her father was unknowingly offering the used garlands to the Lord. But one day the Āzhwār, happening to see her standing with the garlands on, reprimanded her for her profanity and forbade her to repeat the irreverent act. That evening he could not decide whether to offer the garlands, but to his astonishment the Lord appeared before him in a vision and commanded him to offer thenceforth only those garlands that were enriched in their perfume by their contact with the pure *prēma* form of Āṇḍāḷ. Next morning the Āzhwār apprised his daughter of the Lord's behest and requested her to wear the garlands herself before offering them to the Lord. Realizing now her identity with the Divine Mother and Ruler of the universe, he named her "Āṇḍāḷ".

As Āṇḍāḷ grew in age her wisdom and devotion began to ripen day by day until it took the form of a passionate and irrepressible longing to marry God. Unable to bear the agony of separation from her beloved and the pangs of unrequited love, she was driven to the necessity of resorting to the measures taken by the *gopīs* of Vṛindāvana, the love-stricken milkmaids, who were in the selfsame plight with regard to Śrī Kṛishṇa. Her rich and powerful imagination transported her to the pleasant woods of Vṛindāvana and the sweet streams of the Yamunā. There, fancying herself to be a *gopī* pining for the presence of Śrī Kṛishṇa, she rose early in the morning in the auspicious winter month of Mārgaśīrsha (December–January): after bathing and decorating herself she went with the ostensible purpose of fulfilling a vow "in a congregational procession with her own companions, aroused from sleep, to the palace of the sleeping Beauty, to wake Him up and pray for the boon of *parai*".[1] Śrī Kṛishṇa is roused and takes His seat in the audience hall, ready to listen to their petitions. But Āṇḍāḷ, the leader of the party, prays for nothing earthly and craves only the privilege of eternal loving service to Him alone and for His sake alone, bound as they were to Him by inseparable soul-ties for ever. The whole scene is portrayed vividly in her immortal lyric, *Tiruppāvai* ("The Song Divine"), a poem of thirty stanzas, wherein we see a marvellous blending of artistic excellence, metaphysical symbolism and devotional fervour. This poem is sung daily in every Vaishṇava shrine.

But the outpourings of Āṇḍāḷ's divine frenzy for spiritual communion with Śrī Kṛishṇa, as it develops spontaneously from being a fancy to a consuming passion, are depicted autobiographically in her *Tirumozhi* ("Sacred Utterance"), a work of greater length. Herein is a frank and free expression of the varying moods of her profound bridal love—her tender hopes and grave fears; her earnest entreaties and fervent prayers to Cupid, the God of Love, to prepare her for God alone; her confidence and triumph; her keen anguish; her paroxysm of joy when her Beloved married her in a dream; her all-consuming love and utter dejection; her messages to her Lover that would melt even stony hearts; her mild rebukes of her Sweetheart's extreme callousness; her indignation at the refusal of her relatives to carry her openly to the immediate presence of her Divine Lover; and lastly the intense burning sensation in her body that could only be mitigated by contact with the articles that adorned the person of Śrī Kṛishṇa.

Notwithstanding the consoling, mysterious and rapid growth of Āṇḍāḷ's pure devotion to God, her attainment of marriageable age cannot but have filled even her saintly father's mind with anxiety regarding the choice of a suitable human bridegroom for his precocious daughter, the gem of his entire childless family. One day, to sound her own feelings in the matter, he gently queried: "Daughter, whom dost thou choose to wed?" Āṇḍāḷ responded sternly: "If I heard I had to wed a mortal, I could not bear to live." "How then should I proceed?" the father inquired. "I intend to marry the Lord alone" was the bold reply. Periāzhwār then recounted to his darling the

[1] *Parai* is a kind of drum by which the Deity is roused from sleep. Here Āṇḍāḷ considers it a privilege to play the drum and so wake up Śrī Kṛishṇa.

characteristics and Divine glories of each and every one of the various special manifestations of God, and watched her reactions to the glowing descriptions. It was patent to him that her preference was for Śrī Raṅganātha, the Lord of Śrīraṅgam (on the banks of the Cauvery in South India), since the mention of His glories enraptured her beyond all bounds of maidenly control. After this Āṇḍāḷ cherished fond dreams of being united with Him in wedlock.

Yet the Āzhwār's mind again became a prey to misgivings and cares regarding the practicability of the proposal, for it involved nothing short of a rare miracle wrought by Divine grace. However, one night the Lord of Śrīraṅgam, the Bridegroom elect of Āṇḍāḷ, vouchsafed to Āzhwār a vision in which He assured him that Āṇḍāḷ would be accepted by Him as the Divine bride if brought to His presence in the temple. In obedience to the mandate Āṇḍāḷ was taken in the company of Āzhwār and his devotees to the presence of Śrī Raṅganātha. There at the sight of the celestial Cynosure she felt her body, heart and soul irresistibly attracted towards Him. She walked straight to His side and stood by Him—and lo! to the utter astonishment and bitter regret of all the onlookers she vanished from mortal sight. Soon the dazed Āzhwār was awakened by a Divine voice that consoled him saying: "Thou hast become My father-in-law. Worship Me with Āṇḍāḷ by My side in your own home and continue offering garlands in loving service." The Āzhwār returned sorrow-laden to his native town, feeling a terrible void in his home and heart. Yet submitting himself to Divine will he converted his own abode into a fitting sanctuary where he installed Śrī Raṅganātha and Āṇḍāḷ, and continued faithfully to serve the Lord to the end of his life.

Thus ended the drama of the divine bard-mystic Āṇḍāḷ enacted on the human stage. Her name has become a household word in South India, especially among the Śrī Vaishṇavas. She came to earth to resuscitate the path of complete self-surrender, which in her case originated in the overpowering frenzy of pure devotion to God. She led captive the proud Conqueror of her heart, her Divine Lover, by binding Him first with the garlands of flowers that gained a divine perfume by their contact with her person and tresses, and then with the garlands of her immortal lyrics glowing with fervour. *Prēma* (Divine Love) was the food she ate, the water she drank and the betel she chewed, that is to say, her sustenance and her luxury. Day by day, nay, instant by instant, her flawless devotion to God was growing in volume and intensity till it found its culmination in bursting the delicate mortal frame that hid it and merging itself in the Supreme Godhead of which it was a manifestation. Her poems reflect the quintessence of the Upanishads, as also does her immaculate purity, which is confirmed by the singular absence of even a single reference to any lapses, self-accusations or contrition for past misdeeds in her pre-illumination period. Her surrender to her chosen Bridegroom was so complete that there was absolutely no trace in it of self-seeking or jealousy, no single stain or shade of human weakness or impurity. She was a "burning Sappho" endowed with the pure passion of *Kṛishṇa-prēma* (love of Kṛishṇa), and her whole life was a poem of the growth and fulfilment of that divine bridal longing. What a passionate fervour of mystic love for Kṛishṇa is revealed in the following translation of her verses!

1. Ye jewelled damsels dwelling in resplendent Gokula!
'Tis hallowed Dhanus now, with nights of silver blaze.
So hie we hence all bathed and pure to where He lies—
The glorious Son of valorous Nanda, sharp-speared and keen,
The mighty whelp of Yaśodā, the beauteous-eyed,
The azure-hued, the lotus-eyed, whose mien both cool
And fiery becomes. Nārāyaṇa, Lord, who 'lone could grant
The boon of *parai*, which gives the bliss we crave.[1]

2. O glorious, mighty Cupid, God of love! I pray thee understand the penance I perform with body foul, hair dishevelled, eyes pale and a single meal a day. O Lord! to thee I wish to speak a word: just for the sake of preserving my life, grant me the boon that I may touch the feet of Lord Kṛishṇa.[2]

3. O song-bird (*kuyil*)! many a day my bones do soften, my spear-like eyes know no wink. Plunged into the sea of dire distress, I am in a plight, failing to secure a ferry-boat—the Lord of Vaikuṇṭha. Thou too knowest the keen pangs of separation that torment those in love. Can you not call my beloved Lord of golden hue, whose banner bears the royal eagle?

4. Ye clouds compassionate! my lustre and hue, my bangles, mind and sleep have deserted me in my lonely affliction, so that I may

[1] Translated from *Tiruppāvai*.
[2] Passages 2–6 are translations from *Tirumozhi*.

perish. Can I engage myself in singing the auspicious qualities of my Govinda, residing in the Hill of Veṅkaṭa with cool waterfalls, just for preserving my life?

5. The sense of shame is of no avail henceforth, for all and sundry have come to know the fact. If you would without delay find the remedy for restoring me to my past condition and save my life, take me to Gokula . . .

6. Being crushed under the feet of that cruel callous Son of Nandagopa in the world, bereft of all respect, I cannot stir. Fetch me the dust of the place trodden by that brazen-faced Youth, and smear my body with it; for then alone my life will not depart from the body.

This brief sketch is concluded with a tribute from the pen of Sri Devendranath Sen, a Bengali devotee and poet.

O fancy-free and yet not fancy-free!
Like some blest fountain, from the very core
Of thy rich heart, O Saint! didst thou outpour
Thy crystal, holy love in ecstasy
To God! O bird, with wings outspread in glee
Adoration's summit didst thou overpeer,
And earth and sky were glad and ever more
Drink deep thy song's ambrosial melody.
Thy love was not of earth; no woman's soul
For mortal love craved with such a yearning.
So thou didst wed great God Himself! O Goal
Beyond our ken, beyond our dim discerning!
And soul to soul, like sunbeam unto Sun,
Thou didst vanish away, O mystic Nun!

CHAPTER V

AKKA MAHADEVI

THE middle of the twelfth century of the Christian era was a period of profound significance in the history of the Kannaḍa country. It was at this time that the great religious leader and social reformer Basavēśwara[1] and his fellow-workers, like the great mystic and teacher Allama Prabhu, vitalized and re-shaped Śaiva religion and philosophy into a new and abiding form, Vīraśaivism. Among the luminaries of the age, a star of the first magnitude, was Akka Mahādēvī who demonstrated in her life the religious principle "*Śaraṇa*[2] *sati Liṅga*[3] *pati*" (the devotee is the wife and Śiva the husband). "Akka", an honorific added to a personal name in Kannaḍa, means "an elder sister". Mahādēvī was certainly an elder in spiritual attainment and was recognized as such; but actually she was one of the youngest members of the Vīraśaiva religious fraternity. In her intense devotion to Lord Śiva and single-minded quest of Him she spurned the riches and comforts of a palace, cut asunder domestic bonds, and set out as a wandering devotee meeting with and overcoming many hardships on her journey to the final goal. In addition, she had the gift of imaginative expression. A few of the outpourings of her experience are preserved for posterity in the shape of *vachanas*, "sayings" in rhythmic Kannaḍa prose, a type of composition which was widely favoured by the Vīraśaiva devotees of the time and forms their unique contribution to Kannaḍa literature. The *vachana* writers of Kannaḍa are many in number; and among them Mahādēvī is acclaimed, by modern critics as well as ancient admirers, one of the very best. Her *vachanas* are characterized by intense feeling and deep insight. Some idea of her spiritual history, its travail as well as illumination, can be gathered from these "sayings".[4]

[1] See the first footnote under Chapter II, page 10.

[2] The terms *śaraṇa*, *māhēśwara* and *bhakta*, etc., used in Vīraśaiva writings, indicate varying stages of spiritual progress. To put it briefly, a *bhakta* is a devotee of Śiva, a believer. Next higher to him is the *māhēśwara* whose devotion is firmly rooted and who has undertaken special vows in this regard. Very much higher comes the *śaraṇa* who has completely surrendered himself to the Lord.

[3] The Liṅga is the emblem of Śiva; it means Śiva as well.

[4] There is also extant a short collection called *Yōgāṅga Trividhi*, ascribed to Akka Mahādēvī. It consists of sixty-seven three-line stanzas and gives expression, mostly in symbolic language, to the advanced stages of the soul's progress.

Mahādēvī was the daughter of a devoted Śaiva couple,[1] who lived in Uḍutaḍi, a town over which a prince by name Kauśika, was the ruler. Mahādēvī grew up to be a maiden of surpassing beauty. One day while Kauśika was returning in procession from the exercise ground, his gaze fell upon Mahādēvī who was sitting in front of her house. Kauśika was smitten with love for her then and there. He stopped his elephant at the spot, losing all control over himself. The procession stopped too. Mahādēvī, who probably was innocently watching the passing of the royal retinue, now became aware that she herself was the object of Kauśika's attention and swiftly went inside her house. Kauśika's heart followed where his eyes could not. Now his ministers somehow took charge of him and led him away to the palace. But his passion for Mahādēvī was so overwhelming that the ministers saw no way out but to ask Mahādēvī's father to give her in marriage to the prince. They described to him in eloquent terms the love-lorn plight of Kauśika; they also warned him that the prince's wrath would descend upon anyone, high or low, who thwarted his desire. The parents of Mahādēvī, who were simple and timid folk, became genuinely frightened and entreated her to marry the prince and become mistress of his riches. But Kauśika was a *bhavi*, a non-Śaiva; and Mahādēvī rejected the proposal with utter indignation.

Mahādēvī was a devotee of Chenna Mallikārjuna from her childhood. He was the sole Lord of her heart and love. Evidently she had not contemplated marriage with any earthly husband. Who knows if she did not sing the following *vachana*[2] when pressed with such a proposal of marriage?

> I have fallen in love, O mother, with the
> Beautiful One, who knows no death,
> knows no decay and has no form;
>
> I have fallen in love, O mother, with the
> Beautiful One, who has no middle, has
> no end, has no parts and has no features;

[1] Harihara, whose outline of the story of Mahādēvī's life is summarized here, gives the names of Mahādēvī's parents as Śivabhakta and Śivabhakte. According to Chāmarasa they were known as Nirmala and Sumatī. It is not certain if their names have survived in their correct forms.

[2] The English renderings attempted here are but rough and tentative. It is very difficult to reproduce in a foreign language the delicate shades of meaning and the emotional flavour of the original as also the free rhythmic flow of its lines.

I have fallen in love, O mother, with the
Beautiful One, who knows no birth and
knows no fear.

I have fallen in love with the Beautiful
One, who is without any family,
without any country and without any peer;
Chenna Mallikārjuna, the Beautiful, is my husband.
Fling into the fire the husbands who are subject
to death and decay.

When such was her feeling, it was unthinkable that Mahādēvī would consent to the idea of marrying Kauśika—and a *bhavi* to boot.

Let us now return to Harihara's narrative. Kauśika's emissaries went back and reported to him the failure of their mission. They told him that Mahādēvī had no eye for worldly riches, was absorbed in her devotion to Lord Śiva and would not marry anyone, *bhakta* or *bhavi*. This news but fanned the already raging fires of Kauśika's passion. He merely told his ministers: "Bring her by persuasion or bring her by force. Promise her anything she wants. But bring her to me." The ministers came again to Mahādēvī's parental home. They announced that the prince's command was that the parents should be immediately put to death if they refused to give him their daughter in marriage. "Hand her over and live in wealth and happiness." This threat was enough. The parents sank to the earth. Tears welled up in their eyes. "O daughter," they said, "we, an aged couple, are going to meet a dire death owing to your obstinacy. Your *bhakti* is indeed a strange thing. Have not there been examples before of saintly Śaiva women who lived in bonds of marriage with *bhavis*? Why do you condemn us to this dreaded death? Please do as others have done before and accept Kauśika as your husband."

This was a stupendous blow. If it had concerned only herself Mahādēvī would have resisted to the very end; but now she had to think of saving her parents' lives. What she would never have done to protect herself, she resolved to do for the sake of these devotees of Śiva, her parents. An old dictum of the saints came to her memory: "One should protect the devotees of Śiva at any cost. One should undergo every kind of misery and agony to save the *śaraṇas*." Thus fortified in her resolve she decided to make the supreme sacrifice: she would submit her body to the marriage. Now she pacified her parents and told the ministers that she would agree to their proposal provided that they agreed to her conditions: "I shall engage myself in the worship of Śiva as I like. I shall spend my time in the company of *māhēśwaras* as I like. I shall serve my *guru* as I like. I shall be with your prince as I like. And I shall forgive only three violations of these conditions." The ministers all too gladly agreed to these terms and even drew up a document recording them. Kauśika was overjoyed at hearing that Mahādēvī had at last agreed to marry him. He showered riches on her parents and eagerly awaited the auspicious day fixed for the marriage.

The day arrived. Mahādēvī allowed herself to be decked with costly jewels and garments, but grief and despair reigned in her heart. She must have felt very much like a victim submitting to decoration before being led to the sacrificial altar; and her anguish must have been all the keener owing to the very fact that she had voluntarily agreed to the sacrifice. In the marriage hall, at the appointed hour, the unwilling bride was handed over to the over-eager bridegroom, and compelled to live in Kauśika's palace as his wedded wife.

One solace remained to her however. She had somehow saved it for herself when all seemed to be lost. Each day she would engage herself as long as possible in the worship of Śiva. She would fix her eager gaze upon the Liṅga held in her hand, perform all the rites of worship, press it to her heart, sing songs expressing her devotion to Lord Chenna Mallikārjuna, and pray for release from the bonds which bound her to a *bhavi*. Then she would feed the *śaraṇas*, spend some time in their elevating company and sing freshly composed *vachanas* describing mystic experience. But she would not be allowed to remain in this happy state for long. The sun would set and darkness would descend simultaneously upon the world and her spirits. The call would come from Kauśika. Most unwillingly she would send away the devotees of the Lord and address another song to Him expressing anger and shame at thus being compelled to flit to and fro between *bhakti* and worldly life. She would throw away all ornaments, wear a soiled dress, refuse all decoration and go with a heavy heart to the bridal chamber where Kauśika would be eagerly waiting for her.

And Kauśika's passion for Mahādēvī was so consuming that even her aversion was sweet to him. It was as if a statue of *sparśamaṇi* (the miraculous stone which turns all things into gold) touched indignantly an image of iron; the latter gained the golden hue all the same! A *vachana* of Akka Mahādēvī, addressed to Śiva in the throes of her deepest longing for Him, runs as follows:

> O Lord, listen to me if you will, listen not
> if you will not; I cannot rest contented
> unless I sing of you.
>
> O Lord, accept me if you will, accept not if
> you will not; I cannot rest contented unless
> I worship you.
>
> O Lord, love me if you will, love not if you will
> not; I cannot rest contented unless I hold
> you in my arms.
>
> O Lord, look at me if you will, look not if you
> will not; I cannot rest contented unless
> I gaze at you in overpowering longing.
>
> O Lord Chenna Mallikārjuna, I worship you and
> revel in a thrill of pleasure.

While Mahādēvī's passion for the Lord was spiritual, Kauśika's passion for her was earthly. Apart from this, however, Kauśika might very well have addressed similar words to his object of adoration!

How did Mahādēvī herself bear the sufferings of this contrary union? The poet tells us that it was like a union experienced in a bad dream; Mahādēvī's spirit looked upon her body's torture verily like a *sākshin* (a passive witness). Such was the greatness of her dispassion!

Thus it went on for some time. One day some *māhēśwaras* came from afar to the palace and sent word to the queen. But Mahādēvī was resting at the time; and Kauśika sent back the servant, shouting that not a day passed without the arrival of these devotees and that the queen should have undisturbed sleep at least on that day. The clamour awakened Mahādēvī. She got wild with Kauśika for speaking insultingly of the devotees and began to weep at what had happened. This was the first "fault" of Kauśika, and, on his imploring her, Mahādēvī consented to forgive it. The second was soon to follow. One morning when Mahādēvī was seated in ceremonial purity, absorbed in worshipping the Lord, Kauśika came to the place on the sly, just to fill his eyes with the sight of her. He was so smitten with her transcendent beauty that he lost all control over himself, rushed towards her and caught her in his arms. Mahādēvī's mystic communion was disrupted. She turned round and saw the face of Kauśika from which she shrank as from a pointed dagger. In distressed anger she flung hot words at him. How could he, a *bhavi*, come and touch her in the midst of her worship of Śiva? Well, he had committed the second "fault".

On another day, we are told, when Mahādēvī was with her husband in privacy, her *guru* happened to come to the palace. She was not properly dressed at the time, but wanted to prostrate herself immediately at his feet. Kauśika felt humiliated, and losing all patience wrested her garment from her with the taunting remark, "Leave it, leave it alone! What need have you, an outstanding devotee and ascetic, for any clothing?" This was the breaking-point.[1] The count of three "faults" was now complete. In spite of his great passion for Mahādēvī, in spite of every desire and effort to keep her bound to himself, Kauśika had thrice violated the terms of the marriage; he had come between her and the *māhēśwaras*, between her and the *Liṅga*, and between her and the *guru*. The release that Mahādēvī

[1] The *Prabhuliṅgalīle* of Chāmarasa gives a different version. According to Chāmarasa, when Mahādēvī learnt that Kauśika wanted to marry her, she laid down the condition that the prince himself should come and swear before her that he would carry out her bidding before seeking to win her heart. When Kauśika was thus sworn, Mahādēvī accepted his presents and went to his palace. There she stipulated that he should become a *bhakta* first if she was to accept him. Kauśika, however, said that he could not agree to change his religion, to which Mahādēvī replied that she could not agree to live with him. This released her from the bond, and handing back all the garments and ornaments he had given her she left the palace. Kauśika was dumbfounded at this unusual behaviour. He thought Mahādēvī had taken leave of her senses. His passion for her ebbed away and he gave up all idea of forcibly detaining her.

The question whether Mahādēvī actually led a married life with Kauśika for some time is a hotly debated one. Taking into consideration all the factors, many scholars feel that the version found in Harihara's poem deserves credence since it is both early and natural. And it must not be forgotten that the mere fact of Mahādēvī's forced marriage with Kauśika, to which she submitted solely for saving her parents, does not in the least take away from her spiritual greatness. Harihara has portrayed the story of her self-sacrifice in such a masterly way that her deep devotion and ascetic spirit stand out in enhanced splendour.

was longing for was now at hand. She left Kauśika's palace, taking in her palm the *Liṅga* of her worship. The desires of the flesh and the torments of the senses were now to her things of the past. Rejoicing in her new-found freedom she bade farewell to her parents and her *guru*, and left the town alone, a living embodiment of renunciation.

According to Harihara's narrative, Akka Mahādēvī set her intent face right in the direction of Śrīśaila, the holy mountain abode of her beloved Chenna Mallikārjuna. After an arduous journey she reached the goal of her pilgrimage and settled down to the uninterrupted worship and contemplation of the Lord. She would be found near caves and streams, groves and flower-gardens, worshipping Śiva to her heart's content. But the shadows of her former life still pursued her: her parents came to see her and were full of grief over the hard ascetic life that their young daughter was leading. But Mahādēvī would not yield to their pleading. She told them that now at last she was free from the *bhavi's* bonds and had embraced the service of Bhava (that is, Śiva). The parents left her, wonder-struck at her determination. But Mahādēvī's temptations were not yet over. Now the love-lorn Kauśika came to her in a new garb. He thought that he could still win the love of Mahādēvī if he only wore the marks of a Śaiva. Thus he came to her wearing the sacred beads, the sacred ashes and so on, and fell at her feet, announcing that he had now become a *bhakta* and beseeching her to be kind to him. It was on seeing this unexpected turn of things that, according to Harihara, Mahādēvī uttered a well-known *vachana*[1]:

> O Lord, your Māyā does not give me up even when I have given it up. In spite of my resistance it clings to me and follows me.
>
> Your Māyā becomes a Yoginī to the Yogin: it becomes a nun to the monk, it becomes a herald to the saint. It adapts itself to each according to his nature.
>
> When I climbed up the hill, your Māyā too came up; when I entered the forest, your Māyā too entered behind me.

[1] The rendering given here follows in general Harihara's paraphrase of the *vachana*.

Lo, the world does not take its hand off
my back even now!

O, Lord of infinite mercy, your Māyā frightens
me. O Lord Mallikārjuna, bestow your grace
on me.

Mahādēvī had really conquered Māyā. She was now beyond the temptation of all earthly love. She spurned the lustful importunities of Kauśika and told him that she had nothing more to do with him, even if he wore the marks of a *bhakta*. Now Kauśika tried a last remedy. He approached a number of Śaiva devotees with presents and told them that his wife, Mahādēvī, had left him because he was a *bhavi*; but now that he had become a *bhakta* he appealed to them to persuade her to go back to him. The *māhēśwaras* thought this a fair request and sent for Mahādēvī. When the messenger arrived, however, he found the saint completely absorbed in devotional meditation and returned without daring to disturb her. The *māhēśwaras* themselves came to where she was, admired her great spirituality and asked Kauśika to go back since there was no place for him in the passionless heart of Mahādēvī.

After a little while Mahādēvī grew tired of earthly existence and prayed to Śiva for release from the body which had been polluted by contact with a *bhavi*. Her wish was granted and she went to Kailāsa in a new divine body.[1]

Life had indeed dealt harshly with her. Without understanding the needs of her soul the world had condemned her to a dreadful existence. It was only by resolute will and uncommon courage that Mahādēvī had thrown off its shackles. But this did not embitter her spirit against the world as such. On the other hand, its din and disturbance proved to be an invaluable training ground, teaching her the great lesson of equanimity:

[1] Harihara does not tell us much about the spiritual progress and illumination of Mahādēvī after she was finally freed from Kauśika's bonds. He does not mention even her meeting with the great figure of the Vīraśaiva reformation, Basavēśwara. Here the *Prabhuliṅgalīle* and the *Śūnyasampādane* come to our help. According to them, Akka Mahādēvī first went to Kalyāṇa, the abode of Basavēśwara, the headquarters of Allama Prabhu and the nerve centre of the Vīraśaiva movement, before proceeding to Śrīśaila. That there must have been such an interlude in her life is supported by some *vachanas* of Akka Mahādēvī herself.

Having made one's home on the hill-top, how can
 one afford to be afraid of the beasts?
Having made one's home on the seashore, how can
 one afford to be afraid of the surging waves?

Having made one's home in the market-place, how
 can one afford to shrink from its noise?
Hear what I say, O Chenna Mallikārjuna:

Having been born in this world, one should not
 lose one's temper at praise or blame
But maintain the poise of one's spirit.

Mahādēvī had come to Kalyāṇa for spiritual guidance. But the elders found to their great wonder that she was far advanced on the path and that they had little to teach her. Basavēśwara in particular seems to have been moved very deeply by this young saint's spiritual perfection. And it was to him, more than to anyone else, that Mahādēvī turned for advice in finding that elusive Lover, Chenna Mallikārjuna. He and the other elders blessed her resolve to achieve unbroken union with the Lord of her heart. It was as if they had given this daughter of theirs in marriage to the Lord and were now sending her to her husband's home at Srīśaila. And Mahādēvī, while taking leave of them, assured them that she would never bring discredit to her spiritual home:

I received my birth at the hand of my *guru*;
I was nurtured by the kindness of countless
 śaraṇas;
Lo, they fed me on the milk of *bhāva*, the ghee
 of true knowledge and the sugar of *paramārtha*:[1]
On this threefold nectar did you feed and nourish me.
You gave me in marriage to a suitable husband;
And now you have all gathered in countless numbers
 to send me to my husband's home.
I shall serve my Lord to the satisfaction of
 Basavaṇṇa;
Having taken the hand of Chenna Mallikārjuna
 in marriage,
I shall bring only glory and never any shame to you.
Be assured of this and please go back, my elders.
My salutations to you!

[1] The word *bhāva* has many meanings; here it probably means the contemplation of the *Liṅga* in its subtlest form. *Paramārtha* means the highest spiritual value.

Mahādēvī, the spiritual bride, now went all alone to Śrīśaila, hoping to meet there her great Lover face to face. The *vachanas* which express the anguished longing of her mystic love are among the best lyrics in the Kannaḍa language. Oppressed by deep desire this waiting bride called to Him:

> Come to me, O my groom, auspicious-scented,
> gold-adorned and rich-clad.
> Your coming would verily be the coming back
> of my life.
> I am watching the roads, all athirst, hoping
> that Chenna Mallikārjuna will come.

Like the heroine of any romance, Mahādēvī felt unbearable physical agony at the absence of her Divine Lover. The following *vachana* is addressed to the conventional confidant, but the feeling it embodies is anything but conventional:

> My distressed mind has been thoroughly upset,
> O my dear!
> The blowing wind has become a burning flame, my dear;
> The moonlight has turned into the scorching sun,
> O my friend!
> I am wandering up and down like the toll-gatherer
> of a town.
> O friend, appease Him and bring Him to me;
> Chenna Mallikārjuna has turned away in anger from me.

With the mounting of the fever of Love, sanity disappears. Mahādēvī had long before understood that the Lord was immanent in the whole of creation and had prayed to Him to reveal Himself to her in everything:

> All the forest is You,
> All the glorious trees of the forest are You,
> All the birds and beasts that move among the
> trees are You.
> O Chenna Mallikārjuna, reveal to me Your face,
> pervading everything.

This imaginative prayer now yielded place to a frantic appeal to every object that met Mahādēvī's frenzied eye:

O parrots that chirp and prattle, did you,
did you see Him?
O cuckoos that sing on the high note, did you,
did you see Him?
O bees that roam about, did you, did you see Him?
O swans that glide on the lake's edge, did you,
did you see Him?
O peacocks that dance in the mountain caves, did you,
did you see Him?
Tell me, O tell me, where is Chenna Mallikārjuna?

And at long last, after much spiritual travail, the Supreme Vision was granted to Mahādēvī and the following *vachana*, with its rich and characteristic imagery, bears witness to it:

I have seen Him in His divine form,
Him with the matted locks,
Him with the jewelled crown,
Him with the gleaming teeth,
Him with the smiling face,
Him who illumines the fourteen worlds with
the light of His eyes.
I have seen Him and the thirst of my eyes is
quenched.
I have seen the great Lord whom the men
among men serve but as wives.
I have seen the Supreme *Guru* Chenna Mallikārjuna
sporting with the Primeval *Śaktī*,
And saved am I.

That was realization of God in His Supreme Form. But Mahādēvī rose even higher and appears to have experienced mystic union with the Formless Itself. This is how she expresses the inexpressible, and with this *vachana* we may close:

I do not say it is the *Liṅga*,
I do not say it is oneness with the *Liṅga*,
I do not say it is union,
I do not say it is harmony,
I do not say it has occurred,
I do not say it has not occurred,
I do not say it is You,
I do not say it is I,
After becoming one with the *Liṅga*
in Chenna Mallikārjuna,
I say nothing whatever.

CHAPTER VI

LALLESWARI OR LAL DIDDI OF KASHMIR

LALLEŚWARĪ, also known as Lalla Yogīśwarī, Lāl Diddi or Lāl Ded, was a mystic poet of Kashmir who lived in the fourteenth century A.D. Loved by the people of her land, her name continues to be a household word even to this day. She embodied in herself the highest aspirations of her countrymen, and is the best exponent of the idealistic Śaivism prevalent in Kashmir during her time. Śaivism accepts the Advaita (monistic) philosophy of the Vedānta which has been epitomized in the formula "I am He". It asserts that in essence the human soul is one with God and He is the only Reality behind the changing phenomena of the world. He pervades and supports the universe and is also beyond it: therefore He is said to be immanent as well as transcendent. This forms the central theme of Lalla's teachings, and she expresses this one idea with an infinite variety of illustration. Lalla, however, did not preach any creed or dogma, or propound a philosophy in the scholarly sense of the term, but taught from the depths of her own mystic experiences; and when one speaks from the fullness of the heart, life-giving power is imparted to the words and they are carried on the wings of time through the ages. Sir Richard Carnac Temple in the preface to his book, *The Words of Lalla the Prophetess*, gives a quotation from Pandit Anand Koul. The latter says, "The Lāl Wākhi or sayings of Lāl . . . touch the Kaṣhmiri's ear as well as the chords of his heart, and are freely quoted by him as maxims on appropriate occasions in conversation, having moulded the national mind and set up a national ideal". And the author (Temple) continues, "There must be something worth investigation in poems having such an effect on the minds of the people to whom they are addressed".

The life of Lalla is shrouded in miracles and legends. Besides the book of Sir R. C. Temple mentioned above, the Royal Asiatic Society has published as one of its monographs (Vol. XVII) *The Lalla Vākyāni or Wise Sayings of Lāl Ded* (*or Lalla*), a mystic poetess of ancient Kashmir, edited with translation by Sir George Grierson and Dr. Lionel Barnett. Pandit Anand Koul of Kashmir has written a booklet entitled *Lalla Yogīśwarī, Her Life and Sayings*, based mostly on folk-lore and tradition. Besides this scanty information there seems to be little or no literature on so outstanding a personality as Lalla. In spite of this drawback the lamp she has lighted has burnt steadily throughout the centuries, and her sayings have been preserved faithfully from generation to generation. Many archaic forms of expression and many old words, the significance of which has been lost, have thus been retained in her verses; moreover we cannot but assume that the language must have been changed to some extent by repetition. In this way the historian and biographer find themselves at a loss, but the people as a whole care little for cold facts. They instinctively seem to know the truth expressed so eloquently in Sister Niveditā's words when she said, "What are mythologies after all but the jewel casket of humanity by means of which its wealth of dreams and loves and sighs in every generation becomes the unperishing and imperishable treasure of the aftercomers?"[1]

Thus it would be worth while giving a brief life-sketch of Lalla from the material made available to us by Pandit Anand Koul. We may safely assume that she lived in the fourteenth century, since Sayyed Āli Hamadāni, a well-known Ṣūfī Persian saint, visited Kashmir during the years 1379–80, to 1385–86, and was a contemporary of Lalla. It is interesting to note in this connection that between the fourteenth and sixteenth centuries in India there arose a large number of eminent poet-saints, religious teachers and mystics who profoundly affected the life and thought of the people. They were leaders of men in their own times, and are living influences even to this day. The great Rāmānanda, who lived in the fifteenth century, is held to be the first in this line, and he was followed by Tulsīdās, Mīrābāī, Nānak and Kabīr in the north, Chaitanya, Chanḍī Dās and Vidyāpati in Bengal and Vallabhāchārya in the south. But Lalla, although it is not known whether her influence spread beyond Kashmir, preceded them all.

She was born in a Kashmiri pandit family at Pandrenthan, four miles to the south-east of Srinagar. There is a strange, and typically Hindu, legend connected with her birth. It seems that

[1] *The Web of Indian Life.*

in a previous life she was also born as a woman in Kashmir and was married to a man living at Pandrenthan. There, in that life, she gave birth to a son. When the family priest Siddha Śrī Kanṭha came to perform the purification ceremony eleven days after childbirth, she said to him, "How is the new-born baby related to me?" "What a strange question!" replied the priest. "Why, he is your son." "No," said the mother, and when the priest inquired who else he could be, she said she was just about to die and would be reborn as a filly with certain marks, in a particular village, and then she would be in a position to answer his question. The woman died immediately and the priest went to question the foal at the appointed time and place. He found the foal, but it said the same thing to him. It was just about to die and would be reborn as a puppy. Then he went to the puppy who gave the same reply and died immediately after. The priest got tired of pursuing the matter further and gave up this search. Thus after six births in the animal world in quick succession this soul was born as Lalla and married to the same boy to whom she had given birth in her previous human life. The same priest came to perform the marriage ceremony, and she confided her secret to him on the day of the wedding. She was twelve years old at this time and the boy had grown to manhood.

This astonishing legend has a moral. Firstly it seems to indicate that she remembered her past lives, which only one who has self-realization can do. In conformity with Hindu thought, and consistent with the way of life that Lalla was going to adopt, it also has a deep philosophical background. It tries to illustrate what has been repeatedly taught by the wise, that all life is one, and the animal and human worlds are more closely connected than arrogant man would care to acknowledge; and again, just as life on earth is fleeting, so worldly relationships also are of no permanent value. "Life is as momentary as a drop of water on a red-hot iron . . . and the meeting of father, mother, son, brother, wife and other relations is like a herd of animals collected together in order to drink water at a trough, or like floating wood in a river brought together by the current."[1] Instead of treating such stories with intellectual scorn born of a rational mind, to the writer of this article at least it seems but right and proper that the birth of a

[1] *Adhyātma Rāmāyaṇa*, II. iv. 20, 23.

woman of such high spiritual attainments as Lalla should be heralded by a picture of the deep and abiding values of life, even if they be in the form of a legend.

Tradition says that Lalla and her husband never lived together as man and wife. The husband of her former life, and now her father-in-law, had married, and owing to the harsh treatment of this wife and new mistress of the house, her life became extremely difficult and unpleasant. Lalla, however, was a model of patience and submission and behaved with a meekness that was in keeping with her position as daughter-in-law of the family. Even now Kashmiri grandmothers are never tired of repeating stories and anecdotes which show how Lalla bore her lot with a quiet resignation that never stooped to complain.

It is not quite known when her search for God began. But we imagine that it must have been an inborn tendency, and any leanings that she may have had towards marriage and home life must have been nipped in the bud at an early age by the indifference of her husband and the unkind behaviour of the step-mother-in-law. On one occasion when it came to the notice of the father-in-law that Lalla was given insufficient food—the rice in the plate being simply a thin covering over a round stone —he tried to intervene, but it only served to increase the wrath of her step-mother-in-law.

It is said that she lived in the house for twelve years. If she was married at the age of twelve years, then she must have still been very young when, due to her own leanings towards religion and to the harsh treatment of her in-laws, she left home, and became a disciple of a well-known Śaiva saint called Sed Bāyu. According to some sources this man appears to be the same as Sed or Siddha Śrī Kanṭha who was the family priest and was known to her from her previous life. He lived at the village of Pampur and is believed to have been a direct descendant in the line of disciples from Vasugupta, the founder of modern Śaivism in Kashmir. Lalla is said to have excelled her *guru* and often to have beaten him in retort and argument; but the result of his teaching was that she became a Śaiva *yoginī* (mendicant devotee) and, like Gārgī, the famous *brahmavādinī* (knower of Brahman) of ancient Vedic times, wandered about the country in a semi-nude condition. She did not conform to the conventional standard of dress. She was well aware of the ridicule that was showered on her for that reason, but worldly criticism did not in any way disturb her equanimity of mind. Koul relates an anecdote in this connection: one day when, as usual, the children made fun of her, a cloth-merchant took them to task. Lalla then asked the merchant for some cloth which she divided into two pieces of equal weight. She then left the place with a cloth on each shoulder and, according to the respect or disrespect that she met with on the way, tied knots in one piece or the other. In the evening on her return she went to the cloth merchant again and asked him to weigh the cloth on each shoulder. Of course they still weighed the same, and so she pointed out to him that praise or blame balanced each other, and were to be accepted with the same philosophic calm.

Henceforth she roamed about the country singing and dancing in divine ecstasy, and innumerable tales that are told of her greatness testify to the love that the Kashmiri bears in his heart for her. She is said to have died at an advanced age at Brijbihāra, twenty-five miles south-east of Srinagar, just outside the Juma Masjid, and when she gave up her body her soul "buoyed up like a flame of light in the air and then disappeared" (Koul).

The Lalla Vākyāni are composed in an old form of Kashmiri which as a distinct language is much older than her time. In India, side by side with Sanskrit, the language of the learned, there also existed a language of the common people, and thus Kashmir had its own dialect. The script is a corruption of Devanāgarī script, and the pronunciation of the Sanskrit alphabet has acquired a peculiarity suggestive of alien influences. Kashmiri literature is very limited and the sayings of Lalla not only hold a very important place in it, but they could also be favourably compared with the devotional and philosophical literature of any other language.

Lalla starts her teachings by relating her own spiritual experience. She says:

> Passionate, with longing in my eyes,
> Searching wide, and seeking nights and days,
> Lo! I beheld the Truthful One, the Wise,
> Here in mine own house to fill my gaze.

Lalla's sayings are deeply mystical at times, and being a

yoginī, terms of the Yoga system are in constant use. She says that the Supreme is not reached by Yogic discipline alone, but by its practice the seeker comes to know that the universe is unreal. He then tries to go beyond it. By dint of practice the perception of the visible world is lost, as it were, and the human soul becomes one with the Absolute. In this condition consciousness of limited individuality is absorbed into the unlimited pure consciousness of the Absolute, and this state she describes thus:

There nor even Śiva reigns supreme,
Nor his wedded Energy hath sway.
Only is the Somewhat, like a dream,
There pursuing an elusive way.

Recognizing the external world to be nothing but an illusion she justifies her nakedness in the following verse:

Dance then, Lalla, clothed but by the air:
Sing then, Lalla, clad but in the sky.
Air and sky—what garment is more fair?
"Cloth", saith Custom—Doth that sanctify?

Lalla thinks that though the need of the body should be satisfied, the mind should be filled with nothing but the Self. She compares desire to a money-lender, and says that no bond-slave of desire can escape Yama (death). Happy is the contented soul to whom desire refuses to give a loan:

Only is he blessed and at peace,
False hopes abandoned, who ascends
Where the hard loans of desire cease,
Where no debt, nor any one that lends.

Like a true philosopher she disdains the supernatural powers which come as a temptation to the seeker in his quest for God. She asks:

Why cool the flames, Yogi? Stay the stream?
Why dost walk feet upward in the sky?
Why milk a bullock? Why magic dream?
Why these base feats of the juggler try?

The following lines describing the all-pervasiveness of Brahman seem closely akin to the Upanishads:

Thou art the heavens, and Thou the earth:
Thou alone art day and night and air:
Thou Thyself art all things that have birth,
Even the offerings of flowers fair.

Her philosophy of Advaita (Monism) does not, however, prevent her from believing in the doctrine of grace, nor was she one who followed the path of Knowledge without deep devotion to the Divine. With obvious emotion she sings:

Striving and struggling, for the door was tight
Bolted and barred, till she longed the more
Him to behold that was beyond her sight,
Yet she could not but gaze at the door.

Though human beings must strive to the utmost, yet it is ultimately by the grace of God that He can be known. She continues:

Yet as she stood gazing at the door,
Contemplating Him with all her soul,
Lo! He opened it for ever more:
There, within herself she saw Him whole.
Lalla burnt the foulness from her soul,
Famed abroad a prophetess was she:
Freed from desire and her heart made whole,
Knelt she, just there, on her bended knee.

She dwells eloquently on the identity of the Cosmic Soul with the individual soul, and in poetic language sings:

Self of my Self, for Thou art but I,
Self of my Self, for I am but Thou,
Twain of us in one shall never die,
What do they matter—the why and how?

In some of her best known sayings she emphasizes the impermanence of material objects, such as:

Just for a moment a flower grows,
Bright and brilliant on a green-clad tree:
Just for a moment a cold wind blows
Through the bare thorns of a thicket free.

Duty for duty's sake performed without hope of reward and as an offering to God is the famous doctrine of the *Gītā*. Lalla teaches the same truth in her songs:

Yet if I toil with no thought of self,
All my works before the Self I lay:
Setting faith and duty before self
Well for me shall be the onward way.

To labour is to pray, but the labour must be dedicated to the Supreme:

Whatsoever thing of toil I did,
Whatsoever thing of thought I said,
That was worship in my body hid,
That was worship hid in my head.

In the homely metaphor of a cotton-pod Lalla describes the difficulties of a life dedicated to the finding of God. It is at first roughly treated by the cleaner and carder, next spun into thread, then hung up on the warp of a weaver's loom. When it is made into cloth, it is beaten by the washerman on the stone to whiten it, and finally cut by the tailor to be made into a garment. The explanation of each metaphor is uncertain but the various stages towards the attainment of knowledge are indicated.

First, I, Lalla, as a cotton-bloom,
Blithely set forth on the path of life.
Next came the knocks of the cleanser's room,
And the hard blows of the carder's wife.

Gossamer from me a woman spun,
Twisting me about upon her wheel.
Then on a loom was I left undone,
While the kicks of the weaver did I feel.

Cloth now become, on the washing stone,
Washermen dashed me to their content.
Whitened me with earth and skin and bone
Cleaned they with soaps to my wonderment.

Tailors then their scissors worked on me:
Cut me and finished me, piece by piece.
Garment at last, as a soul set free
Found I the Self and obtained Release.

Hard is the way of the soul on earth,
Ere it may reach to the journey's end.
Hard is the path of life in each birth,
Ere thou canst take the hand of the Friend.

The cry of the soul for release from the round of birth and death is depicted in the following poem and will find an echo in the hearts of the pious.

Loose the sugar load upon my back:
Sling and knot do my poor shoulder gall:
Crooked hath my day's work gone, alack.
How can I bear with it, ere I fall?

Seeking my teacher, I heard Him tell
Truths that like a blister hurt my heart—
Pain of lost illusion loved so well.
How can I bear with it, ere we part?

Flocks of my consciousness all are lost,
Gone from the shepherd beyond recall,
Ere the mountain of Release be crossed;
How can I bear with, ere I fall?

Searching and seeking from my inner soul
Came I to the moon of knowledge bright:
Searching and seeking, I learnt the whole
Truth that like shall with like unite.

O Nārān,[1] the All is only Thou.
Only Thee, Nārān, in all I see.
O Nārān, the sports Thou showest now
Are but clear illusions unto me.

Learning myself to be Self Supreme,
I have learnt, Nārān, why Thou dost part:
I have solved the Riddle of the Dream,
Where we twain do as one Self consort.

Here the burden of worldly illusions and pleasures has been compared to a load of sugar-candy, and the knot of the porter's sling that supports it has become loose and galls her. The world is a dream, and creation but the sport of God.

Whatever may be the path we follow, and whatever the creed we subscribe to, in the ultimate analysis the human heart undergoes the same travail and suffering before it finds itself established in God-consciousness. The lack of strength and

[1] The word "Nārān" is from "Nārāyaṇa", another name for the Supreme.

faith which makes the end in view seem mountain high is the despair of all seekers. The joy of realization that Lalla describes at the end of the song is denied to most of us. But we experience poignantly "the pain of lost illusion loved so well", and the wounds of "truths that like blisters hurt my heart" are very often all that we know of this Great Way: and to all such people whose footsteps are faltering, whose vision is blurred, to whom the goal is far off, the words of Lalla come as a message of great hope. Her appeal was not to the learned of her land. In popular verse she conveyed her religion to the masses. In recent times Sir R. C. Temple was led to a study not only of Śaivism but of the whole structure of Indian philosophical thought through his interest in the songs of Lalla. His book contains a long dedication to Lalla which begins with the following verse:

Lalla, though nought but a devotee,
Daughter in truth of thy race and time,
Thine is a song that enslaveth me,
Son of an alien kin and clime.

This eloquent tribute is sufficient proof of the adage that it is the heart that speaks to the heart. Lalla's words are not limited by time and country. They will be valued and cherished wherever they are known, for the appeal of her song is as fresh and new today as it was when originally sung six hundred years ago.

CHAPTER VII

MIRA BAI

THE name of Mīrā Bāī is a household word in Northern India. In her we have a poetess who is universally admitted to have been among the greatest saints of India. Details about her life history are shrouded in mystery. Historians differ with regard to the date of her birth, marriage, death and even about the name of her husband. But all agree that she was a princess who belonged to the Rathors of Mertā. Recently, however, some scholars have tried to string together the various accounts and have woven them into a biographical garland.

According to this account Mīrā was born in A.D. 1504 at Chaukari village in Mertā District of Rājasthān. Her father, Ratan Siṅgh, was the second son of Rao Dudāji, a descendant of Rao Jodhaji Rathor, the founder of Jodhpur. Mīrā's mother died when she was ten years old. She then came to live with her grandfather at Mertā. Dudāji died in 1515 and his eldest son Vikram Deo, who succeeded him, arranged his niece Mīrā's marriage with Prince Bhoj Rāj, the eldest son of Rānā Saṅga of Chittor. This marriage raised Mīrā to a very high social position because the ruler of Chittor was then considered to be the leader of the Hindu princes. But luck did not favour Princess Mīrā. By A.D. 1527 she had lost her father, her husband and her father-in-law as well.

Any other princess in her place would have spent the rest of her life plunged in sorrow, or would have become *sati* as was customary in those days, to forestall further misfortunes. But Mīrā, who had dedicated her life to the Universal Lord, accepted these bereavements as a matter of course. It is said that she died in 1550 at Dwārakā in Saurāshṭra.

Before we proceed to examine the spiritual and religious experiences of our saint, it is better to study the political, social and religious conditions of her time, which helped to mould her spiritual life.

At the time Mīrā was born there was widespread political turmoil in India. The Afghan Empire had miserably broken and the Muslim chiefs were fighting amongst themselves to carve petty kingdoms from the ruins of their empire. The Rajputs, too, were once more trying to establish their supremacy in the north. But unfortunately they were disunited, and internecine wars were a common feature among them. It was also at this time that Baber the Moghul began his invasions to lay the foundation of his empire. All love and respect for human life had disappeared. Bloody conflicts, fought for political aggrandizement amongst her own Rajputs, and between the Rajputs and the neighbouring Muslim chiefs, and frequent deaths amongst her relatives, made young Mīrā ponder. She saw the world even at that young age from a human angle. She could not understand of what avail was all this hatred; why duty, peace and love were sacrificed for personal ambitions and human life was made so cheap. She felt she was a stranger amongst her own people and looked round for a loving and peaceful shelter. This shelter she found in the fold of the Vaishṇava cult.

During the first part of the Afghan rule, the disabilities imposed on the Hindus, and the humiliations to which they were subjected, narrowed their outlook. To preserve their culture and religion they assimilated many false beliefs and customs foreign to their original religious and social beliefs. There was a great stagnation in their spiritual and social life. But all the disabilities and humiliations imposed by a harsh foreign rule had not been able to undermine the spiritual vigour of the Hindus. The Hindu genius though stunted and dwarfed got greater impetus to assert itself. Great reformers and saints like Rāmānanda, Chaitanya, Vallabhāchārya, Kabīr, Nānak and many others flourished to remind the Hindus that their religion and culture had not become sterile. They taught to the people the oneness of God, and that He, as merciful Protector and compassionate but omnipotent Master, incarnated from time to time to destroy the evil-doers and to protect the righteous. Union with God could be attained by love and devotion. These reformers also taught the Hindus that love and respect for all human life irrespective of caste and creed was the first step towards achievement of union with God. This feature of Vaishṇava teaching inculcated in the Hindus a love for the Muslims as well as for their own downtrodden brethren, the Untouchables, and henceforward they tried to create friendship with both.

In these Vaishṇava teachings Mīrā Bāī found what her heart desired. She became enamoured of God who was all love and mercy, and began to worship Him in His Kṛishṇa incarnation. Kṛishṇa has many names and she loved Him as Giridhara Nagar. Her love for the Universal Lord was so great that she spent all the time singing His praises and worshipping Him. When her mother advised her to lead a normal worldly life and learn the etiquette of a royal household, Mīrā replied:

O mother, Giridhara Gopāla married me in a dream. I wore a red and yellow veil, and henna was beautifully applied to my hands. My love for this (divine) Cowherd, who played the flute on the banks of the river Yamunā, is from my very childhood. This love can never be given up. It is eternal.

After her marriage with Prince Bhoj Rāj, Mīrā's love for the Lord, instead of decreasing, increased. She spent most of her time in prayer. She gave interviews to saints and sādhus, and held religious discourses with them. This made her father-in-law and other relatives very angry. She was ordered to abandon her ways and live according to the conventions of the royal household. But Mīrā paid no heed. Thereupon the Rānā imposed restrictions on her movements and she was warned to be careful. This is how Mīrā describes it: "All the dear ones of this household are creating trouble over my association with holy men and are causing great hindrance to my worship. From childhood Mīrā made Giridhara Nagar her friend; this attachment shall never be broken but shall flourish."

When Mīrā became a widow her father-in-law, Rānā Saṅga, thought it was an opportunity to be finished with Mīrā. So he sent her word to become a *sati*. But our saint was so convinced of the integrity and omnipresence of the Universal Soul to whom she was wedded that she replied as follows:

Mīrā is dyed in Hari's colour (God's love), and has set aside all (other) colours (loves). I will sing of Giridhara, and will not become *sati* (because) my heart is enamoured of Hari. The relation of eldest daughter-in-law exists no more, Rānā. Now I am a subject, sire, and you are the king.

On the death of her father-in-law, Rānā Saṅga, Prince Ratan Siṅgh became the Rānā. But he too expired soon after and Prince Vikramāditya became the ruler of Chittor. He commanded Mīrā to refrain from meeting the holy men and to give up dancing and singing before the image of Kṛishṇa. Mīrā now found it difficult to worship in the palace, so strict were the restrictions. She went, therefore, to the public temple and carried on her devotions there. In her spiritual ecstasy she would forget her own self and would feel one with the Lord. In this state she would sing and dance before the image of God. Often she would go into *samādhi* (superconsciousness). People of Mewār began to respect this saintly princess and her fame spread far and wide. Scholars and saints visited her and paid homage to her. But this aroused the anger of the Rānā, his brother princes and his relatives, who could not comprehend the meaning of anything beyond bloody conflicts and their trials, or the comforts of a short-lived peace. So the Rānā subjected Mīrā to many hardships. She was confined to her quarters and was made to sleep on a bed of nails. She was given a deadly snake, hidden in a basket, as a gift. Poison was administered to her. There was no torture to which our young saint was not subjected. But those whom God protects, none can harm. All those men and women who were deputed by the Rānā to inflict hardships on her were won over and converted by her, so great was her spiritual power. Mīrā wrote a number of poems about the ill-treatment she received at the hands of the Rānā. Here is one: "Mīrā is happy in the worship of the Lord; Rānā made (her) a present of a basket, containing a serpent; Mīrā performed her ablutions and, opening it, found the Lord Himself. Rānā sent a cup of poison; after her ablutions Mīrā drank the contents (which) the Lord turned into nectar. Rānā sent a bed of nails for Mīrā to sleep on; in the evening when Mīrā slept on it, it became a bed of flowers. Mīrā's Lord averts all her troubles and is ever a beneficent protector. Mīrā roams about happy in her ecstatic devotions. She is a sacrifice to the Lord."

God protected Mīrā and she passed through all tribulations. But Mīrā was not happy. She could not have the calmness and the peace which were essential for her devotional life. She was also tired of long years of torture. So she decided to leave Chittor and go to Mertā, her uncle's kingdom. Before she left, she firmly and frankly told the people of the Rānā's household:

If the Rānā is angry, what harm can he do to me? I shall continue to sing of the attributes of Govinda (God), friend. If the

Rānā is angry, his own kingdom will give me shelter, but if God is angry, then where can I go, friend? I care not to follow worldly conventions, and shall show the banner of independence, friend. I shall row the ship of God's name and will cross the illusory world, friend. Mīrā has taken refuge with the powerful Giridhara and will cling to His lotus-feet, friend.

After this Mīrā left for Mertā. Her uncle provided her with all the facilities for leading a devotional life. But the political misfortune of her uncle compelled her to leave Rajputana. She went on a pilgrimage, visiting Vṛindāvana, Mathurā and other sacred places. Last of all she went to Dwārakā in Saurāshṭra to settle down for good. She spent most of her remaining life in the temple of Kṛishṇa and died there, at the feet of the Master.

Like a true Vaishṇava devotee Mīrā Bāī worshipped God whole-heartedly and with absolute purity of spirit. She considered herself a *gopī* of Vṛindāvana, mad for Kṛishṇa. She sought no worldly comforts and happiness. Her only object in life was to please her Beloved (God), to whom she had surrendered her body, mind and soul. Her soul was ever yearning to meet the Lord, that is, to attain union with Him. Her verse consequently is full of songs praising the Beloved and describing her own pain and sorrow brought on by separation from Him. Here we give a few examples:

O, great Lord, Sire, do not abandon me. I am a powerless woman, O Master of the world; You alone are the crown of my life. I am bereft of all qualities, O Master of the world, and You are the omnipotent Lord. Having (once) become yours, to whom else can I go? You are the light of my heart. Says Mīrā, I have none else, O Lord; this once at least protect me.

And:

How can I live without Hari, O mother? I am like worm-eaten wood, and have gone mad. Medicines and herbs do not work on me, because my ailment is (divine) madness (for the Beloved).

And again:

For Your (love) I have abandoned all happiness: why do You (unnecessarily) let me yearn (for You)? The fire of the pain of separation is burning in my heart; come and extinguish it. It will not be possible (for You) now to forsake me, (so) be pleased and send for me, Lord.

Sire, Mīrā has been (Your) slave in all her lives. Let her be merged in Yourself.

At last Mīrā's yearning to meet the Beloved ceased, for her separation from Him came to an end and she achieved that bliss and peace which the devotee gets on attaining union with the Beloved. Thenceforward she sang in a different tune, as in the following instance:

All-pervading One, I am dyed in Your colour. When other women's sweethearts live in foreign lands, they write letter after letter. But my Beloved lives in my heart, so I sing (happily) day and night.

When Mīrā had attained union and her reputation and fame had spread all over the country, then her family members and other relatives came and surrounded her. She tells of this in her own words:

I am true to my Lord. Why should I feel abashed now since I even danced (for the Beloved) in public? I lost all appetite in the day, and rest and sleep at night. Now the arrow (of love) has transpierced me and come out (the other side), and I have begun singing of knowledge divine: (so) family and relatives have all come and are sitting (round me) like bees sipping honey. Mīrā, slave of Giridhara, is no more a laughing-stock in the world.

Mīrā wrote in Mārwārī Hindī, her mother tongue, but some of her poetry is found laden with Gujaratī and Panjābī words. Composed in a simple, unpretentious style, it is full of vivacity and feeling. The facility with which she expresses her pious thought and her divine love gives it an additional beauty. Who could express attachment to the divine Lord with greater facility than Mīrā?

O, Hari (God), You are the refuge of my life and soul. Besides You, there is no shelter for me in the three worlds. I have searched the whole world; none else but You alone pleases me. Says Mīrā, I am Your slave; forget me not, I beseech You.

Mīrā was a born poetess and she used her poetic talents to express in a beautiful style her intense and deep love of God. Below is an exquisite example in soul-stirring words of the suffering of Mīrā's soul, separated from the Universal Soul.

O Friend, I am mad with love; none can know my anguish. Only he who has been wounded or he who dealt the blow understands the wounded. A jeweller alone can know the secret anguish of (another) jeweller, or else he who possesses the jewellery. My bed is laid on the guillotine, how can I possibly sleep? The bed of my Beloved is in heaven, what chance have I of meeting (Him)? Smitten with pain, from forest to forest I roam. No physician have I found. Mīrā's pain will vanish only when the Beloved (God) Himself becomes the physician.

Mīrā tells us about the aim of her life in this world, in beautiful and impressive language:

Mine is Giridhara Gopāla, none else. He, on whose head is the crown of peacock feathers, He is my Lord. Father, mother, brother and kin, none are mine. I have flung aside the pride of family; what (harm) can anyone do to me? I have lost all worldly shame by keeping the company of saints. I have torn my veil of many hues and covered myself with a woollen sheet (coarse clothes). Pearls and corals I have cast aside to put on a garland of forest flowers. With my tears I have watered the creeper of Love. Now that the creeper has spread out well, its fruits shall be joy itself. I have churned the milk with great devotion, and butter I have collected: he who wants may have the rest. I was born for devotion's sake, but the sight of the world made me captive. Says Mīrā the maid-servant, O Lord Giridhara, save me now.

The Giridhara Gopāla of Mīrā is the eternal handsome Dancer who showers happiness on the righteous and protects His devotees. She describes Him in simple but forceful words:

Dwell in my eyes, O Son of Nanda; enchanting is Your figure, dusky Your complexion, large are Your eyes. So beautiful looks the flute on Your nectar-like lips; on Your chest is the garland of *vaijanti* (forest weeds). The belt of little bells round Your waist and the trinkets on Your ankles look charming and tinkle sweetly. The Lord of Mīrā bestows happiness on the saints and protects His devotees.

Mīrā's literary work consists of a few hundred poems, set in various *rāgas*. Besides these she is said to have written commentaries on *Gītā-Govinda* and *Rāg-Govind*, but neither of them is traceable.

No poetess enjoys a greater reputation than Mīrā. Her poems have gained a unique popularity and are sung by rich and poor alike, even to this day.

Such was Mīrā, the princess who, renouncing all the wealth and happiness of this world, spent her life singing the attributes of the divine Beloved. She was a great woman saint of India and will ever be remembered.

CHAPTER VIII

MAHARASHTRA WOMEN SAINTS

IN the *Navanīta*, an anthology of Marāṭhī poetry, only three of the women saints of Mahārāshṭra are mentioned: Janābāī, Rājāī, and Goṇāī. Janābāī is famous because of her association with the great saint Nāmadev whose disciple she was. All these saints' lives are given in great detail in the *Bhakta-Vijaya* of Mahīpati, but modern readers are rather sceptical of their historical accuracy.

Janābāī had a great reputation as a saint of Paṇḍharpur, and the sacred God Viṭṭhal was her object of devotion. Janābāī was born in a village called Gaṅgākheḍa situated on the banks of the river Godavari. Her father, of the name of Dāmāji, was a great devotee of Viṭṭhal. He was a Śūdra by caste, but had very great devotion to God and went every year to Paṇḍharpur on a pilgrimage. The name of Janābāī's mother was Karuṇḍ. Janābāī was born of these parents, and when she was a child of about five or six years of age her father took her to the father of Nāmadev and she worked as housemaid in Nāmadev's father's house all her life. That is why she called herself "Dāsī Janī", that is, servant Janī. Dāmāsheṭi, the father of Nāmadev, was a tailor by caste and he also was a great devotee of Śrī Viṭṭhal of Paṇḍharpur and used to take Janābāī with him on his annual pilgrimage. Many miracles are attributed to Janābāī. It is very strange that though illiterate she was able to compose so many verses about God Viṭṭhal. "God cares only for your inmost feeling," she says in a verse, "and He is prepared to leave heaven and meet you when He is so attracted by single-minded devotion. He came to Puṇḍalik and stood before him. Puṇḍalik threw a brick for Him to sit upon, but He would not sit. He is the Ocean of all happiness. To those on whom He bestows His grace, the whole world is kind. They do not look for any return. God Himself suffers all the miseries which are inflicted upon such a person and is never absent from such a man whom He protects on all occasions of difficulty and distress. He does not care for caste. Chokhamela was an outcaste, but had great devotion in his heart and so God became his servant and used to dine with him. Janī is inclined to laugh, because Chokhamela made even God an outcaste like himself." She is supposed to have written about three hundred verses; but Sri Ajgaonkar thinks that only twenty-five of these are genuinely hers. She was not a mere blind devotee but understood the relation of the individual soul and the universal Soul, and the Māyā of the universe.

Rājāī and Goṇāī are not mentioned as saints in Sri Ajgaonkar's book, but a few of their verses are to be seen in the *Navanīta*.

Rājāī was the wife of Nāmadev and Goṇāī was his mother. These two were saints because of their association with Nāmadev, who had no interest in life except God. He was a great devotee of God Viṭṭhal of Paṇḍharpur. There are stray blank verses composed by Rājāī and Goṇāī which are extant. As is only natural, they did their best to prevent Nāmadev as much as they could from neglecting all family affairs as he did. It appears that Nāmadev had travelled all over India and had even been to the Panjab. In his early life he was very wild, but later on he reformed himself and became a saint because of close association with Jñāneśwar monks who came to the Paṇḍharpur temple.

Jñāneśwar is the first great saint with whom the series of successive saints in Mahārāshṭra began. He wrote in A.D. 1290 his *Jñāneśwarī* which is a commentary on the *Bhagavad-Gītā*. Even before *Jñāneśwarī* there was a great deal of Mahānubhāva literature in Marāṭhī. The Mahānubhāva sect was a secret one and it did not flourish well for several reasons.

The first Marāṭhī woman saint, according to Ajgaonkar, is Mahadāisā *alias* Mahadambā, and she lived some time about A.D. 1213. She was of the Mahānubhāva sect and was a disciple of Chakradhara, its founder, who was reputed to have great occult powers. The poetry of Mahadāisā is difficult to understand for those who know current Marāṭhī only, but it has been annotated.

The next saint after her is Muktābāī, the sister of Jñāneśwar. She was a very learned woman and wrote a considerable number of poems. Nivṛitti, Jñānadev, Sopān and Muktābāī were great Marāṭhī saints. Muktābāī was the youngest sister of Jñāneśwar, and she too became a great saint. She was fully conversant with Vedānta and her writings are full of Vedāntic discussions. It appears that she had studied the Yogic cult, and her discipleship, like that of Jñāneśwar, is traced from Machendranāth, Gorakshanāth, Gaihinanāth and Nivṛitti, her eldest brother.

The life of these three brothers and of Muktābāī, though very short, was nevertheless very eventful. At a place called Āpegāon, near Paiṭhaṇ, lived one Tryambakpant, who was in his youth a soldier of repute but later became a devotee of the great cult of Saint Gorakshanāth. Tryambakpant had a son called Govinda, whose wife Nirābāī gave birth to a son of the name of Viṭṭhal. From childhood Viṭṭhal was inclined to a life of austerities, devotion and penance, and while on a pilgrimage he went to Āḷandī, near Poona. There he was married to Rukmiṇī, the daughter of a gentleman of the name of Sidhopant. Even after his marriage he was always immersed in meditation, and Rukmiṇī naturally felt deeply concerned as to how he could be made to take an interest in the normal life of a householder. One day Viṭṭhalpant suddenly left Āḷandī and went to Kāśi (Banāras) and approached the great saint, Rāmānanda. He told him that he was single and had neither wife nor children. Rāmānanda therefore initiated him into *sannyāsa* (the life of renunciation) and gave him the new name of Chaitanyāśrama. In course of time Rukmiṇī came to know about this from pilgrims, but she continued to live in hope and prayer. Twelve or thirteen years later, while on a pilgrimage, Rāmānanda himself went to Āḷandī and there he met Rukmiṇī in the temple and heard about her husband's renunciation. Rāmānanda was deeply grieved: when he returned to Banāras he exhorted Chaitanyā to go back to his wife and live the life of a householder because he had no right to be initiated into *sannyāsa* when he had a wife, and he had secured his initiation by telling a falsehood. So Chaitanyāśrama returned to Āḷandī. But the pharisaical Brahmins of Āḷandī could not tolerate this return to household life of one who had once accepted *sannyāsa*, and Viṭṭhal, his wife and family, which now consisted of his three sons, Nivṛitti, Jñānadev, Sopān and a daughter Muktābāī, were all subjected to a complete social boycott. As desired by the priests and Brahmins, Viṭṭhal and his wife left their children in Āḷandī and went to Prayāg (Allahabad) and drowned themselves in the holy confluence of the Yamunā and the Gaṅgā. According to the Brahmins that was the only expiation of the great sin which Viṭṭhalpant had committed. So Nivṛitti, Jñānadev, Sopān and Muktābāī were left orphans, friendless in the world, and complete social outcasts. Nivṛitti was ten, Jñānadev eight, Sopān six and Muktābāī four years of age. In course of time, because of the extreme learning, brilliance and miraculous powers of Jñānadev, the Brahmins were reconciled and allowed these children to live at Āḷandī, but still they were outside the pale of Brāhmiṇism and nobody would associate with or marry them. They all went therefore to Newase in the Ahmednagar district. Nivṛitti was supposed to have received initiation into the mysteries of the Nāth Panth from Gaihinanāth. He in turn initiated Jñānadev. Sopān and Muktābāī attained sainthood because of their constant association with Jñānadev. Muktābāī composed a very large number of verses in A.D. 1296 at the age of twenty-one. Jñānadev entered into a state of God-absorption and buried himself alive, and to this day people go on pilgrimage to Āḷandī to this place of *samādhi*.

Muktābāī was, it appears, well versed in the Vedānta philosophy as her verses bear witness. "He alone is a saint," she says, "who is possessed of compassion (*dayā*) and forgiveness (*kshamā*) and in whose heart neither greed nor egoism finds a place. These are people who are truly renouncers. They alone can be happy in this and the next world." She taught: "To one whose heart has become pure, God is not far away." She says in another verse: "He is not to be found in the market and bought for money. It is a matter of right life. Who can teach one to realize God? One must find God for oneself."

Muktābāī attained final *samādhi* at Managāon, near Verūla, in A.D. 1297.

The next saint mentioned by Sri Ajgaonkar is Janī, who has already been mentioned above as Janābāī, the great devotee of Viṭṭhal.

The next saint after her is Soyarābāī. She was a Mahar, an Untouchable by caste. Her husband was a famous saint and his name was Chokhamela. She was possessed of great devotion. Following her husband she became a saint herself. She has left considerable literature in the way of blank verses of her own. Chokhamela was a well-known Untouchable saint who is deeply revered even today. Although Soyarābāī wrote a large number of verses, only about sixty-two are now known. "The body only can be impure or polluted," she says, "but the soul is ever clean, pure knowledge. The body is born unclean and so how can anybody claim to be pure in body? It (the body) is full of pollution. But the pollution of the body remains in the body. The soul is untouched by it. Thus says (Mahari) the Mahar wife of Chokhamela."

She used to go to Paṇḍharpur regularly on an annual pilgrimage. She and her husband were persecuted, but they never lost their faith or peace of mind and ultimately they triumphed over the persecution of the orthodox Brahmins. Chokhamela's place of *samādhi* is being reconstructed at Maṅgalveḍā.

The next woman saint is Nirmalā, who was the younger sister of Chokhamela. It is natural that both Soyarā and Nirmalā should acquire great reputation as saints because of their connection with Chokhamela. The fact that a Mahar could be a saint even then speaks volumes for the toleration in those days. As stated above, Chokhamela was born at Maṅgalveḍā, near Saṅgli, where his *samādhi* still exists.

The next woman saint was Kānhopātrā. She was born about A.D. 1470, and her mother was a dancing-girl. She was so beautiful that people wanted her to become the mistress of the Moghul emperor of those days, but she refused and instead, when helpless, she went to Paṇḍharpur. She wanted to know whether God Viṭhobā, who was supposed to be a kind God, would accept her as a devotee. She was told that of course Viṭhobā would accept her because He was very kind and cared for the fallen, He was the God of the people—God of the common man, God of the lowliest men. His temple is now open to all sects including the so-called Untouchables. So Kānhopātrā left Maṅgalveḍā, her birthplace, for Paṇḍharpur, and went to the Viṭhobā temple. It is said that the messengers of the emperor came there to take her away to be his mistress. She said she would first go to the temple; she went in and, embracing God Viṭhoba's image, died at His feet.

Premābāī was a widow. She is more famous as a poet than as a saint. She has, however, written much devotional poetry. Little is known about her personal life, but some of her verses survive.

The next saint was Bahiṇābāī who was born in the third decade of the seventeenth century and died in A.D. 1700.[1]

After Bahiṇābāī, who has left considerable literature behind, we have Veṇābāī who was the disciple of Rāmadās, the great saint of the seventeenth century. Veṇābāī is also known as Veṇāswāmī Rāmadāsī. She was so devoted to Rāmadās that

[1] See next chapter for details.

she underwent a great deal of persecution both in her husband's family and in her parents' for having to desert them in order to follow Rāmadās. The probable year of her birth is A.D. 1620. The Rāmadāsī research scholar, Sri Sankar Shikrishna Deo, has mentioned her, and there is no doubt that she was utterly devoted to Rāmadās who was a great saint himself. He wrote the *Dāsabodh* and other sacred literature.

After Veṇābāī, there was another woman saint, Baiyābāī *alias* Bayābāī Rāmadāsī. She lived for eighty-four years, and had a great reputation. She had a disciple called Giridhar. She knew Urdu as well as Marāṭhī, and has written a good deal of Urdu poetry in praise of God. No details of her personal life are available.

CHAPTER IX

BAHINABAI

OVER three centuries back, in A.D. 1628, the curtain of time opens to reveal the life-story of Bahiṇābāī, in the town of Devagāon, a place near Verūla, the site of the famous Ellora Caves. It is known as the City of gods. The river Śiva flows near by, and the place is unsurpassed by any other holy bathing-place. It was significantly called Laksha-tīrtha. Sage Agastya, the leader of the ancient Āryas, had blessed the place to the effect that whoever might bathe therein and perform austerities would realize his desires.

The scribe of the town was a Brahmin named Aooji Kulkarṇī. He was simple and highly fortunate. His wife Jānakībāī nobly performed her marital duties. This couple was childless. They performed austerities at the Laksha-tīrtha, wishing to be blessed with a child.

In a thrice-repeated dream, Aooji saw a holy Brahmin blessing him with a daughter and two sons. Within a year, in A.D. 1628, a girl was born to them. They named her Bahiṇā.

According to the Hindu custom, an adept Brahmin astrologer named Viśweśwar prepared the horoscope of the girl, foretelling her greatness.

Bahiṇā was betrothed at the age of four to Gaṅgādhar Pāṭhak, a relative of the Kulkarṇī family, who lived in Śivpur. He was then thirty years old.

Four years passed peacefully, but her parents were distressed by poverty and domestic troubles caused by a quarrel between Aooji and his relatives over the family property. Gaṅgādhar came to their aid. He studied the situation and found that there was no other way than to leave the place. At dead of night the family left Devagāon. They had to suffer many hardships on their journey and beg as they went along. The path of righteousness is never smooth. On their way the family saw many holy places and rivers. Whenever she visited such places, Bahiṇā felt keen attachment for them. They spent five days and nights in Paṇḍharpur, the Banāras of Mahārāshṭra. Bahiṇā was delighted at the sight of the image of Pāṇḍuraṅga. Thence they reached the Mahādeo forest, a place sanctified by the presence of God Śankara. Being Brahmins by caste they accepted only uncooked food grain while begging, and hence they were compelled to shift and settle in Rahimatpur. Fortunately Gaṅgādhar was appointed to officiate as a priest of the town in the absence of the permanent one.

Bahiṇā was now eleven, but she felt a strong desire to be associated with the saints and to listen to the stories of the gods. While the girls of the neighbourhood used to come to play with her, Bahiṇā was thinking of God. The unfulfilled desire of her previous births was manifest in the events of her daily life: passion for God was her only play.

On the return of the permanent priest from Banāras, Gaṅgādhar was relieved and he had no other means of livelihood. The family then moved to Kolhāpur, an exceedingly holy place. The real epic of Bahiṇā's life story begins here.

In Kolhāpur there lived a Brahmin, Bahirāmbhaṭ by name. He was well versed in the Vedas and the Śāstras, and was kind enough to offer shelter to the family. In his house they had a chance to listen to his readings from the Purāṇas, and to *Hari-kīrtanas*.[1] In the same city there was one Jairām Swāmī who used to relate stories from the *Bhāgavata Purāṇa*. Listening to him Bahiṇā used to feel a great urge for meditation.

Once during a festival Bahirāmbhaṭ received a jet black cow as a gift. Her horns were gilded, her hoofs were silvered, and she was covered with a yellow silken robe, all these making her a typical gift in those days. A similar jet black calf was born to the cow. Ten days after its birth, Bahirāmbhaṭ was inspired to offer the cow and the calf to Gaṅgādhar. The whole family was happy over this gift. The calf had great attachment for Bahiṇā. It moved with her. It would not accept food or drink from anyone but Bahiṇā. When she went to draw water from the well, the calf would bawl loudly and with its tail erect follow her. Bahiṇā could understand every action of the calf as a child understands the language of its pet. If you have love enough to understand, you can interpret every movement of the animals. Bahiṇā saw in the calf a sort of devotion for holy *kīrtanas*, because whenever she attended them the calf followed her. It would listen intently to the religious services without disturbing the audience. Bahiṇā and others discerned

[1] Singing in praise of Hari (God).

in the calf the soul of a *yoga-bhrashṭa*—of one who had fallen from *yoga* in a previous life.

In Kolhāpur the *kīrtanas* of Jairām Swāmī had become very popular and Bahiṇā never missed them. She with her calf became the talk of the town. Though her husband was a religious mendicant, he was a man of angry disposition. He did not like his wife to become a target of social criticism. Once, being irritated, he rushed home, caught hold of his wife's hair and started beating her. Bahiṇā was greatly distressed. The cow and the calf moaned aloud. Bahiṇā, then a girl of eleven, could do nothing to her husband, a man of thirty-seven. In what duty towards him had she failed? Even her parents were unable to appease him in his rage. They asked him the reason for his brutal behaviour. The jealous husband replied: "What special greatness did she find in Jairām Swāmī? Who cares for *Hari-kīrtana*? I'll give her a beating for the second time if she persists in going there again." Since that time he used to beat her every now and then.

Finally Bahirāmbhaṭ, the head of the household, could bear it no longer: he asked Gaṅgādhar to quit the house that very moment. Matters went smoothly after that. A fortnight passed peacefully. All of a sudden the calf became very ill. Everybody lost hope of its recovery. No pains were spared to save it. Its lips were quivering. Bahiṇā, with her intense love for the calf, could hear its parting words. To her child-mind they seemed to utter a last prayer to the Almighty. The next day the calf died peacefully. This incident was taken to heart by Bahiṇā, who remained unconscious for three days, but on the fourth day she had a vision. A Brahmin appeared to her and said, "Bahiṇā, awake! Begin to think! Let your mind awake!"

And awaking she saw that the lamp was burning. It was midnight and her parents, husband and brother were sitting anxiously by her side. In the vision of the Brahmin she saw the reflection of Pāṇḍuraṅga of Paṇḍharpur. Now her memory retained only the images of gods and saints, their stories and verses. She craved to see Tukārām, whose fame as a saint had already spread throughout Mahārāshṭra, the province of the Marāṭhas. She declared Tukārām to be her *guru*, without whose guidance she felt like a fish out of water.

She remembered how he, just to please a Brahmin, threw the manuscript of his verse into the river and how he recovered it intact from the holy waters after thirteen days: how he alone of all the seers, gave to the common people the substance of Vedānta in the Marāṭhī language. The intensity of her thoughts about him made her unconscious, and on the seventeenth day after the calf's death, Tukārām appeared in a vision, comforted her and gave her the *mantra*—"Rāmā-Kṛishṇa-Hari".

Tukārām instructed her in spiritual knowledge. While she was in this condition, Jairām Swāmī visited her. Sitting beside her bed he fell into a trance for a moment. But Bahiṇā clearly heard the voice of Tukārām, who was saying: "I have come to visit Jairām, but I have noted your passion for salvation. Do not stay here any longer; strive for self-knowledge and enlightenment." She now had repeated visions of Tukārām: but to most people she seemed insane. They came in crowds to inquire after her. Some marked her saintly behaviour. Gaṅgādhar was cruel and jealous. He did not like people crowding to see his wife. He did not like it that Tukārām, a Śūdra, should be accepted as *guru* by the wife of a Brahmin, such as he was. He thought that his home life was shaken to its roots by Tukārām. He feared her popularity and the disrespect they showed him in her presence. His manly pride refused to surrender to a woman's glory. It became impossible for him to stay in the house wherein his influence was fast waning.

One day he said very politely to his father-in-law: "My wife, who is your daughter, is now advanced in pregnancy. I have, however, decided to leave her with you and go on a pilgrimage. As she has a passion for God and an undue respect for her *guru* Tukārām, I shall not return and see her face again. Who is going to suffer humiliation at the hands of his wife?"

Suddenly, on the day of his departure from the house, Gaṅgādhar became severely ill. For seven days he was bed-ridden with high fever. He rejected food and medicine. Bahiṇā was at his side day and night. He suffered immense pain. He repented at last, and attributed his sufferings to the insult of God Pāṇḍuraṅga and his devotee Tukārām. While in this condition somebody—maybe his conscience—was saying: "Why do you wish to die? If you wish to live, accept your wife. What wrong has she done to you? She is a real devotee of Hari and you should also join her in spiritual life." All this conversation took place in the presence of Bahiṇā. Afterwards, to her surprise, her husband regained his health. He felt himself reborn, and he determined to give himself fully to the worship of Hari. He told his father-in-law to return to Devagāon, and asked for permission to go to the forest for meditation with his wife.

The whole family of Bahiṇā now decided to go to Dehū, a holy place near Poona, to pay their respects to Tukārām. The cow followed them. After bathing in the sacred river Indrāyaṇī, they all paid their respects to Tukārām, who was performing worship in the temple. Bahiṇā rejoiced to meet the saint whose form she had seen in her vision at Kolhāpur. At the very sight of him, her emotions were transformed. Everything seemed changed. The idea of duality disappeared. Her mind became concentrated, sight fixed, tongue speechless, heart passion-free. She says of this moment, "My pride and the burden of the sorrows of worldly life were removed when I met Tukārām".

At Dehū a Brahmin named Kondāji promised them food, but could not offer them shelter. Māmbāji Swāmī lived next door. He had a spacious house, but when Gaṅgādhar asked for shelter he drove him away with his stick. They then settled in the pilgrim quarters of the temple. Here they passed their time peacefully listening to the *Hari-kīrtanas* of Tukārām.

Māmbāji was hot-tempered, jealous and arrogant. He considered himself a prominent citizen of Dehū. Seeing the crowds of people flocking to the door of Tukārām, who did not boast of mastering any sciences, roused his hatred. He requested Gaṅgādhar and his wife to become his disciples, but when he was told that they had accepted Tukārām as their *guru*, he roared with anger at the top of his voice: "Brahmins as you are, how on earth can you accept Tukārām, a Śūdra, as your *guru*? Can a Śūdra attain Knowledge? You will be ostracized, remember." After that they were on his black list. He took every opportunity to insult and harass them. Bahiṇā said, "God makes us suffer in many ways, just to test us". She was right: everywhere we find that saints have to undergo trials and sufferings. Tukārām was no exception.

Unable to bear the ascendancy of Tukārām, a Śūdra, Māmbāji wrote to one Appaji Swāmī of Poona, how Tukārām, a mere Śūdra, went so far as to hold *kīrtanas* in the temple, and how he received honour even from the Brahmins residing there. He even mentioned the names of Bahiṇā and Gaṅgādhar, and requested him to inflict some punishment upon Tukārām.

Appaji Swāmī was greatly angered to hear such an unheard-of thing—a Śūdra being the *guru* of a Brahmin. He threatened Bahiṇā's family with ostracism. Māmbāji continued in his hostility and ordered Bahiṇā's family to leave the place.

The family had the cow with them, and one day Māmbāji, just to harass them, stole their cow, hid her and tied her securely in the remote part of his house. For three days she was given neither food nor drink. He used to beat the poor beast to express his anger. Bahiṇā became restless and Gaṅgādhar spared no pains in search of her. The cow appeared in Tukārām's dream and prayed for relief. Whenever the cow was beaten, a swelling appeared on Tukārām's body on account of his realization of the oneness of souls.

All of a sudden a fire broke out in Māmbāji's house. People rushed in and put it out. There they found the cow, moaning in distress. They rescued her from the fire. There were marks of beating on her back, and they were astonished to find similar marks on the back of Tukārām. They identified Tukārām with Pāṇḍuraṅga, the all-pervading supreme Spirit.

At this time Bahiṇā gave birth to a daughter. She named her Kāśībāī. She thought that it was the calf reborn to her. To a woman the birth of a child is really an occasion for rejoicing, but Bahiṇā felt habitually depressed. Being born a woman, she thought, she was unable to discard all worldly things and take to spiritual life, for which she had the utmost craving. She was surrounded by worldly relatives and friends who were averse to spiritual endeavour. Her husband, though a Vedāntin, had no real love and devotion for God. Unable to bear such a profane atmosphere, she thought of committing suicide. Her soul had a great longing for liberation. Suicide, she thought, was the only way of ending her mental anguish. She felt like throwing herself into fire or drowning herself in a river. In her growing agony she prayed to God: "Thou art causing me irritation through my husband, but I will not leave Thy worship even though it mean death to me. Help me, O Lord, to see the Infinite One with the eye of spiritual knowledge. If in distress I were to commit suicide the fault would be Thine! Protect Thy child!"

She longed to sit in meditation for three days, but did not get an opportunity to leave her husband, except one day when Gaṅgādhar had to go on business to Poona. Thus she got a chance to meditate for hours together, with Rāmachandra in her heart and the image of Viṭhobā before her eyes. With closed eyes, in sleep and while awake, she saw the form of Tukārām blessing her with poetic power, telling her that it was her thirteenth and last birth, as she had accomplished all her desires, and worked out the last vestige of her *karma*. The son who was to be born was her companion in her previous birth. She felt the saint's touch, and her senses ceased to function. She felt the presence of God. In this state of contemplation, her soul dancing with joy, she bathed in the river Indrāyaṇī and worshipped the image of Viṭhobā in the temple. To her surprise, she found she was inspired with poetry. She composed five verses and dedicated them to Viṭhobā in the temple. They were her first verses of poetry.

The family left Dehū and settled in Shiur. In this period of her life she observed a vow of silence; she was too much engrossed in her spiritual life to take an interest in worldly matters. No particular events took place: life passed smoothly with Bahiṇā. Nobody knows of the death of her husband and parents. In 1649 Tukārām left for his heavenly home. When Bahiṇā heard of it, she was deeply grieved at the loss of her *guru*. She came to Dehū and fasted for eighteen days. Her desire was fulfilled: Tukārām appeared to her and blessed her.

Those were the flourishing days of Mahārāshṭra. Śivaji's fame was in the ascendant. In his efforts to establish the empire of Mahārāshṭra he was assisted by such religious masters as Tukārām and Rāmadās. Bahiṇā felt the need of some virtuous company. In Rāmadās she found her heart's desire. She paid him respects, but when Rāmadās also passed away in 1681 she returned to Shiur with a heavy heart. Not much is known of her later years, as they were filled with mental struggle and unrest.

Bahiṇā was now seventy-two years old and could hear the approaching footsteps of death. Her daughter-in-law, Rukmiṇī, had died, and Viṭhobā, the husband of Rukmiṇī, had gone to Śukleśwar on the river Godāvarī to perform the last religious rites when he received a letter from his mother asking him to return with the greatest possible speed. She wrote to him, "Five days from now my expected end will come, but I am awaiting it with self-control". On reading this letter he chose a place for her *samādhi* on the banks of the Godāvarī, and rushed to see her. He told her how he had dreamt of her approaching death, and when he read the contents of her letter he jumped as if with fairy wings to her side. But she preferred for her *samādhi* a place blessed by the confluence of holy waters. She said to him: "Listen to me, my son! We have performed our religious duties together during our previous twelve births, and you are my son in this thirteenth birth. This is my last birth because the desires that necessitate rebirth have ceased." Viṭhobā was astounded by what she told on her death-bed. She was quite conscious. He could not disbelieve her who had never uttered a single lie during her whole life.

"Mother!" he said, "I have a doubt."

"What is it, my dear?"

"You have told me about our previous births, but can you relate to me their details?"

"Yes, my son: though I should not reveal them to anybody, I shall tell you." So saying she told him how she had passed through twelve lives and was reborn for the thirteenth and last time.

As death approached, Bahiṇā asked her son to call Brahmins and recite Vedic *mantras*. She could now hear the resounding music in the air. Then she gave the minutest details of the hour of her death and instructions as to the disposal of her body.

In 1700, at the age of seventy-two, this noble woman left the world peacefully for her divine abode, after struggling in her thirteen births for salvation.

Bahiṇā was a poetess of no mean order. Her autobiography abounds in poetry. Her style is exceedingly lucid but elliptical, after the manner of her *guru* Tukārām, whose *abhaṅga* metre she had adopted throughout her poetry. Spontaneity is its distinguishing mark. Her poems deal with a variety of subjects, such as the philosophy of Ātman, life, religion, the Sad-guru, sainthood, Brahmanhood, devotion and so forth. They contain also teachings on moral and domestic life which are inspiring to the ordinary reader. With her intense passion for spiritual life and renunciation of worldly matters, this woman has unique observations on domestic life; especially are her thoughts on wifely duties worth mentioning, as they reveal the social status of Indian women over three hundred years ago, when a woman had no existence apart from her husband. Bahiṇā says: "A dutiful wife carries on her household duties and her religious duties simultaneously. Such a wife bears even the heavens in her hands. She is a dutiful wife who holds no anger or hatred in her heart, who is free from pride of learning, who avoids evil, who is obedient, who has control over her sexual appetite, who is ever ready to serve saints, and fulfils her husband's commands without questioning. Such a wife gains victory over her worldly life and secures a place for herself in heaven. A wife must make her domestic life happy by accepting her husband's wishes in a noble spirit, and, though it may even mean death to her, she should not transgress them. Blessed is she, her caste and her family!"

We women in the twentieth century, quarrelling over our emancipation and our equal rights with men, would curl our lips at these thoughts. But Bahiṇābāī preached the ideals of character-building and humanity in the social context of her time and in the light of the Vedānta.

The story of her life is thus a twofold guidance in the philosophy of religion and life.

CHAPTER X

GAURIBĀI

IT was not the custom in India to write biographies of saints, or for that matter, of any notabilities. Court poets used to write verses or books extolling the virtues, wealth and prowess of kings and princes. But as they were mostly composed with an eye to the fatness of the reward expected for the labour, these were grossly exaggerated and gave no true picture of the sovereigns or their surroundings. During the Muslim rule some historical biographies written by Muslim scribes throw light on the important aspects of contemporary life and statecraft. But the facts dealing with a saint's life have to be gathered from legends and information handed down from generation to generation.

In the case of Gaurībāī, the poetess-saint of Gujarāt, it is fortunate that we are not too far removed from her to get some definite information about her life and work. When her biography was written in the last century, two members of her family were alive and were able to give some facts concerning their saintly ancestor. Of course, as in the case of all saints in every country, here also many legends are intertwined with facts, and it is no easy task to give an authentic picture.

Gaurībāī was born about Samvat 1815 (A.D. 1759) in Giripur (also known as Duṅgarpur) situated in Vagad, on the borderline of Gujarāt and Rājpuṭāna. She belonged to the community known as Vaḍnagara Nāgar Gṛihastha. This small community is ranked as the foremost in Gujarāt, and it is to their credit that there has been one hundred per cent literacy even among its womenfolk for hundreds of years. The community boasts many Persian scholars and Gujarāti literary lights, and once it was their prerogative to hold high office in both Muslim and Hindu states.

Little is known of Gaurībāī's parents; but it is certain that she had a sister named Champu who had a son, Fulśankar, and two daughters, Chāturī and Jamnā. Of the two, Chāturī became a widow after a year of married life. Jamnā was married to one Belśankar, and had two sons named Prabhāśankar and Rūpśankar, and a daughter, Tuljā. Of these, it is known that

Prabhāśankar married one Majhukuṇver and had two sons named Vrijlāl and Kṛishṇalāl who were living at Banāras, and some of the time in Gujarāt, in the latter half of the nineteenth century. They have helped to provide Gaurībāī's biographer with some details of her life and work.

According to the then prevailing custom, Gaurībāī was married[1] at the tender age of five or six. Four days before her marriage she developed eye trouble, so the eyes had to be tied up in bandages and she was married in that state. But a greater misfortune was to follow. Scarcely had a week elapsed when the bridegroom was seized by some deadly disease and he died within a few hours of contracting it. The whole place was stricken with grief, and the family's woe knew no bounds. But Gaurībāī, though young, never thought fit to make capital of her misery. Whenever someone pitied her for the loss of her husband, she philosophically replied, "God is my lord, and my life is dedicated to Him". According to the prevailing custom of her community she stayed with her parents.

Gaurībāī was very intelligent. There were no schools for girls in those days, but she quickly learnt to read and write at home. As was thought fit for a young widow, she spent her time in worshipping the household deities, reciting devotional songs and reading sacred literature. Her faith in God Almighty was strong and unshakeable. She began to compose a few poems in praise of the Lord.

Among the higher strata of Hindu society, it is not considered proper for a widow to remarry, and she is expected to lead a chaste, religious life. At the very tender age of thirteen Gaurībāī understood that it was best for her to avoid company and remain immersed in religious practices. She spent her time at home, reading scriptures and concentrating on the worship of God.

Giripur at that time was ruled over by Rāja Śivasiṁhji, a righteous, learned and dutiful prince. He had abolished all unjust taxes. When he knew that the public were being cheated by the traders' adopting various standards of weights and measures, Rāja Śivasiṁhji put an end to these and enforced one standard weight known as "Śivasai tol" throughout the state, which is still in force. He spent large sums of money in constructing wells, tanks, free caravanserais for travellers,

[1] Means 'betrothed' in such cases.

temples and so forth. His name is still remembered for these charitable acts.

This Rāja heard of the pure life led by Gaurībāī and went to her house to have her *darśana* (purifying sight). He had religious discourse with her, during which he was greatly impressed by her knowledge of sacred lore and spiritual vision.

Highly gratified by her purity and devotion, the Rāja built a beautiful new temple in her honour and also had a step-well constructed near it. Gaurībāī took her household images to this shrine, and the consecration ceremony was held on the sixth day of the bright half of the month of Māgh in Samvat 1836 (A.D. 1780) with great pomp.

Gaurībāī left her home and family life for ever and came to reside in the temple, making the worship of God her sole aim in life. Her widowed niece Chāturī also went to live with her. After some time the other niece Jamnā and an old relation named Hariyan joined them.

Gaurībāī took great pains to keep the shrine clean and attractive, and its fame spread far and wide. Pilgrims, saints and scholars came in crowds to visit it. Religious discourses were held there, which helped to increase Gaurībāī's knowledge of sacred lore. Her natural gift for writing poetry gained impetus in such surroundings, and she began composing religious songs.

Rāja Śivasiṁhji had established a *sadavrat* (free kitchen) for mendicants in the temple premises. Hundreds used to flock there to take advantage of the charity. Once a learned sādhu came there and, observing Gaurībāī's devotion and knowledge of sacred lore, he remarked: "You are an incarnation of Saint Mīrābāī. Mīrābāī, though a great devotee, had not so much knowledge as one would desire in a saint. You are born to correct that defect. I have come to instruct you and give you the necessary additional knowledge." He took her aside and instructed her in *Brahmajñāna* (knowledge of Brahman) and *Ātmajñāna* (knowledge of the Self). He showed her the right path for a saint and blessed her. Presenting her with a small idol of Bālamukunda (the infant Kṛishṇa) he went away and never returned.

Gaurībāī's knowledge increased and so did her detachment from worldly affairs. It is said that she would become absorbed in *samādhi* (superconsciousness) which sometimes used to last for fifteen days at a stretch, during which period she touched neither food nor drink. So deep was her meditation that she lost all consciousness of her surroundings and remained seated in a closed room.

It is recorded that the old woman Hariyan, who had made her home with Gaurībāī, suspected that the *samādhi* was only feigned and not true superconsciousness. In order to test this she once went secretly to where Gaurībāī was seated deep in *samādhi* and pressed needles into her limbs. It is said that Gaurībāī never felt the pricks; she did not even wince a little. Leaving the needles in the body, Hariyan ran away. After the period of *samādhi* was over, Chāturī found the needles in Gaurībāī's body when bathing her. Inquiries were started to find out who the culprit was, but no one admitted the crime. After some time Hariyan was seized with leprosy—a just punishment for her crime, according to the chronicler. She fell at the feet of Gaurībāī and, making a full confession, asked for pardon. The saintly lady was very generous. She told the culprit that only white spots would remain where the leprous scars showed, and the disease would disappear.

Gaurībāī was credited with foretelling events. And with her devotion and sacred knowledge her poetic genius increased. She is said to have composed thousands of devotional songs and prayers.

Besides outward beauty, she had also a very attractive personality. She forsook all worldly pleasures and spent her time in worship and the pursuit of knowledge. Virtuous, wise and kind-hearted as she was, she never lost her temper, however great the provocation might be. She usually sat with downcast eyes, as was thought fit for a devotee of God. But whenever she had occasion to lift her eyes, the onlooker was staggered by their lustre. She used to dress in plain white, and the only ornaments that adorned her body were strings of sacred *tulasī* beads. Since her experience of *samādhi*, she ceased taking solid food and lived upon milk alone.

Thus Gaurībāī spent her life till Samvat 1860 (A.D. 1804). Then she thought of spending the rest of her days in the holy Vraja Bhūmī (Gokula and Vṛindāvana). When the Rāja knew of it, he came to the temple personally and tried to persuade her to remain in Giripur. He even offered her various expensive gifts. But Gaurībāī did not covet such worldly goods and remained firm in her decision. She entrusted the worship of the chief deity to some deserving sādhu, and taking her personal images with her, set out for Vṛindāvana with her nieces.

When the party came near Jaipur, the ruler of that state went to receive them personally, as he had already heard of the fame of the saintly woman. The party were entertained as state guests. The Mahārānī of Jaipur came to have the *darśana* of the saint and offered five hundred sovereigns at the latter's feet. But Gaurībāī refused to accept such a princely gift, saying that she was an ascetic and as such did not require worldly goods. On the royal couple's persisting in their request to accept it, Gaurībāī gave it to a follower accompanying her and asked him to distribute it among deserving Brahmins.

The Mahārāja of Jaipur was much impressed by Gaurībāī's abstemious habits and learning. He however wished to test her nearness to God, having heard tales of the Lord manifesting Himself personally before her. The story goes that he ordered the priest of his private shrine to decorate the image of Govindaji elaborately and then had the doors closed. He invited Gaurībāī to the shrine and made her sit in the outer hall under the pretext of listening to the reading of the sacred *Bhāgavata*. When it was over, the Rāja told Gaurībāī of his desire to test her power, and asked her to describe the dress and ornaments of the image within the closed doors. Gaurībāī was hurt at this and said that she was as much a mortal being as the Rāja and the rest, and she made no claim to any supernatural powers. But she said that God was kind to his devotees and would help her in the present issue. She then meditated and composed a prayer which she sang. It is said that she then described the dress and ornaments of the image in detail, and said, "The only flaw is that there is no crown on the head". The Rāja and others were much surprised at this as the image of Śrī Kṛishṇa is never without a crown. When the doors of the temple were opened, it was found that Gaurībāī's statement was correct. The crown had slipped off the head of the image because the priest had not secured it properly. The Rāja was very much mortified and asked to be forgiven. Of course in Gaurībāī's heart there never was any rancour towards anyone and she forgave him.

The Rāja requested Gaurībāī to stay in Jaipur as his

permanent guest, and offered her as a present the palace where she was staying, and undertook to meet the expenses of its maintenance. But the saintly woman refused the offer as she had done before and expressed her desire to proceed to Vṛindāvana. On the Rāja's persisting in his request, she agreed to leave her image of worship in the palace and asked her royal host to arrange for its worship, which he did.

After spending some time in Mathurā, Gokula and Vṛindāvana, Gaurībāī went to Kāśi (Banāras) with her nieces. The ruler of Banāras, Mahārāja Sundersiṁha, also had heard of the saintliness of Gaurībāī and offered her hospitality. He was also fond of composing devotional songs, and both he and Gaurībāī used to sit together and conduct religious discourses through songs and poems, composed extempore. She showed him how to practise meditation, and was accepted by the Rāja as his *guru*.

Rāja Sundersiṁha pressed Gaurībāī to accept a sum of fifty thousand rupees from him. She used twenty thousand rupees of this to settle the differences that had arisen in her own community in Banāras, and the rest in charity when she made a pilgrimage to Jagannāth Purī.

After returning from Purī, Gaurībāī made her home in Kāśi. Once she remained in *samādhi* for seven days, and then told her niece that her end was near. She wished to die on the banks of the Jamunā where, according to the Purāṇas, the boy Dhruva had performed his great penance. She prophesied that her death would take place on Rāmanavamī, Rāma's birthday. Rāja Sundersiṁha arranged to send her to the place she desired. There she remained in *samādhi* for a few days and then went to eternal peace on Rāmanavamī in Samvat 1865 (A.D. 1809), at the age of fifty.

One may or may not believe in the supernatural powers attributed to Gaurībāī, but one cannot help admiring her simplicity, devotion and learning. She had undying faith in the omnipotence and benevolence of God Almighty. Her heart was magnanimous; she did not know what hatred or jealousy was The devotional songs attributed to her reveal her character. Her detachment from worldly affairs and attachment to the Deity pervade her poems.

Most of her poetry is written in the Gujarātī language, though it contains some Rājasthānī words, her birth-place being on the borderline of the two provinces. She has composed a few songs in Hindī also, which may be a result of her long stay in Vṛindāvana, Gokula and Banāras.

One of her followers has truly compared Gaurībāī to the river Ganges, which purifies all those who are devoted to her.

CHAPTER XI

SOME WOMEN SAINTS OF KERALA

THROUGH the ages India has clung to religion and philosophy, and its very life consists in contributing inspiring ideals of religion to the sum total of human culture. From the Vedic period of the pre-historic past up to modern times, India has given birth to religious leaders who were capable of giving vivifying ideas and ideals to the whole world. Buddha, Śaṅkara, Chaitanya and Rāmakṛishṇa, to name but a few, are great figures in the world of religion and philosophy.

Women have distinguished themselves as much as men in this field from the earliest times. Viśwavārā, who wrote some of the finest hymns of the *Ṛig-Vēda*;[1] Gārgī, the virgin philosopher of Upanishadic fame who could challenge the great thinkers of her time and win respect from them; Maitrēyī, who chose the knowledge leading to immortality and for the sake of that rejected the wealth and possessions offered to her by her husband, the sage Yājñavalkya, a prominent figure in the *Brihadāraṇyaka Upanishad*; and Mīrā Bāī, the sweet singer who enjoyed the company of Śrī Kṛishṇa and spurned royal honours due to her as queen—these will always command the homage of every sincere devotee.

South India has not been behind in this respect. Śrī Āṇḍāḷ, who wanted to be the bride of Śrī Kṛishṇa and was merged in the Lord, is a shining example. Some of her soul-ravishing songs have been rendered into English by no less a poet and mystic than Śrī Aurobindo.

Kēraḷa has had its great religious heroes among men and women alike. Rāmānujan Ezhuttachchhan, who created a grand religious literature in Malayāḷam; Nārāyaṇa Bhaṭṭatiri, the great poet and devotee whose *Nārāyaṇīya* thrills the hearts of scholars and devotees as it beautifully summarizes the *Bhāgavata* and is at the same time a masterpiece of devotion; and Pūntanam whose ecstatic *bhakti* was declared by the Lord Himself to be superior to the wonderful scholarship of his contemporary, Nārāyaṇa Bhaṭṭatiri—these are household names in Kēraḷa.

[1] See the first footnote under Chapter II, page 10.

Among the women devotees of Kēraḷa who attained God-realization, three names stand prominent: Chaṅkrottu Amma, Vaḍakkēḍattu Naṅga Peṇṇu and Kurūr Amma. Fragments alone of their life stories are available through tradition, though they suffice to reveal something of their intense devotion and God-intoxication.

The first-named of these lived in a house still known as Chaṅkrottu House, thus recalling her memory. The house stands just west of the famous temple of Śrī Vallabha (Vishṇu), at Tiruvella (in Travancore), a temple eulogized even in the works of some of the great Vaishṇava Āzhwār saints of South India. As the temple was established in her time and is mentioned by Nammāzhwār whose date has been assigned to the ninth century A.D., she must have been born in the eighth century A.D.

From her childhood she was a great devotee of Vishṇu and her days were spent in prayer and worship of the Lord. The *Ēkādaśī* fast of every eleventh day of the waxing or waning moon is the most sacred fast observed by devotees, and is undertaken without any ulterior motive at all. Chaṅkrottu Amma would not even sip a drop of water throughout that holy day. On the next day she would have her bath and prayers, prepare food, offer it to the Lord and feed a Brahmin, and only then take her own meal. The fast was thus rigorously observed by her without a break for many years. But on one occasion she could not find any Brahmin whom she could feed on the day succeeding the *Ēkādaśī* fast. The ardent devotee was in a fix and finally resolved on fasting to death since she could not observe the fast for once in all its details. Suddenly, Vishṇu, the Lord who hastens to relieve his true devotees in distress, appeared before her in the garb of a *brahmachārin*. She was carried away with joy and served Him with food in the sheath of an areca-nut tree. The Lord was greatly pleased with her simple devotion and strong faith, and graciously accepted her humble and yet devoted offering. Before He disappeared, the Lord blessed her with *mukti*, the supreme release from the bonds of constant birth and death. The people of the locality came to know of this extraordinary incident and erected a grand temple of Vishṇu on the spot and installed His image. This is the traditional origin of the famous temple of Śrī Vallabha in Tiruvella. To perpetuate the memory of that event, the food is still served in the sheath of the areca-nut tree. The pious lady had no descendants and so her property was dedicated to the service of the temple.

While Chaṅkrottu Amma had the vision of God in her old age, Naṅga Peṇṇu attained God-vision even when she was but a maiden. She belonged to a respectable Malayāḷi Brahmin family of Vaḍakkēḍattu Illam at Ṭrippūṇittura, the seat of the Royal House of Cochin. From her childhood[1] she had unbounded devotion to the Lord Vishṇu whose image was installed in the temple there. She would regularly go to the temple and offer her heart's devotion which would be unabated even when she returned to her house. Her days were spent in constant remembrance of the Lord and repetition of His holy name with faith and devotion. The other members of the family could not understand her. They thought that she was worshipping God to be blessed with worldly happiness. But her heart was above all such selfish considerations. She loved the Lord with pure and untainted devotion.

When she attained age, her parents arranged for her marriage. The proposed bridegroom was a very handsome and wealthy youth. All preparations on a grand scale had been completed in the house of the bride on the auspicious day fixed for the marriage: the bridegroom was brought to the house in a procession with musical accompaniments and other festivities in the time-honoured customary fashion. When the exact propitious moment for the marriage was at hand, Naṅga Peṇṇu, the maiden devotee, proceeded to the temple to bid the Lord farewell. Her heart was sorely distressed at the thought that she would now have to stay permanently in the house of her husband and hence would no more have an opportunity for her regular visit to the temple, to be blessed with the sight of the Lord of her heart. Tears filled her eyes at the thought. Restraining herself with great difficulty, she entered the temple and prostrated before the image in the anguish of her heart. She was standing there and had at that time no thought of returning home. "From the morrow, I cannot have this blessed vision. How can I live without seeing the Lord? I have no other desire here or hereafter except the vision of the Lord. Deign to merge me in Thyself, O Lord, even now." Such was her ardent prayer and the Lord granted it. The maiden saw the

[1] No materials from which her date of birth can be fixed are available.

Lord emerging from the image, coming to her, catching hold of her hands and entering the sanctum again. The news of this incident soon spread over the whole place. The wonder and amazement of the people can very well be imagined. The proposed bridegroom felt ashamed and left the house hurriedly without taking leave of anyone. The parents were bewildered. Even to this day, the memory of the event is kept alive by the annual celebration in that temple of a festival known as Naṅga Peṇṇu Festival. The most important item in the festival is the splendid procession of the Lord to the paternal house of Naṅga Peṇṇu, where a feast is given to the Lord Himself and clothes and other presents are given to the members of the family.

While the two devotees mentioned above got the vision of the Lord and *mukti*, liberation from worldly bonds, simultaneously, Kurūr Amma, the last of the devotees treated in this article, enjoyed the almost uninterrupted vision of her Chosen Deity, the Baby Kṛishṇa, and lived for many years on earth. She could see the Lord of her heart whenever she desired it.

She belonged to a respectable Brahmin family of Kurūr Illam, which has survived to the present day. It is about four miles from Trichur, a famous city of Cochin State. As she was an elder contemporary of Nārāyaṇa Bhaṭṭatiri and Pūntanam, who were born in the beginning of the seventeenth century A.D., she must have flourished in the last half of the sixteenth century. It is remarkable to note that the simple devotion of Kurūr Amma is regarded as surpassing that of even Pūntanam himself. Her devotion grew to that supreme love in which the lover, the Beloved and love become One. By the power of that Love, the Lord was ever ready and willing to do as she wished.

Many stories have gathered around the hallowed name of Kurūr Amma, testifying to her unsurpassed devotion. Once an old Brahmin came to her house seeking food. There was no male member in the house at that time and the orthodox women used to observe strict *purdah*, which did not permit them to appear before men. So she told the stranger that food would be ready but that he would have to serve himself. To the astonishment of all, the Lord Himself came in the form of a boy *brahmachārin* as soon as food was ready and served the stranger-guest who, being a great devotee, recognized the boy as the Lord. On another occasion a saint who used to be blessed with the vision of the Lord whenever he meditated ardently, called on his Chosen Deity, Śrī Kṛishṇa, for a long time, but to no purpose. It was only after a long time that he had his usual vision. When he asked Śrī Kṛishṇa the reason for the delay, the Lord explained that He had been imprisoned by the pure and intense love of Kurūr Amma who had released Him only just then!

Nārāyaṇa Bhaṭṭatiri was on his death-bed when Kurūr Amma came to enquire about him. He was very much delighted to see her at that time. He told her, "Revered sister, my last moments have come and I shall soon merge in the Lord. I would like you to stay with me till the end." She replied, "No, Nārāyana, there is no such hurry. I have to return home today; but I shall be with you during your last moments as you desire." Still Nārāyaṇa Bhaṭṭatiri was insistent and said: "I shall pass away even today. So, if you go away now, my desire will remain unfulfilled." But Kurūr Amma was confident and replied: "I shall be with you at the proper time. I am certain that you cannot pass away before I come to you again." Even then Bhaṭṭatiri was not hopeful though he allowed her to have her own way. Kurūr Amma gently reassured him and left the place. On the third morning she returned. Nārāyaṇa Bhaṭṭatiri was still alive though utterly prostrated. She roused him with these words: "Nārāyaṇa, the time is up. Prepare for it. Repeat the name of the Lord, Nārāyaṇa. May He bless you." Accordingly, that devotee repeated the Lord's name thrice and passed away in peace and bliss, cheered and encouraged by the presence of the woman saint. It is said that she also followed him soon after in full possession of God-consciousness and devotion.

Tradition has it that Kurūr Amma was a contemporary of Vilwamaṅgala Swāmī, a renowned sage and devotee, whose wonderful transformation as a *bhakta* is celebrated in a famous drama of Girish Chandra Ghosh, one of the great devotees of Śrī Rāmakṛishṇa. Once, during the period of menses, Kurūr Amma was repeating "Nārāyaṇa", the name of the Lord, when the Swāmī happened to go there. He was surprised and asked her whether it was proper to repeat the Lord's name in her state of bodily impurity. Her pertinent reply satisfied the Swāmī completely. She said: "Can anyone have the firm assurance that one will not die in the state of physical impurity?"

The love of Kurūr Amma for the Lord was that of a mother for her beloved child. It is said that while she would be at her devotions, the Lord would sit on her lap or ride on her back or play childish pranks.

The prayer she used to repeat constantly is given below:

Komalaṁ kūjayan veṇum
Śyāmaloyaṁ kumārakaḥ
Vēdavēdyam Param Brahma
Bhāsatām pūrato mama.

"May this dark-complexioned Boy (Kṛishṇa), who is really the Supreme Brahman known by the Vedas, deign to appear before me, sounding His sweet flute."

CHAPTER XII

TARIGONDA VENKAMAMBA

VEṄKAMĀMBĀ'S[1] life was one of utter simplicity and constant devotion to Śrī Kṛishṇa. She is one of the fairest flowers of Indian spiritual culture. As is usual with most Indian saints, she has not left behind any autobiography and, since not even a proper biography is available, we have to depend upon stray references in her writings and upon tradition for a connected account of the incidents of her life.

Veṅkamāmbā, or Veṅkammā as she is popularly known, was a contemporary of Śrī Rāmakṛishṇa. Sir C. P. Brown in his famous English–Telugu dictionary records that she was living in 1840. She was the daughter of one Kṛishṇayya, an orthodox Brahmin of the Nandavarīka sect, who belonged to the family of Kanali and the line of Vasishṭha. Her mother's name was Maṅgamāmbā. Her (Veṅkammā's) native village was Tarigoṇḍa, or, as some call it, Tarikuṇḍa, four miles to the north of Vayilpāḍu in the Chittoor District of Madras province in South India.

According to the custom of her community she was betrothed at an age when she hardly knew what marriage was. But she remained a devoted wife. At the end of her *Bhāgavata-purāṇa*, an exquisitely beautiful poetical composition, she says that she wrote it keeping in her heart of hearts the hallowed feet of Veṅkaṭāchalapati, son of Timmayya, of the family of Nuñjēṭi and the line of Śrīvatsa. Evidently this Veṅkaṭāchalapati was her husband. Shortly after her betrothal or marriage he died.

Veṅkammā was a woman of high courage and independent spirit; she refused to bow down to all meaningless customs and traditions. For instance, as a widow she was required to remove her hair, but she stoutly refused to do so. The villagers began to press her and her father to get her hair removed, but she replied to her father: "Dear father, heed not the opinions or the prattle of the worldly-minded. Whom are we going to please? What is the good of removing this God-given hair, and what is the infamy in retaining it? So long as our inclinations are pure, the merciful Lord will not be offended with us

[1] See the first footnote under Chapter II, page 10.

even when we set aside worldly customs and manners. And if our inclinations are impure, though we may pay all homage to customs and manners, the Lord will not spare us. So please leave me alone." Knowing the immaculate purity of the character of his daughter, Kṛishṇayya kept silent.

At this juncture, the chief abbot of the Pushpagiri Pīṭha happened to visit Tarigoṇḍa and the villagers bitterly complained to him about the behaviour of Veṅkammā, urging him to force her to remove her hair. Oh, what a storm in a tea-cup! So much agitation about the hair on an innocent widow's head! The chief priest called for the father of Veṅkammā and on pain of being ostracized demanded the immediate removal of her hair. With folded hands Kṛishṇayya pleaded, saying: "Holy father, it is not my fault. Let Your Holiness speak to her directly."

Ushered into the presence of the abbot, who curtly conveyed to her his mandate, Veṅkammā respectfully said: "Revered Swamiji, you are a Jagad-Guru (world-teacher). I am less informed than Your Holiness. Please tell me in which Veda it is enjoined that a widow should not keep her hair. Why should a woman be disfigured by shaving her head? Do not our scriptures maintain that where women are not honoured, there all works and efforts come to naught? When a widow's inclinations are pure, what is wrong in her keeping her hair or even wearing ornaments? This hair, which is the gift of the merciful God right from birth, will it not grow again after it is once shaven? If Your Holiness has the power to prevent it from growing again, you can have it shaven right now. I deem it wrong to abuse the gifts of God." Veṅkammā's protest was a protest of womankind, nay, of humanity, against priestcraft. Enraged at her reply, the chief priest called for a barber then and there and by force got her head shaven. Overcome by devotion rather than shame or sorrow, Veṅkammā went to a river near by, and offering prayers to her chosen Deity, Śrī Kṛishṇa, she took a dip in it, and lo, when she came out her head was adorned as usual with long beautiful hair. The chief priest and the rest were stupefied at this miraculous turn of events and began to stammer out their apologies to her. Here was an instance of the arrogance of authority and learning being subdued by the humility of devotion and wisdom.

Veṅkammā's sentiments are echoed in the most effective

manner in the words of Swami Vivekananda. He declares: "Educate your women first and leave them to themselves; then they will tell you what reforms are necessary for them. In matters concerning them, who are you?

"Liberty is the first condition of growth. It is wrong, a thousand times wrong, if any of you dares to say, 'I will work out the salvation of this woman or child'. I am asked again and again, what I think of the widow problem and what I think of the woman question. Let me answer once for all:—Am I a widow that you ask me that nonsense? Am I a woman, that you ask me that question again and again? Who are you to solve women's problems? Are you the Lord God that you should rule over every widow and every woman? Hands off! They will solve their own problems."

The reasons for the rude interference of the so-called pandits and the priests with the rights and privileges of women are not far to seek. In the decadent period of Indian history there arose the Smṛitis or codes with a somewhat narrow attitude towards women and the masses. But in the period of the Vedas and the Upanishads, conditions were vastly different. Then the social and religious status of women was in no way inferior to that of men. Among the Vedic Ṛishis we find the names of such glorious women as Viśwavārā, Apālā, Lopāmudrā and Ghoshā. In the *Taittirīya Upanishad*, almost at the beginning of his instructions to the disciple on the completion of his studies, the teacher exhorts: "Let thy mother be thy God." And the *Chaṇḍī*: "She (the Divine Mother) when pleased becomes propitious and becomes the cause of the freedom of man."

However, Veṅkammā's tender heart received a rude shock from the behaviour of the villagers and the abbot. Her passion for God-realization was fast developing and she managed to obtain spiritual initiation from a renowned *guru* called Rūpāvatāram Subrahmaṇya Śāstri, a native of Madanapalle in the Chittoor District. In her *Veṅkaṭāchala-māhātmya*, an excellent poetical composition, Veṅkammā pays homage to her master saying, "I bow down to the lotus-feet of my *guru*, Subrahmaṇya, who taught me to look upon the principle of intelligence as Brahman or the Supreme Spirit". In search of a lonely place for her spiritual practices, she went to the temple of Nṛisiṁha in her native village, and at length in a quiet spot behind the image of Hanūmat, she took her seat and was absorbed in meditation. In that state she remained regardless of bodily comforts or physical needs. Occasionally she would break her meditation to eat a little sacramental food. One day the priest of the temple saw her and with a shower of abuse drove her away from the place. Veṅkammā, in a mood of complete resignation to the will of the Lord, did not utter a single word of protest. As she had already left her home, she now left her native village once for all, and proceeded to Tirupati to take refuge at the feet of the presiding Deity there, Veṅkaṭēśwara, whom she believed to be the God of the present Iron Age, the Kali-yuga. In her *Veṅkaṭāchala-māhātmya* she gives a glowing description of the town with its sunlit golden temple towers, chariots, monasteries, gardens, elephants, peacocks and parrots. It is a town built on a mountain with seven hills, one leading to the other, a romantic spot where the sublime beauties of nature mingle with the artifices of civilization.

This Tirupati, then known as Veṅkaṭāchalam, with such sublime temples crowning the mountain, is indeed symbolic of the soul's pilgrimage of life leading to its destination, namely the unification of the soul with the Divine. Daily hundreds of pilgrims from all over India visit Tirupati.

Reaching there, Veṅkammā paid homage to the presiding Deity and was soon in search of a proper place for her spiritual practices. The people and the temple authorities were much impressed with her religious fervour, and she was given a small dwelling-place and a daily portion of some rice. Further, she obtained permission to render some special services to the Deity which to this day are continued in her name. However, in the course of time, she had to pay for her popularity, and this came in the form of the wrath of some jealous priests who began to harass her in various ways; but she overcame all such impediments by her wonderful love and devotion. Desire for solitude once more arose in her heart, and in a valley known as Tumulurukoṇa, amidst picturesque scenery, she found a suitable solitary place where she began to practise divine communion. Lofty hills with peaks, as if penetrating the very mysteries of heavens, valleys and meadows covered with fruit trees and flower plants wafting their fragrance over a wide area, the sun, moon and stars with the outstretched hands of their rays, kissing and embracing everything on earth and in heaven—such natural phenomena as these were very dear to Veṅkammā with her profound aesthetic sense, for later on we find her describing these natural beauties in a very striking manner. Here she carried on her spiritual practices for about six years and was blessed with many visions and realizations of a very high order. Thence she proceeded to a small pavilion to the north of the lake called Swāmi-pushkariṇī and began to give to the world through her writings the benefits of her realizations.

Veṅkammā found that for the regeneration of both men and women in her motherland, Āndhra-dēśa, the spread of ethical, religious and philosophical teachings in a simple style was of paramount importance. Books in those days were generally in a high-flown style more for the pleasure of the educated classes than for the use of the masses. With a view to gaining honour and money such books were often dedicated to kings and zemindars. But Veṅkammā's motive was service to God through service of man. She dedicated all her writings to her chosen Deity. At the end of every chapter in her *Vāsishṭha-Rāmāyaṇa*, she says: "O Lord Veṅkaṭēśwara, manifesting Thyself as Nṛisiṁha of Tarigoṇḍa, I dedicate it to Thy graceful lotus-feet. Whosoever whole-heartedly copies or reads or hears it, may he or she cross the ocean of *saṁsāra* with all its miseries and attain *nirvāṇa*".

Veṅkammā's works, which are mainly poetical, cover different forms of poetry, such as the epic, lyric, ballad, song and drama of various kinds. At the end of her *Bhāgavata-purāṇa* she gives a list of her works; but it seems she wrote a few other books subsequently. Among her books *Veṅkaṭāchala-māhātmya*, *Rāja-yoga-sāra* and *Vāsishṭha-Rāmāyaṇa*—all three based on the Sanskrit originals—have been published.

The *Vāsishṭha-Rāmāyaṇa* is an epic in Sanskrit; it is a huge volume, running into thousands of pages, the central theme of which is the teaching of Vasishṭha to Śrī Rāma. It has been appraised as a unique and important contribution not only to Indian wisdom, but to the thought of the world as well. Veṅkammā has popularized the teachings of this great work through her beautiful poetic compendium, *Vāsishṭha-Rāmāyaṇa*. Setting aside prolonged passages in the original dealing with theories of creation and abstruse philosophical argumentations, she confined herself in her compendium for the most part to stories to illustrate sublime truths in a very homely manner.

She knew very well that what is expressed in sweet and graceful language with appropriate similes and illustrations goes directly to the heart of the reader and expands there like a drop of oil on the surface of water. Like the jasmine which, though not very imposing in appearance or striking in colour, smells sweet, her style, reflecting her personality, is simple yet graceful and effective. But she always cared more for loftiness of feeling than for beauty of expression. Poetry to her was the handmaid of philosophy. She considered that rules of prosody were for the poet and not the poet for them. She felt that rules were her servants and not her masters. We find her here and there violating grammatical and metrical rules. Wherever it is desirable, she uses colloquial language freely. In many of her works we find her using a metre called *dwipada* which is akin to blank verse. Celebrated poets like Pālkuriki Somanātha have praised this metre highly.

Many of Veṅkammā's songs have become folk-lore. Famous Telugu poets and critics like Vīrēśaliṅgam Pantulu and Prabhākara Śastri have sung high praises of her works.

Veṅkammā was an inspired poetess. If "out of the fullness of the heart the mouth speaketh", out of the fullness of love and devotion she burst forth into poetry. In every sense of the term poetry was a gift of God to her. In her *Veṅkaṭāchala-māhātmya* she says, "I did not learn in my younger days even the alphabet from any teacher. I have not studied even the rudiments of prosody, nor have I read any literary works. Like a stringed instrument in the hands of a musician I sing. As the Lord, out of His infinite grace, dwelling upon my tongue—verily as He makes me sing, I sing. I have absolutely no claim to originality."

I am ever bound in gratitude to Saraswatī, the Goddess of learning, who, one blessed noon, appeared before me and showed me the Primeval Being and my *guru*. . . . When I was overcome with weariness She came down from the heavens and revealed Herself to me in the form of glowing lines of letters. . . .

I adore my Lord Śrī Kṛishṇa, who, having approached me in His bewitching form, commanded me to compose poems (about his amorous exploits) in veiled and amorous language, and when I expressed my inability, looked at me in a fit of anger, and, on my prostrating before Him, Himself composed them in these words.

Great masters teach more through their own example than

through precepts. As art conceals itself, true teaching does not appear as teaching at all. Rulers may urge and command, friends may argue and advise, while one's sweetheart imperceptibly and sweetly suggests and persuades. Through her dramas, songs and poems, which are like the suggestions of one's sweetheart, and above all through her own life, Veṅkammā imparts her ideas and ideals to people.

Moral discipline is the basis of all spiritual endeavour and achievement. If Veṅkammā performed any miracles, they were as we have already pointed out, by-products of her sainthood. The test of sainthood is not the performance of miracles but purity of character. A juggler may perform miracles, but he may not be a saint. Veṅkammā points out this truth in the following manner:—

Some, practising different *yogas* such as Mantra-yoga, Haṭha-yoga and Laya-yoga with a view to obtaining *siddhis* (powers) begin to roam about, demonstrating their miracles to the ignorant. This is, after all, superficial *yoga*, and these are false *yogis*. Saints who are adepts in the knowledge of God never hanker after such things as making the body immune from disease, old age and death. (*Rājayoga-sāra*)

Saints or godly men are those who, giving up inertia and desire for ephemeral things, are steadfast in goodness, truthfulness, purity, peace of mind and kindness to all living beings. (*Veṅkaṭāchala-māhātmya*)

Yoga must be practised uninterruptedly (for a long time). Without constant practice the mind becomes the hotbed of vices like lust and anger.

One who practises discrimination, renunciation, control of the mind and the senses, endurance, abstinence from sensual enjoyment, tranquillity, faith in the words of the teacher and the scriptures; one who considers another man's wife as his mother, who does not hanker after others' wealth, . . . who takes refuge at the feet of the Lord, . . . such a one alone is fit for illumination and liberation in this very life. (*Rājayoga-sāra*)

"The mansion of liberation" is guarded by four gate-keepers, namely Tranquillity, Contentment, Company of the Wise and Reflection. (*Vāsishṭha-Rāmāyaṇa*)

Among Hindu philosophical books none lays so great a stress upon human endeavour as the *Yoga-Vāsishṭha*, otherwise known as *Vāsishṭha-Rāmāyaṇa*. Veṅkammā has very ably presented the central teaching of *Yoga-Vāsishṭha* in her compendium, which recalls the words of Beaumont and Fletcher:

> Man is his own star; and the soul that can
> Render an honest and a perfect man
> Commands all light, all influence, all fate;
> Nothing to him falls early, or too late.
> Our acts our angels are, or good or ill,
> Our fatal shadows that walk by us still.

To show how work is to be performed and what is true renunciation, Veṅkammā, in her characteristically simple and effective manner, tells the story of Chūḍālā and Śikhidhwaja at considerable length in her compendium. She describes how the queen attained liberation while living a busy home life and ruling over a kingdom, whereas the king could not, even when he had left home, kingdom and society; and how the wife, becoming the husband's friend, philosopher and guide, led him to liberation. The moral of the story is obvious. Woman is in no way inferior to man in her capacity to rule or to attain the highest spiritual knowledge and liberation. As the Sanskrit words *ardhāṅgī* (half of the husband) and *saha-dharmiṇī* (she who performs religious rites and duties along with the husband) indicate, man and woman are helpmates in the pilgrimage of life and fellow-travellers on the path of spirituality. There is no question of inferiority or superiority entering into their mutual relations and attitude.

In the life and writings of Veṅkammā we find a satisfactory solution to many of the problems of the modern age. Her name is associated with one of Tirupati-Veṅkaṭeśwara's annual festive celebrations, the Brahmotsava. Even today there exists a caravanserai on the Tirumalai hill which perpetuates her saintly memory.

CHAPTER XIII

SRI SARADA DEVI

THE HOLY MOTHER

IN the whole range of religious biography we do not come across the life of a woman seer and teacher like Śrī Sāradā Devī. There were great holy women in the past who did not want to marry but chose to move on their souls' pilgrimage alone and without a companion. There were also great and holy women who had married in their youth but later renounced their hearth and home in search of God and attained Him. Some of them had to struggle hard against unfavourable social environments and family circumstances but succeeded in the end in breaking those shackles under which they had been chafing. Some others had the misfortune to live with husbands who had neither understanding sympathy nor common sense, and who were utterly devoid of devotion to God; these ill-treated their noble-minded wives who possessed whole-souled devotion to God and were compelled finally to leave their husbands to their fate. Some others again became widows but availed themselves in the best manner possible of a God-given opportunity to shake off the bondage and limitations of a domestic life devoid of the freedom in which their godly endeavour could become fruitful. Sāradā Devī was like none of them. She was betrothed, but she and her "husband" did not live *en maritalement*. She stands apart as a solitary example of a woman who seemed even in her girlhood to have come into this world with a message. She experienced God as the Divine Mother and saw Her in herself and in her "husband": he also saw God the Mother in himself and in his "wife". The world had not seen such a couple before, nor witnessed such lofty spiritual experiences as theirs. They both have become symbols of moral and spiritual perfection for men and women, for the married and the unmarried, for the laity as well as the monks and the nuns.

ŚRĪ SĀRADĀ DEVĪ
(*Known as the Holy Mother*)

BIRTH AND PARENTAGE

Śrī Sāradāmaṇi Devī, known as the Holy Mother, in commemoration of whose birth-centenary this volume is published, was born of Brahmin parents on December 22, 1853, in the quiet little hamlet of Jayrāmbāṭī, in the district of Bankura in Bengal. With its setting of green pastures, untrimmed meadows and grazing cattle, with the river Amodar, and ponds, trees and shrubs, the hamlet, which consists of hardly more than a hundred mud houses, breathes a typical rural atmosphere. It has become a place of pilgrimage today, visited by hundreds of devotees, and on special occasions by thousands, to pay their homage to the memory of Sāradā Devī.

Her parents, Rāmachandra Mukhopādhyāya and Śyāmāsundarī Devī, were deeply religious, though poor. Though Rāmachandra's sole income was derived from the cultivation of a few acres of paddy fields, performance of priestly duties, and the making and selling of sacred threads, he lived up to the ideal of a Brahmin's life and would not accept gifts without discrimination. He was generous: in times of famine or scarcity of food he would not care to keep the surplus stock of food grains for the use of his family, but would spend what he had in feeding the hungry and destitute.

The life of Sāradā Devī seems to have been set in a web of mystical experiences and divine influences. Once Rāmachandra and Śyāmāsundarī had a vision foretelling the birth of a divine being as their daughter. They both considered it a blessing indicating rare good fortune. In due course, when little Sāradā was born, their affection for her was mingled with feelings of gratitude to the Divine Dispenser and of an unearthly felicity.

Sāradā lived the simple life of an Indian village girl. She used to play, but she was found to be too serious for childish games. She had playthings in her doll's house, but was more interested in the clay models of Kālī and Lakshmī, which she worshipped with flowers and *vilwa* leaves. Feeling a sense of identity with the Divine Mother she meditated on Her with very deep concentration. She was thus going through her lessons in the kindergarten of religion. In about a decade her spiritual tendencies, of which one could get only an inkling, began to bloom. Even in her early life she had experiences and mystic visions, which even a Hindu saint in his advanced stages of discipline would consider a blessing. While she was at Kāmārpukur in the heyday of her youth and had to proceed hesitatingly and alone to a neighbouring tank for her bath, she used to see a bevy of eight girls of her age coming from she knew not where, and escorting her there. Indeed one is apt to wonder how she could thus secure Divine favour and protection from above.

Her education was not of the bookish sort. As a girl of tender age she began to learn the alphabet of her language, and was also admitted to the village *tol*; but unfortunately nobody took any trouble to teach her or to ensure her regular attendance at the school. She had a keen desire to study, but being the eldest child of her family she underwent home training, which is a part of the education of almost all Hindu girls, and began to help her mother in the performance of her duties. Thus she joined her in cooking and occasionally, when necessary, took her place in the kitchen. She also had to do sundry odd jobs of the household.

India's culture cannot be acquired through literacy. The country devised methods of its own for imparting the best of the national heritage in higher culture, religion and philosophy. Celebrating the temple festivals, reciting the epics, playing the village dramas, participating in the daily domestic worship and, as occasions arose, in the more important family functions in which all the members of the family joined—all these provided ample opportunities for developing character harmoniously, unlike the system of education in colleges and universities. Those who imbibed the ideals and ideas could practise them. Śrī Sāradā drank deep of the fountain of culture and spirituality, religious lore and traditions, and her spiritual instincts were quickened thereby. Further, circumstances were destined to bring her even at the tender age of six into contact with another soul—a mighty one—who was to guide and teach her and mould her life into a pattern of perfection.

Betrothal

In accordance with the then prevailing custom, little Sāradā was betrothed at the age of six to Śrī Rāmakṛishṇa, who was then twenty-three. The betrothal, which took place in May,

1859, was arranged by his parents. Rāmakṛishṇa was then practising severe austerities at Dakshiṇeśwar. He was born in 1836 in the village of Kāmārpukur—five miles from Jayrāmbāṭī—in the district of Hooghly. As he was very backward in his studies at school and was therefore a source of anxiety to his elder brother, the latter got him appointed as a priest at Dakshiṇeśwar so that his earnings might add to the income of the joint family. Rāmakṛishṇa began his spiritual disciplines seriously at the age of seventeen. In about seven months he developed such strange moods and other-worldly behaviour that the people about him, who did not know what longing for God was, took him for a madman. His mother and brother brought him to Kāmārpukur for treatment. They were grieved to see that he had become completely indifferent to the world and had a restless hankering for something unseen, occasionally crying piteously, "Mother, O Mother!" It was at this time that they decided to arrange for his marriage in the hope that it would be the best means to bring down his mind to normal worldly life and duties. They were, however, disappointed at not being able to find a suitable bride of proper age. It is usual that when a man is deeply religious or has attained some spiritual progress, he is unwilling to marry or to be tied down in any other way with the responsibilities of domestic life. Śrī Rāmakṛishṇa, however, did not feel worried at the arrangements that his mother and brother were making for his marriage. Further, when their attempts to find a suitable girl resulted in failure, he said to them one day in an inspired mood, "Vain is your search in this place and that. Go to Jayrāmbāṭī, and there in the house of Rāmachandra Mukhopādhyāya, you will find her who is marked out for me".

The betrothal took place at the time when dates ripened, and Śrī Rāmakṛishṇa stayed in his village for nineteen months. In December of this period, in 1860, Sāradā was just seven. According to the custom Rāmakṛishṇa visited his father-in-law's house, and when he returned to his parental home he took Sāradā to spend some days with his mother. On his return to Dakshiṇeśwar she returned to her parental home.

Several years passed, and little Sāradā was growing under the care of her parents. She was helping them in their domestic duties in all possible ways. Śrī Rāmakṛishṇa visited Kāmārpukur again. She was then fourteen years old, and she spent three months in the company of Rāmakṛishṇa at his home. He was very kind, tender and cordial to her. He taught her many things, from cookery, household management and the discharge of her duties and responsibilities in the world, to meditation on God, living the spiritual life and attaining its goal. Now she was sufficiently grown up to realize that she was betrothed. She felt very happy in his company and found in him a man with an exalted love of God and immaculate purity of body and mind, yet quite normal and human in other respects. Referring to those days which she remembered, she used to tell her women disciples, "I then felt as if a pitcher of bliss was kept in my heart. It was a constant experience with me then. It is very difficult to convey an idea of this experience to others".

Four years more passed and Sāradā grew to be a young woman at the age of eighteen. Her memory of Rāmakṛishṇa was sweet, and when she came of age she felt a strong urge to be with him. Her heart told her that he who was so very kind to her four years earlier would not forget her, but would in good time call her to his side. She gave no expression to her inner feelings and tried to forget her anxieties and longings in doing household work, and in helping her mother and father as much as possible.

She had already become aware of the rumour that Rāmakṛishṇa had become insane. Indeed, when her neighbours would visit her parents, some of them would express their sympathy for her, saying: "O dear me, Śyāmā's daughter has been married to a lunatic". Sāradā herself would avoid meeting them lest they should have occasion for such talk. It was but natural that she felt a stronger urge than before to see Rāmakṛishṇa and to find out for herself the exact truth of what people were saying about him. She therefore decided to go to Dakshiṇeśwar where he was living.

When her father came to know of her wishes, he agreed to take her there. In the absence of railway or steamer service to Calcutta she was taken in a palanquin for a short distance, and then the party began to walk. As she had not been accustomed to long walks, she fell ill on the third day and developed a high temperature. In the evening Sāradā and party rested at an inn where she obtained unexpected relief of body and mind as the result of a significant vision at night. She described it in her own words in later years:

I was lying unconscious owing to fever, without even any sense of decorum. Just then I saw a woman, pitch dark in complexion, sitting by my side. Though she was dark, I have never seen another so beautiful as she. She stroked my aching head with her soft cool hands, and I felt the heat of my body subsiding. "Where are you from?" I asked her. And she replied, "From Dakshiṇeśwar". At this I was speechless with wonder and exclaimed, "From Dakshiṇeśwar! I too am going to Dakshiṇeśwar to see my husband. But this fever has unfortunately detained me on the way". To this she replied, "Don't worry. You will soon be all right to see your husband at Dakshiṇeśwar. It is for your sake that I have kept him there". I said to her, "Indeed! Is it so? But who are you to me?" "I am your sister", she replied. I was much astonished to hear this. After this conversation I fell asleep.

In the morning she found that her fever had gone. The party then resumed their journey on foot.

At Dakshiṇeśwar

When Sāradā first met Rāmakṛishṇa on arrival at Dakshiṇeśwar, she went straight to his room and could see for herself how kind he was. "Ah! You are here!" he said to her, and asked someone to spread a mat on the floor. As the long journey had been too wearisome for her and the effect of the fever still persisted, he arranged for her treatment and nursing. Now her worst fears were allayed: she could see for herself that the rumour about the condition of his mind was only the idle gossip of worldly-minded people who could not understand his spiritual greatness and knew not what they were saying.

The Holy Mother stayed at Dakshiṇeśwar till 1885, except for short periods which she spent at her village home. During the early days of her stay she could see that Śrī Rāmakṛishṇa used to pass into high states of spiritual consciousness even at night. She knew that he was a man of God who could throw himself into high *samādhi* (superconsciousness) on hearing the temple bells, or listening to a hymn, or taking part in the discussion of any divine topic. Referring to the happy and blessed days of her stay at Dakshiṇeśwar, she used to say:

The divine state in which the Master used to be absorbed passes all description. In ecstatic moods he would smile or weep, or at times remain perfectly still in deep *samādhi*. This would sometimes continue throughout the night. In that divine presence my whole body would tremble with awe, and I would anxiously await the dawn. For I knew nothing of ecstasy in those days. One night his *samādhi* continued for a very long time. Greatly frightened, I sent for Hriday.[1] He came and began to repeat the name of the Lord in the Master's ears. When he had done this for a little while, external consciousness reappeared. After this incident, he came to know of my difficulty, and taught me the appropriate divine names that should be uttered in the ear in particular states of *samādhi*. Thenceforth my fear was much lessened, as he would invariably come to earthly consciousness on the utterance of the particular divine names. But even after this, I sometimes kept awake whole nights, as there was no knowing when he would fall into *samādhi*. By degrees he came to know of my difficulty. He learnt that even after the lapse of a considerable length of time I could not adjust myself to his *samādhi* temperament. So he asked me to sleep separately in the *nahabat*.[2]

The Divine Mother in Sāradā Devī

Śrī Rāmakṛishṇa had by now finished practising all the disciplines of Hinduism and attained a variety of experiences; nay more, he had realized the truths of other religions as well as the underlying harmony of all faiths. He was then thirty-five years of age.

After the betrothal, when Sāradā was growing into womanhood, he had fervently prayed to the Divine Mother to remove all traces of carnality from her mind so that she might remain pure and immaculate. During the early days of her stay at Dakshiṇeśwar he once asked her whether she had gone there to drag him down to worldly life, but she replied: "Why should I do it? I have come only to help you in the path of religious life".

It was during these early days of her stay in the same premises with Rāmakṛishṇa that he performed a form of worship known as Shoḍaśī Pūjā. On the seat intended for the Divine Mother he asked Sāradā Devī to sit. The worship began at about 9 p.m. with the usual ritual and *mantras*. She was in a mood of spiritual fervour throughout. After sprinkling holy water on her several times, he invoked in her the Divine Mother by addressing the following prayer:

[1] A nephew of Śrī Rāmakṛishṇa.

[2] Concert house, which was later set apart for the residence of Rāmakṛishṇa's old mother and Sāradā Devī.

O Divine Mother, Thou Eternal Virgin, the Mistress of all powers and abode of all beauty, deign to unlock for me the gate to perfection. Sanctifying the body and mind of this woman, do Thou manifest Thyself through her and do what is auspicious.

All through the worship Śrī Sāradā Devī was in a state of semi-absorption, and when the worship was over she went into deep *samādhi*. It was a transcendental union of the worshipper and the worshipped who realized their identity of being as the One Brahman.

A long time passed in that state of spiritual absorption. Late in the second watch of the night Śrī Rāmakṛishṇa regained a little of physical consciousness. Then he resigned himself completely to the Divine Mother and, in a supreme act of consecration, offered to the Deity manifest before him, the fruits of his austerities, his rosary, himself and everything that was his. He then uttered the following *mantra*:

O Goddess, I prostrate myself before Thee again and again—before Thee, the eternal Consort of Śiva, the three-eyed, the golden-hued, the indwelling Spirit in all, the Giver of refuge, the Accomplisher of every end, and the most auspicious among all auspicious objects.

In the course of ritualistic worship it is usual for the worshipper to invoke the Deity in him and when the worship is over, to pray to the Deity to mingle again with the universe from which It came. Though the worshipper feels his identity with the Deity for a while, he is soon overpowered again by worldly consciousness and completely forgets his identity. When Rāmakṛishṇa invoked the Divine Mother in Sāradā Devī, she attained a high state of spiritual experience. When she came to, she did not lose sense of her identity with the Divine but retained it throughout her life. Further, the worship symbolized her participation in Rāmakṛishṇa's life, in the fruits of his own austerities, and in his spiritual ministry. Henceforth her body and mind became the instruments of that Energy which is known as the Divine Mother and which played through the body and mind of Rāmakṛishṇa. They saw in each other only the Divine Mother. Their minds never once came down to a lower level. She was holy as he was holy. He was the "divine man", and she the "divine woman". She was a mother to his disciples, and to their disciples in turn, as much as to her own. Nay, she was more than a mother, for through her that Energy known as the Mother, whom Rāmakṛishṇa worshipped and realized, was made manifest. It is no wonder that she is known today as the Holy Mother—a name which at once evokes mingled feelings of love and reverence.

It is a traditional teaching among the Hindus that the Hindu woman should cultivate a spiritual attitude in her domestic life by looking upon her husband as a symbol of divinity. Rendering him selfless service in the proper frame of mind sublimates the human into the divine and ensures spiritual progress. Śrī Sāradā Devī was singularly fortunate as her "husband" was the holy Rāmakṛishṇa, the God-man of this age. It was thus easy for her to transmute service into worship. His teachings had a profound effect on her receptive mind. She spared no pains to practise the highest spirituality. We get a glimpse of her inner life from her own words:

During my days at Dakshiṇeśwar, I used to get up at 3 o'clock in the morning and sit in meditation. Often I used to be totally absorbed in it. Once, on a moonlit night, doing *japa*,[1] I was sitting near the steps of the *nahabat*. Everything was quiet. I did not even know when the Master passed that way. On other days I would hear the sound of his slippers, but on this, I did not. I was totally absorbed in meditation. . . . On this day the cloth had slipped off from my back owing to the breeze, but I was unconscious of it. It seems "son Yogen"[2] went that way to give the water-jug to the Master and saw me in that condition.

Ah! the ecstasy of those days. On moonlit nights I would look at the moon and pray with folded hands, "May my heart be as pure as the rays of yonder moon!" If one is steady in meditation, one can clearly see the Lord in one's heart and hear His voice. The moment an idea flashes in the mind of such a one, it will be fulfilled then and there. One will be bathed in peace. Ah! what a mind I had at that time. Brinde, the maidservant, one day dropped a metal plate in front of me with a bang. The sound penetrated into my heart.[3]

In the fullness of one's spiritual realization, one will find that He who resides in one's heart resides in the hearts of others as well—

[1] Repetition of the *mantra* given her by Śrī Rāmakṛishṇa.

[2] Swāmī Yogānanda (Yogen), a monastic disciple of Śrī Rāmakṛishṇa.

[3] The Holy Mother, who was then meditating in the *nahabat*, felt the sound like a clap of thunder and burst into tears. According to Patañjali, the great teacher of Yoga, when the mind gets deeply concentrated, even a slight sound is heard like a peal of thunder.

the oppressed, the persecuted, the Untouchable and the outcast. This realization makes one truly humble.

No less a person than Śrī Rāmakṛishṇa himself bore testimony to Sāradā Devī's moral and spiritual perfection. "Had she not been so pure," he told his disciples in later years, "who knows whether I might not have lost my self-control? After betrothal I prayed to the Divine Mother, 'O Mother, remove even the least taint of carnality from the mind of my wife'. When I lived with her I understood that the Mother had really granted my prayer".

Indeed, both of them were great. They saw the Divine Mother in each other! So completely different from other men and women they were! It is worth remembering that when Rāmakṛishṇa passed away in 1886, she who had been serving him for nearly thirteen years wept and cried, "O Mother, where hast Thou gone leaving me behind?"

He also saw in her the same Divine Mother that she saw in him. One day while massaging his feet, she asked him frankly, "How do you look upon me?" At once came his reply: "The Mother who is the Deity in the temple, the mother who gave birth to me and now lives in the *nahabat*—even she is now massaging my feet. I look upon you in that light, as the embodiment of Motherhood".

Śrī Sāradā Devī practised her spiritual disciplines according to the instructions of Śrī Rāmakṛishṇa; of these, *japa* and meditation formed an important part. Service to him, such as cooking and serving, which she did with meticulous care almost every day until his passing away, and other forms of personal service, gave her opportunities of communing with the great Teacher with whose life hers had become intertwined. As a result she used to attain high states of spiritual concentration and divine consciousness.

During these days of intense spiritual practices and exalted divine realizations, Śrī Rāmakṛishṇa knew that the Holy Mother was destined to continue his spiritual mission. He told her, "The people round about live like worms in darkness. You should look after them". He taught her the great *mantras*, instructed her how to initiate people in them and be a guide to those who sought spiritual refuge. She said in later days, "I have received all these *mantras* from the Master himself.

Through these one is sure to achieve perfection". During the days of his illness at Kāśipur he asked her very feelingly, "Well, won't you do anything? Am I to do all?" To this she replied: "I am a woman, what can I do?" And he said: "No, no, you have much to do".[1]

Her purity was immaculate like that of her husband. Her relinquishment of wealth and other possessions clearly showed how successfully she had practised the ideal of renunciation.[2] Indeed, she was eminently fitted to carry on the work of spiritual teaching after his passing away, and to guide hundreds of disciples in later years.

In Her Village Home

She first returned from Dakshiṇeśwar to Jayrāmbāṭī in October, 1873, and stayed at her home for some months. Her father passed away in March, 1874. In this bereavement she was a tower of strength to her mother.

She returned to Dakshiṇeśwar in April, 1874. As Śrī Rāmakṛishṇa was then suffering from dysentery she had to nurse him. He recovered, but she in turn suffered from the same illness. When she improved, she went again in 1875 to her home where she had a severe relapse. All remedy failed and Śrī Rāmakṛishṇa felt very anxious. She, therefore, decided to try to obtain divine aid by fasting and appealing to the Deity at the temple of the Divine Mother in the aspect of Siṁhavāhinī. The Holy Mother herself observed that within a short time the Goddess revealed two medicines—one was revealed to her mother for the dysentery and the other to herself for a malady of her eye. Both the medicines were accordingly tried and proved successful.

The Holy Mother again fell ill, this time suffering from an enlargement of the spleen. When she was cured, she went to Dakshiṇeśwar for the third time in January, 1877. In the meantime, Chandra Devī, the mother of Śrī Rāmakṛishṇa, had passed away. Sāradā visited Dakshiṇeśwar again in February,

[1] Meaning her rôle as a *guru*.

[2] One day a rich Marwari gentleman proposed to lodge Rs. 10,000 in the bank to the credit of Śrī Rāmakṛishṇa so that he might be placed beyond want. Rāmakṛishṇa did not accept the proposal as it was incompatible with his ideal. He, however, suggested that he might ask the Holy Mother, and the money might be invested in her name. She also stoutly refused the offer, as it would be the same as Rāmakṛishṇa's accepting the money. Rāmakṛishṇa was delighted to see that she jealously guarded her ideal.

1881, but did not stay for more than a short time. In 1884 and 1885 she returned to Dakshiṇeśwar. During one of these visits she had to pass through a wilderness while travelling from Jayrāmbāṭī to Dakshiṇeśwar. It was infested with dacoits. She went with a party, but as she was rather slow, she did not keep pace with it, and was lagging behind. When the party was out of sight, she met a dacoit and his wife; realizing her danger, terror-stricken as she was, she kept a cool head. Speaking to them in an appealing tone as though they were her father and mother, and she their daughter who had lost her way, she won them both over to escorting her through the dangerous area. Her womanly grace and sweetness, her simplicity and utter resignation, appealed to their hearts, and they took her to Tārakeśwar where she rejoined her companions of the party. The two dacoits then disappeared.

Śrī Rāmakṛishṇa was suffering from cancer of the throat. He was first brought to Śyāmpukur in September, 1885, and three months later to Kāśipur. The Holy Mother busied herself in nursing the Master, cooking suitable food for him and attending to his needs.

When Śrī Rāmakṛishṇa's illness continued unabated in spite of medical care and devoted nursing, the Holy Mother sought divine aid at the temple of Śiva at Tārakeśwar. She fasted two days, taking neither food nor drink, and prayed for a divine remedy. During the night of the second day she was startled to hear a sound, and the idea flashed in her mind, "Who is husband and who is wife? Who is my relative in this world? Why am I about to kill myself?" She said: "All my attachment for the Master was gone and my mind was filled with the sense of utter renunciation. When I returned to Kāśipur the next morning, the Master asked me, 'Well, did you get anything? In truth, everything is unreal, isn't it?' "

The Master dreamt at the same time that an elephant had gone out to fetch him medicine and was digging the earth to get it. The Holy Mother also saw in a dream that the neck of the image of Kālī the Mother was bent to one side. She described it thus: "I asked her, 'Mother why do you stand with the neck bent?' The Deity replied, 'It is because of this (pointing to the cancer in the throat of Śrī Rāmakṛishṇa). I also have it in My throat' ".

Śrī Rāmakṛishṇa passed away on August 16, 1886. Her

heart was filled with despair and grief. The cremation over, she was removing her ornaments as Hindu widows do on the death of their husbands. When she was about to do this, Śrī Rāmakṛishṇa appeared in a vision and asked her, "What are you doing? I have not gone away, I have only passed from one room to another". After this vision she felt greatly consoled.

Pilgrimage

Two weeks after the Master's passing away Śrī Sāradā Devī began her pilgrimage through North India. She started from Calcutta on August 30, 1886, and was accompanied by a party of two women disciples—Lakshmī-Didi, a niece of Śrī Rāmakṛishṇa and Golāp-Mā—and three monastic disciples,—subsequently known as Swāmī Yogānanda, Swāmī Abhedānanda and Swāmī Adbhutānanda—as well as the householder disciples, Mahendranāth Gupta and his wife.

The party halted on the way at Deoghar and Banāras. At Banāras, while she was attending evening service at the Temple of Viśwanāth, she attained a state of ecstasy. She visited also Ayodhyā, associated with the life and doings of Śrī Rāmachandra, the divine hero of the *Rāmāyaṇa*. While she was proceeding to Vṛindāvan by train, she was sleeping with her arm exposed on which was tied Śrī Rāmakṛishṇa's amulet. He then appeared to her in a vision which she described in these words: "I saw him look at me through the window of the railway carriage and warn me with the words, 'You have my gold amulet with you. See to it that you do not lose it' ". She got up at once and kept the amulet safe in the box in which she carried his photograph. Later on when she returned to Calcutta, she handed it over to the Belur Math.[1]

At Vṛindāvan her remembrance of Rādhā's passionate grief at her separation from her beloved Kṛishṇa created so poignant a longing for the Divine and stirred her pent-up feelings to such an extent that she used to burst into tears. Then again she had a vision in which Śrī Rāmakṛishṇa appeared before her and assuaged her grief with the words: "Why are you weeping so much? Here I am. Where have I gone, after all? I have passed only from one room to another".

[1] The monastery at Belur on the bank of the Ganges, established by Swāmī Vivekānanda. In the temple dedicated to Rāmakṛishṇa his relics have been deposited.

Her life at Vṛindāvan was one of deep meditation, fervent prayer and profound experiences. In her residence at Kāla Bābu's house she used to attain the highest contentless consciousness called the *nirvikalpa samādhi* (superconsciousness in which the ego is transcended). It was here that she began her rôle as *guru*, and it came about in a strange manner. Yogen (who became Swāmī Yogānanda) had not been given Tāntric initiation by Śrī Rāmakṛishṇa. The Master appeared in a vision before her on three consecutive nights and told her that he had not initiated Yogen, and asked her to give him initiation, even telling her the *mantra* she should give him. The Master appeared also before him and bade him receive his initiation from her. Accordingly she performed worship, entered into *samādhi*, and initiated Yogen.

The party returned from Vṛindāvan to Calcutta before August, 1887.

At Kāmārpukur

On her return from Vṛindāvan the Holy Mother went to Kāmārpukur, the birthplace of Śrī Rāmakṛishṇa, accompanied by Golāp-Mā and Swāmī Yogānanda. The latter returned to Calcutta in three days, but Golāp-Mā stayed with her for nearly a month.

Western readers would find it difficult to understand what an uproar of criticism among the village women was occasioned by the Holy Mother's presence at Kāmārpukur. To their painful surprise they saw a Hindu widow wearing bracelets and a red-bordered *sāri*, which are used only by women whose husbands are alive. The Holy Mother wanted, therefore, to remove the bracelets, but she again had a vision of Śrī Rāmakṛishṇa. She described it in these words:

> One day I saw to my great surprise that the Master was coming towards the house from the direction of Bhuti's canal. He was followed by Naren and other disciples. . . . He then said to me, "Don't take off the bracelets. Do you know the Vaishṇava Tantras?" I said, "What are they? I don't know anything about them". Thereupon he said, "Gaur-Maṇi will come here this afternoon. She will tell you about them". That very afternoon Gaur-Maṇi arrived, and I learnt from her that to a woman, her husband is *Chinmaya* (Pure Spirit).

After Golāp-Mā's departure from Kāmārpukur there was none to help the Holy Mother, none whom she could ask to fetch such necessaries of life as food and vegetables, for she observed *purdah* according to custom and would not leave the house, nor had she any money for her expenses. She had, therefore, to take a spade and dig the earth to cultivate some greens. She prepared rice out of the paddy that had been left in the granary, offered it to Śrī Rāmakṛishṇa, and ate it without any condiments, curry or even salt. On hearing of her return to Śrī Rāmakṛishṇa's village, her widowed mother offered to take her to Jayrāmbāṭī, but the Holy Mother spent only a day with her and returned to Kāmārpukur. She was absolutely lonely,[1] her future seemed to be dark, and she began to brood over it. She said in later days, "While staying alone at Kāmārpukur, I thought to myself, 'I have no child. There is no one in this world whom I can call my own. What will happen to me?' Thereupon the Master appeared to me and said, 'Well, do you want a son? I have given you so many jewels of sons. And in course of time you will hear many many more people addressing you as Mother' ". She became convinced more and more that the Master had some definite work for her to do.

At last news reached the lay and monastic disciples of Śrī Rāmakṛishṇa that the Holy Mother needed their care and attention, and they took it upon themselves as their spiritual duty to invite her to Calcutta and arrange for her stay.

In 1888 we enter another phase of her life and activities. From this year onwards she used to stay in Calcutta in the house arranged for her by the disciples and devotees, and later in the home known as "The Mother's House" where Swāmī Sāradānanda, a direct disciple of Śrī Rāmakṛishṇa, made permanent arrangements for her stay and comfort as long as she lived.

Austerities and Ecstasy

In 1893 she performed a severe form of austerity known as the "Austerity of the Five Fires",[2] with a view to removing some

[1] Sometimes at her request Prasannamayī of the Lāhā family used to send an old maidservant to stay with her at night.

[2] This is called *pañchatapaḥ*, in which four fires are lighted on four sides; the sun burning overhead constitutes the fifth fire. In the midst of these prayer and meditation are practised. After the practice she did not have any further disturbances.

psychic disturbances which took the form of frequent visions. In these visions she used to see a monk who requested her to practise the austerities, and see also a girl. She used to have very rare spiritual experiences to which Yogīn-Mā and other women disciples of Śrī Rāmakṛishṇa bore witness. She could transcend body-consciousness at will. Once while meditating on the roof of Balarām Bābu's house in Calcutta, she fell into a state of *samādhi*. She then had a rare experience which she described in the following words: "I found in that state that I had travelled into a distant country. Everybody there was very affectionate to me. My beauty was beyond description. Śrī Rāmakṛishṇa also was there. With great tenderness they made me sit by his side. I cannot describe to you the nature of that ecstatic joy. When my mind came down from that exalted mood, I found my body lying there. I thought, 'How can I possibly enter into this ugly body?' I could not at all persuade my mind to do so. After a long while, it did, and the body became conscious again". When she had a similar experience in the house of Nīlāmbar Mukherji, set apart for her stay near the Belur Math, she took a long time to come to. When she began to gain traces of body-consciousness, she began to say, "O Yogīn, where are my hands? Where are my feet?" Yogīn-Mā, who was meditating in her company, pressed her limbs and said to her, "Why, Mother, here are your hands and here are your feet". However, it took the Holy Mother a long time to become conscious of her whole body.

An increasing number of people began to flock for guidance, instructions and spiritual initiation, as her spiritual greatness came to be known more and more.

Domestic Life

Her mother Śyāmāsundarī Devī passed away in 1906, and she became virtually the head of the family. She had four brothers of whom Abhay Charan was the youngest and brightest. Unfortunately, not long after qualifying as a medical practitioner he died in 1899, leaving behind his widow, Surabālā, whom he committed to the Holy Mother's care. Stricken with grief over her husband's premature death, Surabālā became insane. In 1900 she gave birth to a posthumous daughter who was called Rādhārānī, or more familiarly Rādhu. The Holy

Mother had a deep affection for Rādhu who was not properly cared for by her sickly and insane mother, and played the part of a mother to the child. This little girl and her mother proved a constant source of trouble and anxiety to her, but never for a moment did she give up her love for the child and the mother in spite of the offensive behaviour to which she was subjected. She used to console herself by saying: "Perhaps I worshipped Śiva with *vilwa* leaves having thorns. Therefore I have got such a thorn in this life".

If Rādhu's mother was a thorn, Rādhu when she grew up proved herself to be another thorn not less prickly! She was weak in body and mind, and had a dogged obstinacy and an incurable perversity which never left her, but became worse with the showering of love and affection by her illustrious aunt. In June, 1911, the Holy Mother arranged for the marriage of this girl. Years passed, but Rādhu would not visit her husband's house, with the result that both she and her mother became part of the Holy Mother's household! The girl's evil qualities became worse with the appearance of insanity which she inherited from her mother. Rādhu had a baby, but she would not take care of the child. The Holy Mother had, therefore, to entreat her and occasionally reprimand her. On one such occasion Rādhu in her anger threw a large egg-plant from the vegetable basket at the Holy Mother. It struck her heavily; she bent her back in pain, and a swelling appeared. The Holy Mother became anxious for the welfare of Rādhu, for Hindus believe that if a foolish and ignorant person insults a spiritually advanced man or woman, the offender will have to suffer in life or meet with an evil fate. So the Holy Mother turned to the photograph of Śrī Rāmakṛishṇa and prayed: "Lord, please forgive her mistake; she is senseless". Then she blessed Rādhu and said, "Rādhu, the Master did not even once utter a word of remonstrance to me, and you afflict me so much. How can you understand where my place is? You think nothing of me because I live with you all". At these words Rādhu burst into tears: but such tears were momentary.

Rādhu never changed. The Holy Mother had to meet all the expenses of Rādhu and, though pressed for money, she could not ask any devotee for help, for it would be against the injunction of Śrī Rāmakṛishṇa.

Her mind was absolutely pure and unselfish; she gave

herself away in the service of all. As the Holy Mother used to get spiritual absorption, which developed into *samādhi* very often, there was nothing in this world to attract her and bring her mind down to world-consciousness. Highly spiritual persons who have no attachment to this world or love of their physical body may pass away in *samādhi* even in early life. The Holy Mother felt and became convinced that the Lord Himself had provided an entanglement so that she might continue to live to fulfil the mission which Śrī Rāmakṛishṇa had left for her to do. She herself said:

How the Master has entangled me through Rādhu! . . . After the passing away of the Master I did not at all relish anything in life. I became utterly indifferent to worldly things and kept on praying, "What shall I achieve by remaining in this world?" At that time I saw a girl of ten or twelve, dressed in a red cloth, and walking in front of me. The Master pointed her out to me and said, "Cling to her as a support. Many children (disciples) will come to you". The next moment he disappeared. I did not see the girl any more. Later on I was seated in this very place (her house at Jayrāmbāṭī). At that time Rādhu's mother was stark mad. She was clutching some rags pressed under her arm, and Rādhu crawled behind her weeping. Seeing this, I felt a peculiar sensation in my heart. At once I ran to Rādhu and took her in my arms. I said to myself, "Well, if I do not look after this child, who else will take care of her? She has no father, and her mother is that insane woman". No sooner had I taken the child in my arms than I saw the Master. He said, "This is that girl. Cling to her as your support. She is Yoga-māyā, the Illusive Power".

She herself used to say, "You see, my doting on Rādhu is a delusion that I have superimposed upon myself". And she sometimes would add, "My mind does not dwell on Rādhu in the slightest degree. I force it on her. I pray to the Master saying, 'O Lord, please divert my mind a little on Rādhu. Otherwise who will look after her?' ".

That the Holy Mother's mind dwelt on God in spite of all these distractions caused by Rādhu and other relatives is beyond doubt. An ordinary man or woman who is attached to relatives young or old, children or grown-ups, can hardly bear the pang of separation from them at the time of death. But the Holy Mother, who was so fond of Rādhu, asked her attendant again and again to send Rādhu and her cousins back to Jayrāmbāṭī.

Even when their little ones approached her bed, she would ask for them to be taken away from her, saying that she had once for all detached her mind from them, and that their presence by her side was unwelcome.

As *Guru*

Next to Śrī Rāmakṛishṇa the Holy Mother received the highest reverence from the Rāmakṛishṇa Order and its devotees. She was his first disciple and was identified with him, and he was identified with her. He bade her continue his mission after his passing away and wanted his disciples not to make any distinction between himself and her. His spiritual presence and power manifested through her, and she was fitted to play the part of a *guru* on his passing away. To be a *guru* is a great responsibility, but she accepted it in full whenever she initiated anybody. She observed:

> The power of the *guru* is transmitted through the *mantra* to the disciple. That is why the *guru* at the time of initiation takes on himself the sins of the disciple and suffers so much from physical maladies. It is extremely difficult to be a *guru*; for he has to take the responsibility for the disciple's sins. He is affected by them. A good disciple, however, helps the teacher. Some disciples make quick progress, and some do it slowly; it depends on the tendencies of the mind acquired by one's past deeds.

Her motherly love and tenderness for one and all never allowed any consideration of personal suffering to stand in the way of giving spiritual refuge to those who sought it. Once, Swāmī Premānanda, a great disciple of Śrī Rāmakṛishṇa observed, "We are sending to the Holy Mother the poison we could not take ourselves. She is giving refuge to everybody, accepting the sins of all and digesting the same". On Tuesdays and Saturdays, when she was staying at her Calcutta residence, several hundreds of disciples and devotees would bow down before her and touch her feet. She then used to feel a severe burning sensation all over her body on account of her vicarious sufferings; so she would wash her feet again and again with Ganges water, for she received great relief thereby. When a woman disciple of Śrī Rāmakṛishṇa warned her not to do so lest she should catch cold, the Holy Mother replied:

Well, Yogīn, how can I explain it to you? Some people touch my feet, and that refreshes me wonderfully. Again there are others whose touch gives me a terrible burning sensation. I feel it like the sting of a wasp. Only by applying Ganges water do I get some relief. Once, in the absence of an attending disciple, a rather elderly man came here. . . . Seeing him from a distance, I entered my room and sat on my bed. He was very anxious to salute me by touching the feet. I protested and shrank back, yet he did it. From that time I have been almost at the point of death through an unbearable pain in the feet and the stomach. I washed my feet three or four times, still I cannot get rid of this burning sensation.

Though she knew that she would have to suffer vicariously for her disciples' sins, she would not let it prevent her from exercising her motherly love. When a disciple once hesitated to touch her feet because it might cause her suffering, she said, "No, my child, we are born for this purpose. If we do not accept others' sins and sorrows and do not assimilate these, who else will do so? Who else will bear the responsibilities of the sinners and the afflicted?" During her last illness, when her body had become very emaciated and she could no longer get up without help, her monastic disciples were speaking amongst themselves about her extreme suffering. One of them said, "If the Mother recovers this time, we shall ask her not to give initiation any more. She is suffering so much because of taking upon herself the sins of so many types of people". On hearing this, the Holy Mother smiled and said, "Why do you say so? Do you think that the Master came only to take *rasagollas*?"[1] Once she said to a disciple, "My child, several among those who come here have been up to everything in life. No type of sin has been left undone by them. But when they come here and address me as mother, I forget everything and they get more than they deserve".

Her Hospitality

The hospitality of the Holy Mother was unique. It was characterized by a rare motherly care and solicitude. Those who had the privilege of visiting her would not be sent back without being treated as guests as long as they stayed. If a disciple attending on her had to go out on business to a neigh-

[1] Bengali sweetmeat.

bouring village and returned late, the Mother would not take her food at the usual time, but would wait for her. When the devotees went to her village home at Jayrāmbāṭī, she would always insist on their taking rest there for at least two or three days. She knew that people had to undergo much hardship to reach Jayrāmbāṭī. She said, "It is easy to visit Gayā or Banāras, but not this place". In the last years of her life the number of devotees who used to visit her in her Calcutta residence was so large that she got tired with the rush and went for rest to her village home; but there also many devotees from Calcutta used to go, some of them arriving at odd hours without any warning. They all received, however, the same warm and cordial hospitality.

Her Powers

"The Mother had the power of weaning people from evil ways by a sheer effort of will. Thus she cured one who was an inveterate drunkard of his vicious habit. She changed the mind of a girl who was trying to seduce a young man, and she converted to holy living a young wife who was going to ruin herself in the disappointment caused by her husband's taking to a life of renunciation."[1] Some of the devotees had mystical experiences after their contact with the Holy Mother. Some dreamt of her as a goddess in human form though they had never seen even her picture before. Others received their initiation wholly or in part from her in dream, and when they asked for initiation, they found that she gave them the same *mantra* that they had received from her in dream. Girish Chandra Ghosh, the father of the Bengali drama, saw the Holy Mother in a dream when he was nineteen years old, and when he met her many years after, he found to his astonishment that it was the same person that he had seen in the dream. She, however, continued to be simple in her everyday life and seemed like an ordinary woman. Besides initiating spiritual aspirants in a *mantra*, she also used to bless the young novices of the Rāmakṛishṇa Order, by conveying to them the inner meaning of the vows of *brahmacharya* or of *sannyāsa*. She also gave the *brahmachārin's* white dress or the *sannyāsin's gerrua*-dyed cloth as the case might be, by way of benediction.

[1] *Śrī Sāradā Devī, the Holy Mother:* Rāmakṛishṇa Math, Mylapore, Madras.

Pilgrimage Again

In 1888 the Holy Mother, accompanied by Swāmī Advaitānanda, went to Gayā on a pilgrimage. There she performed funeral rites in memory of Śrī Rāmakṛishṇa's mother. She also visited Bodh Gayā. In the same year she visited the great temple at Purī. She went to Gayā and Purī, because Rāmakṛishṇa had not visited them on the ground that he would be so much overwhelmed by divine ecstasy that he might pass away.

In 1894 she visited Banāras and Vṛindāvan a second time. In 1901 she went again to Purī. In 1910 she left for Rāmeśwar, halting on the way at Berhāmpore. She stayed at Madras for about a month and initiated many people. She was delighted to see a large number of educated ladies there. On her way to Rāmeśwar she halted at Madurā and visited the temple of the Divine Mother in that city. At Rāmeśwar the Rāja of Rāmnāḍ, a great admirer of Swāmī Vivekānanda, gave her special facilities for worship, such as have been enjoyed by no other pilgrim before or since. From Rāmeśwar she went to Bangalore. On her way back to Calcutta she halted for a day at Rājahmundry and took a bath in the holy Godāvarī. She also stopped at Purī for a couple of days and reached Calcutta in April, 1911.

She went to Banāras for the third time in November, 1912, staying two months and a half in that holy city. There she visited the well-known Chameli Purī—a brother disciple of Tota Purī, the *guru* of Śrī Rāmakṛishṇa—who was then over a hundred years old. She also saw Sārnāth before returning to Calcutta.

The Mother's House at Calcutta

In May, 1909, the Holy Mother moved to what is known as the Holy Mother's House[1] in Calcutta. While staying there, a number of women[2] disciples of Śrī Rāmakṛishṇa used to stay with the Holy Mother—Golāp-Mā, Yogīn-Mā, Lakshmī-Didi and Gaurī-Mā being the best known. All of them were widows except Gaurī-Mā who was a virgin. They all lived holy lives

[1] This is one of the publication centres of the Order of Rāmakṛishṇa and is also known as the Udbodhan Office, the *Udbodhan* being a Bengali bimonthly published there.

[2] See the next chapter.

of meditation and service. The wives of several of Śrī Rāmakṛishṇa's householder disciples like Balarām Bose, Mahendranāth Gupta ("M" of *The Gospel of Śrī Rāmakṛishṇa*) and others used to visit the Holy Mother and invite her to their homes.

Last Days

In January, 1919, the Holy Mother went to Jayrāmbāṭī and stayed there for over a year. During the last three months of her stay her health seriously declined. On her lunar birthday in December, 1919, she had black fever, and afterwards suffered from it every now and then. Her strength was greatly impaired. Swāmī Sāradānanda, therefore, arranged to bring her to Calcutta on February 27, 1920, and she came "in a pitiable condition", looked like "a skeleton covered with skin" and appeared "black as soot". For the next five months she continued to suffer. Sometimes the temperature shot up to 103°. She suffered also from an intense burning sensation all over the body.

A month before her passing away she had the picture of Śrī Rāmakṛishṇa moved from her room to an adjoining one, and her own bed made on the floor. Even in that wretched state of health whatever food she could eat she would eat only after offering it to the Master. A few days before her passing away she withdrew her mind entirely from Rādhu and the little child of Rādhu, both of whom had been dear to her. Swāmī Sāradānanda and others then knew that the Mother would not live much longer.

She was fast sinking. Owing to anaemia the legs began to swell, and she could not even get up from her bed. A few days before the final event, a woman prostrated and sobbed saying, "Mother, what will happen to us hereafter". The Mother consoled her in a low, almost inaudible voice: "Why do you fear? You have seen the Master". After a pause she added, "But I tell you one thing—if you want peace of mind, do not find fault with others. Rather see your own faults. Learn to make the whole world your own. No one is a stranger, my child: this whole world is your own!" Perhaps this embodies her last message to the world also.

During the last three days she was almost silent and would

not talk to anyone. She once called Swāmī Sāradānanda, and said, "Śarat, I am going—Yogīn, Golāp and the rest are here. Look after them".

She passed away after a final ecstasy at 1.30 a.m. on July 20, 1920. Her body was brought to the Belur Math and cremated. Several thousand people and devotees as well as some of the disciples of Śrī Rāmakṛishṇa were present.

Her Spiritual Greatness

The Holy Mother's simple and unostentatious life is so profound that its extraordinary nature is not easily appreciated. She lived very near us in point of time: what is known of her is not the outcome of legend and tradition which have grown round the names of many saints and sages of olden days in the mist of antiquity. The world has not seen a woman who lived with her husband like the Holy Mother, and whose life resembles hers. The Holy Mother was in constant communion with God, but she so completely veiled her spiritual greatness that she looked like an ordinary woman. She was so *sāttwic*, so serene, so brimful of the spirit that there was almost no external expression of her greatness and spiritual power. Śrī Rāmakṛishṇa and his disciples identified her with the Primordial Power Herself who is known as the Divine Mother. Śrī Rāmakṛishṇa once said, "If the being who is residing at the concert house (meaning the Holy Mother) is cross with one for some reason, it is beyond even my power to save him". "In her, Indian womanhood fulfils, nay, transcends, its purely Indian character and assumes a world significance."[1] Sāradā Devī was neither wife nor mother. Yet she was a mother in another and higher sense: when we think of her, we think of God as the Divine Mother; the Holy Mother and God are inseparable.

Her Teachings

No one can read the story of the Holy Mother's life without being convinced that God dwelt in her heart. Her teachings are not those of a scholar or savant but are the revelations of a Saviour. Being the fruits of her own direct experiences, they

[1] *Great Women of India* (Advaita Ashrama, Calcutta): Dr. Sir S. Radhakrishnan in his Introduction.

possess an irresistible power like those of the great World Teachers. The more one studies and ponders over them, the purer in heart and therefore the more peaceful one becomes. We give below a selection of her teachings which may give the reader a glimpse of the beauty of her soul.

SPIRITUAL PRACTICE

1. If you do not pray to God, what is that to Him? It is only your misfortune.

2. The conjunction of the day and the night is the most auspicious time for calling on God. The mind remains pure at this time.

3. The *mantra* purifies the body. Man becomes pure by repeating the name of God. So repeat His name always.

4. Practise meditation, and by and by your mind will be so calm and fixed that you will find it hard to keep away from meditation.

5. One cannot escape from the effect of one's past *karma*. But if a person lives a prayerful life, he gets off with only the prick of a thorn in the leg where he was to suffer from a deep cut.

6. You should work, no doubt. Work saves the mind from going astray. But prayer and meditation also are necessary. You must sit for meditation at least once in the morning and once in the evening. That will be like the helm of a boat. When one sits in meditation in the evening, there is self-examination in respect of the work done in the course of the day.

7. Ordinary human love results in misery. Love for God brings blessedness.

8. Many take the name of God after receiving blows in life. But he who can offer his mind like a flower at the feet of the Lord right up from childhood is indeed blessed.

9. An unmarried person is half free whether he prays to God or not. He will advance towards Him with rapid strides when he feels a little drawn towards Him.

10. You can practise *prāṇāyāma* a little, but not much, otherwise the brain will get heated. If the mind becomes calm of itself, what is then the necessity of practising *prāṇāyāma*? The practice of *prāṇāyāma* and *āsana* often brings occult powers, and occult powers lead one astray.

11. First offer to God whatever you eat. One must not eat

unoffered food. As your food is, so will be your blood. From pure food you get pure blood, pure mind, and strength. Pure mind begets ecstatic love (*prema-bhakti*).

12. The goal of life is to realize God and to be always immersed in thought of Him.

13. Everything depends on the mind. Nothing can be achieved without purity of mind. It is said, "The aspirant may have received the grace of the *guru*, the Lord and the Vaishṇavas; but he comes to grief without the grace of 'one' ". That 'one' is the mind. The mind of the aspirant should be gracious to him.

14. What else does one obtain by the realization of God? Does one grow two horns? No, the mind becomes pure, and through a pure mind one attains knowledge and awakening.

15. The mind is everything. It is in the mind alone that one feels pure and impure. A man, first of all, must make his own mind guilty and then alone can he see another man's guilt.

16. As clouds are blown away by the wind, the thirst for material pleasures will be driven away by the utterance of the Lord's name.

17. Don't puzzle the mind with too many inquiries. One finds it difficult to put one single thing into practice, but dares invite distraction by filling the mind with too many things.

CAUTIONS IN SPIRITUAL LIFE

18. I tell you one thing. If you want peace of mind, do not find fault with others. Rather see your own faults. Learn to make the whole world your own. No one is a stranger, my child; this whole world is your own. When a man sees defects in others, his own mind first gets polluted.

19. One should not hurt others even by words. One must not speak even an unpleasant truth unnecessarily. By indulging in rude words one's nature becomes rude. One's sensibility is lost if one has not control over one's speech. Śrī Rāmakṛishṇa used to say, "One should not ask a lame person how he became lame".

20. Give up this dry discussion, this hodge-podge of philosophy. Who has been able to know God by reasoning?

21. Money always taints the mind. You may think that you are above money and that you will never feel any attraction

for it. You may further think that you can leave it behind at any moment. No, my child, never harbour this thought in your mind. Through a tiny little loop-hole it will enter into your mind and then, quite undetected, strangle you gradually.

22. As long as a man has desires, there is no end to his transmigration. It is desires that make him take one body after another. There will be rebirth for a man if he has even the desire to eat a piece of candy.

23. One must have devotion towards one's own *guru*. Whatever may be the nature of the *guru*, the disciple gets salvation by dint of his unflinching devotion towards his *guru*.

24. One should not trifle with a thing, though it may be very insignificant. If you respect a thing, the thing also will respect you. One should perform even insignificant work with respect.

25. However spiritual a man may be, he must pay rent for the use of the body to the last farthing.

DIVINE GRACE

26. *Q*. Mother, I have practised austerities and *japa* so much, but I have not achieved anything.

A. God is not like a fish or vegetables that you can buy Him for a price.

27. *Q*. Mother, I am coming to you so frequently and I hope I have received your grace, but I do not feel anything.

A. My child, suppose you are asleep on a bed, and some one removes you with the bed to another place. In that case, will you know immediately on waking that you have come to a new place? Not at all. Only after your drowsiness clears away completely will you know that you have come to a new place.

28. *Q*. How does one get the vision of God?

A. It is only through His grace. But one must practise meditation and *japa*. That removes impurities of the mind. One must practise spiritual disciplines such as worship and so forth. As one gets the fragrance of a flower by handling it, or as one gets the smell of sandalwood by rubbing it against a stone, in the same way one gets spiritual awakening by constantly thinking of God.

29. Repeat the name of God always from the innermost core of your heart, and in all sincerity take refuge in the Master. Do not bother to know how your mind is reacting to things

around. And do not waste time in calculating and worrying over whether or not you are progressing in the path of spirituality. It is *ahaṁkāra* (vanity) to judge progress for oneself. Have faith in the grace of your *guru* and *Ishṭa*.

30. A child might not give a thing to a person who asked for it a hundred times, whereas he might give it away to another even at the first request. In the same way the grace of God is not conditioned by anything.

ON ŚRĪ RĀMAKṚISHṆA

31. How attached the Master was to truth! He used to say that truth alone is the austerity of the Iron Age (*Kali Yuga*). One attains to God by sticking to truth.

32. Śrī Rāmakṛishṇa left me behind to manifest the Motherhood of God to the world.

33. If you pray to him constantly before his picture, then he manifests himself through that picture. The place where that picture is kept becomes a shrine.

HOPE

34. Even the injunctions of destiny are cancelled if one takes refuge in God. Destiny strikes off with her own hands what she has written about such a person.[1]

[1] The short account of the life and teachings of Śrī Sāradā Devī, the Holy Mother, given in this chapter, is based on the books on the subject published in Bengali by the Udbodhan Office, Calcutta, and *Śrī Sāradā Devī, the Holy Mother*, in English, by the Ramakrishna Math, Madras.

CHAPTER XIV

SOME HOLY WOMEN FIGURING IN THE LIFE OF RAMAKRISHNA

THE life of a great Teacher inspires millions of people. When a tidal wave rises and flows, the rivers and streams, reservoirs and tanks, pools and hollows, all get filled with water, each receiving it according to capacity. Men and women who come into contact with a God-man receive spiritual impetus from him, and those few who follow in his footsteps in a spirit of complete dedication become saints.

It is natural that Śrī Rāmakṛishṇa should have inspired not only many men, some of whom became monks and others householders, but also many women. Of these, several lived the holy life as nuns, and others the life of devout householders.

One of the great women who met him was older than he, and became one of his *gurus*. Another was a profound mystic who had rare experiences of the Divine Boy Gopāla. His niece became a disciple, and the rest of his women disciples were either householders or nuns who embraced the ideals of Śrī Sāradā Devī, the Holy Mother, and were associated with her, like his niece.

Yogeśwarī Bhairavī Brāhmaṇī

The woman *guru* of Śrī Rāmakṛishṇa was known by the name of Yogeśwarī Bhairavī Brāhmaṇī. An adept in Yoga, she also practised Vaishṇava and Tāntrik disciplines. She was born probably in the second decade of the nineteenth century, for she was nearly forty-five years of age when she met Rāmakṛishṇa in 1861. He was then about twenty-five years old. Her parents were Brahmins who lived in the district of Jessore in Bengal. She was a lifelong virgin, and had acquired great mystic powers as a result of Yoga practices.

In 1861, in the course of her wanderings, the Bhairavī Brāhmaṇī came to Dakshiṇeśwar. When she met Śrī Rāmakṛishṇa she shed tears of joy and told him very affectionately, "My child, you are here! Knowing that you were somewhere on the banks of the Ganges I have been searching for you for a long time, and now I have found you". Rāmakṛishṇa felt drawn to her as a son to his mother and asked, "How could you know about me, mother?" She then replied, "Through the grace of the Divine Mother I had come to know that I was to meet three of you. I have already met two—Chandra and Girija—in East Bengal, and I find you here today".

In those days Śrī Rāmakṛishṇa was practising strenuous spiritual disciplines and having rare experiences of different kinds. He sat close to the Bhairavī Brāhmaṇī and taking her into confidence like a boy, recounted his spiritual visions and realizations. He described his loss of outer consciousness at the time of meditation, the burning sensation which he felt all over the body, his lack of sleep, and his utter other-worldliness, which he had during the days of his spiritual disciplines. He repeatedly asked her, "Can you tell me what these things might be? People say I am mad. Do you think I have really become insane?" While listening to his anxious words describing his wonderful experiences the Brāhmaṇī was transported with joy that he should have been fortunate enough to attain them. She replied, "Who calls you mad, my son? This is not madness. You have attained a rare and blessed spiritual state called *mahābhāva*, which is attended by nineteen external characteristics such as tears, tremor of the body, hair standing on end, and perspiration. One who has not experienced such a state can hardly understand it, and that is why men of the world call you insane". She also said that Śrī Rādhā and Śrī Gaurāṅga experienced the same state. On hearing her words Rāmakṛishṇa felt greatly consoled.

In the evening after cooking, the Brāhmaṇī offered the food to Raghuvīra, her chosen Deity, whose stone emblem she always carried tied round her neck. In the course of her meditation she had a significant vision. In the meantime Śrī Rāmakṛishṇa felt an uncontrollable urge to proceed to the Pañchavaṭī, the grove of five sacred trees, and went there in a high spiritual mood. Like a man possessed he began to eat the offerings placed before the stone emblem. When the Brāhmaṇī came to and opened her eyes, she was thrilled to see Rāmakṛishṇa eating the offering, for she had just seen this in her vision and was delighted to see him actually doing so. Rāmakṛishṇa was not his normal self at that time, and when he finished eating he apologized to her, saying, "I do not know what makes me do such things in a semi-conscious state". The Brāhmaṇī replied, "You have done well, my son. It is not you but the One that is within you that has done this thing. I realized at the time of meditation who did it and why. I have now come to the conclusion that I no longer need any ceremonial worship, which has at last borne fruit". So saying she took the remnants of the food as *prasād* (dedicated food), and consigned to the Ganges the sacred emblem of Raghuvīra, which she had devoutly worshipped for years, for she was convinced that Raghuvīra was embodied in the person of Rāmakṛishṇa.

The Brāhmaṇī was now fully convinced that Śrī Rāmakṛishṇa had attained his extraordinary experiences as the result of his deep love of God and successful practice of spiritual disciplines. She identified his experiences with those of Śrī Chaitanya. It was significant that Śrī Rāmakṛishṇa had a vision of two luminous boys coming out of his body on his way to Sihor, and she recognized them as Chaitanya and his comrade Nityānanda. The severe burning sensation which he felt all over the body she cured by a simple prescription. Once Śrī Rāmakṛishṇa was seized by an unappeasable hunger which no amount of eating could satisfy. She knew that those who are advanced in spirituality occasionally pass through such peculiar states, and prescribed a remedy by following which he was cured in three days and became normal again.

The Brāhmaṇī taught Śrī Rāmakṛishṇa the different disciplines mentioned in the sixty-four principal Tantras. He said later on, ". . . The infinite grace of the Divine Mother enabled me to pass unscathed through those fiery ordeals. Some of them were so dangerous that they very often caused the aspirant to lose his foothold and slip into moral turpitude."

It was the Brāhmaṇī who first discerned in Rāmakṛishṇa the signs of an Incarnation. She, therefore, boldly declared her conviction. Mathurnāth Biswās, the son-in-law of the proprietress of the Temple of Dakshiṇeśwar, invited Vaishṇava Charaṇ, Paṇdit Gaurīkānta Tarkālaṅkār and others, who were highly respected for their scholarship and spirituality, in order that she might discuss the matter with them. Paṇdit Gaurīkānta asserted unequivocally before Śrī Rāmakṛishṇa, "I am firmly convinced that you are that mine of infinite spiritual power, only a small fraction of which appears in the world from time to time in the form of Incarnations. I feel it in my heart, and scriptures are in my favour. I am ready to prove my contention to anyone who challenges me in the matter".

The Bhairavī Brāhmaṇī spent most of her last days exclusively in meditation and other spiritual disciplines. While Śrī Rāmakṛishṇa was at Banāras on pilgrimage, he met her there and advised her to spend the rest of her life at Vṛindāvan. She accordingly accompanied him to that place of pilgrimage, where she passed away shortly after.

Aghormaṇi Devī
(Known as Gopāla's Mother)

Aghormaṇi Devī was a profound mystic with rare spiritual experiences. One feels thrilled on reading an account of her life and spiritual attainments.

She was born in 1822 of Brahmin parents at Kāmārhāṭī. Her father Kāśīnāth Bhaṭṭāchārya got her betrothed at the age of nine to a young man of humble status in the village of Pāighāṭī, near Bodrā, in the district of Twenty-four Parganās, but unfortunately she became widowed almost immediately after the betrothal. She was then too young to know what married life was. After a short stay in the home of her father-in-law, she returned to her father's home. Her elder brother, Nīlmādhav Bhaṭṭāchārya, was a priest in the Temple of Śrī Rādhāmādhava in the village. Aghormaṇi Devī slowly felt drawn to the temple with its flower-garden and orchard. There the widow of the devotee Govinda Chandra Dutta, who built the temple, was living. Soon young Aghormaṇi became acquainted with her and began to reside in the temple garden permanently. She had a small abode in the garden just on the bank of the Ganges. Here she grew in devotion and spirituality.

She received initiation from a Vaishṇava *guru*. Baby Kṛishṇa was her life's ideal, the object of her heart's adoration. In her room she continued for thirty long years such devotional practices as telling beads and meditation. So fervent were these that she eventually realized God as the Divine Child.

She went to Dakshiṇeśwar in 1884 accompanied by the widow of Govinda Dutta and met Śrī Rāmakṛishṇa for the first time. He received them with great affection and invited them to come again. From the day of her first meeting Aghormaṇi was deeply attracted to Rāmakṛishṇa. She went to Dakshiṇeśwar again and became more and more drawn to him. He felt like a child in her presence and pestered her for sweets and other delicacies as young Gopāla[1] used to do when he was growing in the home of Yaśodhā. It is difficult to describe the sweet and tender relationship that developed between her and Śrī Rāmakṛishṇa, or the hair-raising experiences of this great woman mystic who lived, moved and had her being in a divine realm of which it is not given to ordinary mortals to have even a glimpse. One day after finishing her *japa* she surrendered the fruits of her austerities to her chosen Ideal, but lo! she found to her utter amazement Śrī Rāmakṛishṇa sitting on her lap with a smiling face and his right hand clenched; she then stretched her hand to touch him but the figure vanished, and in its place she saw the Baby Kṛishṇa crawling forward to her and raising one arm begging for butter! Narrating this vision she said:

> I was so surprised! I cried in an excess of joy and said to him, "Alas! I am a poor widow. Where shall I get butter and condensed milk for you, my child?" But Gopāla would not listen. "Give me something to eat", he said again and again. With tears in my eyes, I got up and brought for him some dry sweetened coconut balls which I had. Gopāla sat on my lap, snatched away my rosary, jumped on my shoulders and moved about the room, so that all my efforts to carry on further repetition of the *mantra* were baffled.

She started the next morning for Dakshiṇeśwar with the Baby Gopāla clasped to her bosom and his tiny ruddy feet dangling gracefully. The object of her heart's devotion was realized that day as a reality. She walked her way in a state of spiritual absorption with dishevelled hair and staring eyes and the hem of her cloth trailing the ground. As soon as she sat in Rāmakṛishṇa's room, the latter in an ecstatic mood sat like a little child on her lap and she talked to him in a manner quite unintelligible to ordinary people. She said, "Here is Gopāla on my lap. . . . Now he enters your body. . . . There, he has come out again. . . . Come, my darling, come to your poor mother". Thus overpowered by emotion she entered the super-conscious state. From that day onwards she used to be called "Gopāla's Mother" by Śrī Rāmakṛishṇa and others. By her spiritual disciplines and attainments this virgin widow became

[1] Another name for Śrī Kṛishṇa.

spiritually transformed as the Mother of the Divine Child Kṛishṇa! Śrī Rāmakṛishṇa detained her the whole day and made her bathe and take food. When her spiritual emotions had subsided a little, he sent her back to her village. There also the same divine sport continued. Rāmakṛishṇa once said to her, "You have achieved the impossible. Such a realization as yours is rare in this age".

Śrī Rāmakṛishṇa's passing away in 1886 was a blow to her. She was now advanced in age but her visions in which she used to see the Baby Gopāla never left her. Sometimes she used to see him manifest everywhere and as everything.

In 1904 she fell ill and was removed to the house of Balarām Bose in Calcutta. Sister Niveditā served her with the love and devotion of a daughter. The Holy Mother used to see her now and then. Before she passed away she was taken to the bank of the Ganges, and just prior to her final breath her feet were kept touching the sacred water of the river. She passed away on July 8, 1906, her face full of divine sweetness and peace.

Lakshmīmaṇi Devī
(*Known as Lakshmī Didi*)

Lakshmīmaṇi Devī, familiarly called Lakshmī Didi ("sister Lakshmī"), was a niece of Śrī Rāmakṛishṇa. She was the daughter of his second elder brother, Rāmeśwar Chaṭṭopādhyāya, and became a very saintly woman. Born at Kāmārpukur on February 11, 1864, she was thus about ten years younger than Śrī Sāradā Devī, the Holy Mother. Her elder brother was Rāmlāl, who sometimes used to take care of Śrī Rāmakṛishṇa, and her younger brother was Śivarām.

Lakshmī had not the benefit of a literary education at school. She, however, learnt how to read in later years and made good use of her knowledge of reading by going through the *Rāmāyaṇa*, the *Mahābhārata* and other similar books in Bengali.

She was very reticent by nature and would not speak with anyone except her nearest relatives. Even at an early age she cultivated a deep devotion for the gods and goddesses of the Hindu pantheon, of whom Sītalā and Raghuvīra were her favourites. When she was nearly nine years old, she lost her father Rāmeśwar. She was betrothed at the age of twelve. A couple of months later her elder brother Rāmlāl informed

Śrī Rāmakṛishṇa of her betrothal. Rāmakṛishṇa immediately fell into a trance and said: "She will soon be a widow". His nephew Hṛiday, who was by his side, was shocked, and asked him why he spoke those tragic words instead of words of blessing. Rāmakṛishṇa replied, "What could I do? It was the Divine Mother who spoke through me. Lakshmī is a manifestation of Mother Sītalā, a very spirited goddess, while her husband is just an ordinary mortal. Lakshmī can never be the mate of such a being. . . . She cannot help being a widow". Indeed Lakshmī's husband soon left his house in search of a job, and no more was heard of him. His relatives searched for him in vain for twelve years, and as no trace of him could be found, the usual funeral rites which had so long been put off were performed. Lakshmī, however, did not claim her husband's property, in deference to Śrī Rāmakṛishṇa's wish.

When Lakshmī was fourteen years of age, she visited the Holy Mother. She was initiated by Śrī Rāmakṛishṇa into the Vaishṇava disciplines. For thirteen years, from 1872 to 1885, she lived mostly in the company of Śrī Rāmakṛishṇa and the Holy Mother, and her life was moulded in their holy presence. She used to say:

> Many a day I lived with the Holy Mother in the concert house, in a small room stuffed with articles for daily use and consumption. The Mother used to cook, and I helped her in her devoted service. At that time there was a ceaseless flow of devotees at all hours of the day, and we had to prepare most untimely dishes, to suit their individual tastes. Seeing our power of adjustability, Śrī Rāmakṛishṇa used to call us both *śuka* and *sarī*, birds of the same feather, and likened the concert house to a cage, so small and narrow was the space wherein we dwelt. But what a joy it was to live in such a divine atmosphere and to learn from day to day all manner of work from the Mother and to drink deep of the cascade of spirituality that flowed in an incessant stream from the living gospels of the Master and the Mother!

During Śrī Rāmakṛishṇa's illness she helped the Holy Mother at Śyāmpukur and the Kāśipur Garden, and served him. After his passing away in 1886 she went on a pilgrimage, and at Vṛindāvan devoted a year in the Holy Mother's company to spiritual disciplines. When the Holy Mother went to Purī she accompanied her. She also visited other important places of pilgrimage such as Gaṅgāsāgar, Navadwīp, Triveṇī at Allahabād, Gayā, Banāras and Haridwār. Lakshmī Didi lived with the Holy Mother whenever possible, and at other times she lived at Kāmārpukur. When her brother Rāmlāl lost his wife, he invited Lakshmī to live with him. And she mostly lived with him at Dakshiṇeśwar for nearly ten years.

In October, 1922, she again went to Purī where a plot of land was secured for her from the municipality and a house built for her. She occupied it in February, 1924, and spent her last days at Purī. On February 24, 1926, at the age of sixty-two, she left this mortal coil, leaving behind a large number of disciples.

Says Sister Niveditā in her book, *The Master as I saw Him:*

Sister Lucky, or Lakshmīdidi, as is the Indian form of her name, was indeed a niece of his,[1] and is still a comparatively young woman. She is widely sought after as a religious teacher and director, and is a most gifted and delightful companion. Sometimes she will repeat page after page of some sacred dialogue, out of one of the *yātras*, or religious operas, or again she will make the quiet room ring with gentle merriment, as she poses the different members of the party in groups for religious tableaux. Now it is Kālī, and again Saraswatī; another time it will be Jagaddhātrī, or yet again, perhaps Kṛishṇa under his kadamba tree, that she will arrange, with picturesque effect and scant dramatic material.

Yogīndra Mohinī Biśwās
(*Known as Yogīn-Mā*)

Yogīndra Mohinī Biśwās was born in north Calcutta on January 16, 1851. Her father, Prasanna Kumār Mitra, was a successful physician and held a chair in the Medical College of Calcutta.

When she was six or seven years of age, Yogīn was betrothed to Ambikā Charaṇ Biśwās, a rich handsome man of the *zemindar* family of Khardāh in Twenty-four Parganās. Her married life was most unfortunate. Her husband lived a life of vice and squandered all his wealth in a few years. She had only a daughter. When the daughter was married, Yogīndra Mohinī's responsibility was over and she felt free to leave her husband's house and return to her father's home at Bāghbāzār where her widowed mother was staying. It need hardly be said that a

[1] Rāmakṛishṇa's.

young mother like Yogīndra Mohinī spent years in anguish and loneliness.

In these days of mental distress Balarām Bose, a householder disciple of Śrī Rāmakṛishṇa, who was also a distant relative of hers on her father-in-law's side, took her to his residence on the occasion of Rāmakṛishṇa's visit to him. Slowly her life began to change, and her hankering for spiritual peace was gradually satisfied. She had already been initiated in the path of the Divine Mother, and Rāmakṛishṇa just confirmed the *mantra* and consented to be her guide. He said of her, "Yogīn is not an ordinary bud blossoming quickly, but the bud of a thousand-petalled lotus opening slowly".

At Dakshiṇeśwar she met the Holy Mother who at once felt that a companion for life had come. Yogīn-Mā—by which name she was called by the disciples of Rāmakṛishṇa—used to visit Dakshiṇeśwar about once a week and spend the night with the Holy Mother. They loved each other deeply.

The life lived by Śrī Rāmakṛishṇa and the Holy Mother spurred Yogīn-Mā on to higher and higher spiritual practices and enhanced her fervour for God-realization. She also studied the *Rāmāyaṇa*, the *Mahābhārata* and the chief Purāṇas, as well as the life of Śrī Chaitanya. A keen memory enabled her to narrate correctly the incidents mentioned in these holy books. She was thus able to render valuable help to Sister Niveditā in preparing one of her books entitled *Cradle Tales of Hinduism*.

In July, 1885, Śrī Rāmakṛishṇa paid a visit to her home and on that occasion she begged him to place his feet in her bedroom and take refreshment there; for such was her faith in him that she believed that the room would thereby become as holy as Banāras, and that if she died there, she would attain liberation. Śrī Rāmakṛishṇa graciously granted her wish.

Śrī Rāmakṛishṇa's passing away in 1886 came as a shock to Yogīn-Mā, who was then practising austerities at Vṛindāvan. She was deeply grieved at not having been able to see him during his last days. She met the Holy Mother when the latter went to Vṛindāvan, and shared her distress at separation from Śrī Rāmakṛishṇa. But both were consoled by a vision in which he appeared before them and said, "Why do you weep so much? Here I am. Where have I gone? It is just like passing from one room to another."

Once, while meditating at Lālā Bābu's temple, Yogīn-Mā

attained a state of *samādhi* (superconsciousness) with the result that the Holy Mother, who was at her residence, became anxious over the unusual delay in Yogīn-Mā's return. The latter was found seated in deep *samādhi*; referring to this she said afterwards: "Then my mind had plunged so deep into meditation that I had totally forgotten the existence of the world. . . . I could see the presence of my Ishṭa (chosen Deity) everywhere. This lasted for three days."

She had a similar experience while staying at her paternal home. Once Swāmī Vivekānanda said to her, "Yogīn-Mā, you will pass away in *samādhi*, for once a person experiences this blessed state, the memory of it is revived at the time of his death". She worshipped the Child Gopāla with fervent devotion. "One day", she said, "while I was engaged in worship, two exquisitely handsome boys came smiling and threw their arms round me. Patting me on the back they said, 'Do you know who we are?' I said, 'Certainly I do: you are the valiant Balarāma, and you are Kṛishṇa'. The younger of the two said, 'You won't remember us'. 'Why?' I asked. 'On account of them', he replied, pointing to my grandsons." Really, after the death of her daughter, she was for a time kept so busy taking care of her three helpless grandsons that her meditations became less deep.

Her life was very austere. Some of the spiritual disciplines which she practised were most rigorous. She performed along with the Holy Mother "the austerity of the five fires"[1]. She was formally initiated at Purī into Tāntrik *sannyāsa* (monasticism of the Tāntrik school) by Swāmī Sāradānanda, a direct disciple of Śrī Rāmakṛishṇa. However, she put on the saffron robe only at the time of worship.

The Holy Mother used to say, "Yogīn is a great *tapaswinī* (performer of austerities)", and, "She is a *jñānī* (possessor of wisdom) among women". She passed away on June 4, 1924.

Golāp Sundarī Devī
(Known as Golāp-Mā)

Golāp Sundarī Devī, who later came to be known as Golāp-Mā, was born about 1864 of an orthodox Brahmin family in north Calcutta. Her married life was unhappy. While she

[1] See footnote in the section, "Austerities and Ecstasy", in the previous chapter.

was young, her husband died leaving behind him a son and a daughter. Shortly after, the little son also died. Her only daughter, Chaṇḍī, who was married to Saurindra Mohan Tagore of Pāthuriāghāṭā in Calcutta, also passed away. Golāp had none to call her own and was utterly disconsolate.

Yogīn-Mā happened to be her neighbour and took her one day to Dakshiṇeśwar. Golāp's meeting with Śrī Rāmakṛishṇa slowly wrought a change in her life. She burst into tears before him. He listened to her words of sorrow with the deepest sympathy and told her that she was fortunate in having none but the Lord to think of. She felt greatly consoled. Śrī Rāmakṛishṇa introduced her to the Holy Mother who was living at that time in the concert house in the temple premises. She soon became an intimate companion of the Holy Mother.

Once Śrī Rāmakṛishṇa visited the old dilapidated brick-built house where she was staying with her brothers and sister. She was so overwhelmed with joy at his visit that she said that all her grief was gone. He asked the Holy Mother to take particular care of Golāp-Mā who, he said, would follow her like a shadow throughout her life. Golāp-Mā served the Mother with unflagging zeal for thirty-six years till the latter passed away. Golāp-Mā was with her at Śyāmpukur and the Kāśipur Garden to help her serve Śrī Rāmakṛishṇa during his last illness. After his passing away she accompanied the Holy Mother to Banāras and Vṛindāvan in North India, and to Madurā and Rameśwar in the south. She was a constant watchful attendant of the Mother.

Her daily life was simple. She used to get up at four in the morning and practise *japa* and meditation in her own room. Then she would dress the vegetables and go to the Ganges for a bath in the company of the Holy Mother. When the worship of Śrī Rāmakṛishṇa by the Holy Mother was over, she would distribute the offered food among the devotees and servants. In the afternoon she would read the *Mahābhārata* and study the *Bhagavad-Gītā*, as well as the teachings of Rāmakṛishṇa and Vivekānanda. After vespers she would do her *japa* and meditation till about half-past nine at night. Thereafter she would have supper and go to bed. The Holy Mother used to say, "Golāp has attained Illumination through *japa*".

Golāp-Mā loved the poor. Half of her income was spent to meet their needs.

She outlived the Holy Mother by four years. She passed away at about the age of sixty on December 19, 1924.

GAURĪMAṆI DEVĪ
(*Known as Gaurī-Mā*)

Gaurīmaṇi Devī was born in 1857 as the fourth child of Śrī Pārvatī Charaṇ Chaṭṭopādhyāya in Śibpur, Howrah. Her religious-minded mother, Giribālā Devī, was well versed in Bengali and Sanskrit, and knew a little of Persian and English.

Mṛiḍānī, as Gaurīmaṇi Devī was known in her girlhood days, was admitted to the local Missionary School. Miss Maria Milman, sister of the then Bishop of Calcutta and one of its organizers, liked the girl so much that she was willing to arrange for her higher education in England, but the young pupil became disgusted with the attitude of the Christian teachers towards her religion and left school once for all. She had by now learnt by heart many Sanskrit hymns, as well as the *Gītā*, *Chaṇḍī*, many passages of the *Rāmāyaṇa* and the *Mahābhārata*. She also had an elementary knowledge of Sanskrit grammar.

Even as a girl Mṛiḍānī was highly spiritual-minded. At about ten years of age she received initiation from a Brahmin preceptor who visited her home. She also devoted much of her time to the worship of Śrī Dāmodara,[1] through a sacred stone emblem given her by a woman devotee. She kept this emblem with her for life.

Her mother and other relatives became alarmed at the rapidly rising spiritual fervour of the girl and hurriedly made arrangements for her marriage when she was only thirteen. She, however, warned her mother by saying, "I shall only marry that bridegroom who is immortal", meaning thereby that she would accept only Śrī Kṛishṇa as her Lord. On the day preceding that fixed for the marriage she was confined to a room lest she should leave the house. However, she was too clever for her relatives and succeeded in escaping at night. Though she was found and brought home, she was never afterwards pressed to marry.

She soon felt that home life was not for her. At the age of eighteen, while going on a pilgrimage to Gaṅgāsāgar along with a party of relatives, she departed unnoticed. She then journeyed to Haridwār with some up-country monks and nuns. She

[1] A name for Śrī Kṛishṇa.

avoided the society of householders, travelling sometimes in dense forests and meeting hardships. Her spirit was unbending, the Deity represented by the stone emblem of Dāmodara tied to her neck being her only protection. The *Gītā*, a few other sacred books, and pictures of Śrī Gaurāṅga and Kālī the Mother, were her sole possessions other than a few articles of everyday use. She succeeded in visiting such sacred places as Kedārnāth, Badrīnārāyan, Jwālāmukhī, Amarnāth, Vṛindāvan, Dwārakā and Purī. During her pilgrimages and travels through mountains and in the plains she used to put on the *gerrua* cloth. Sometimes, in order to hide her identity, she covered her body with clay or ashes, or dressed herself as a man with a flowing garment and a turban, or even posed as a lunatic. At Dwārakā she had wonderful spiritual experiences.

In 1882 she returned to Calcutta where she stayed with Balarām Bose of Bāghbāzār, a well-known householder disciple of Śrī Rāmakṛishṇa. One day he took her with his wife and a few other devotees to Dakshiṇeśwar and introduced her to Śrī Rāmakṛishṇa. Rāmakṛishṇa asked her to come again, and the next morning she went alone to Dakshiṇeśwar. He kindly took her to the concert house and introduced her to the Holy Mother. After that, Gaurī-Mā used to live with her now and then, and became a disciple of Śrī Rāmakṛishṇa.

One early morning when Gaurī-Mā was plucking flowers in the temple garden, Śrī Rāmakṛishṇa told her, "Gaurī, I am pouring the water; you knead the clay." She took this in a literal sense, but he said smiling, "Oh, you entirely misunderstand me. What I mean is, the women of this country are in a sad plight. You must work for them." Gaurī-Mā then understood what he meant, but she did not care for the suggestion of work in noisy and crowded cities. However, she expressed her willingness to train, if necessary, young girls in a quiet retreat, according to Śrī Rāmakṛishṇa's ideal. His words were definite and emphatic, for he said, "You must work in this very city for the education of women. You have had enough of spiritual practices. Now this life of penance should be devoted to the service of women." In this manner he gave her his inspiration and most precious blessings for her future work for women and girls.

In 1886, at the suggestion of Śrī Rāmakṛishṇa, she began a certain form of hard spiritual exercise at Vṛindāvan, which lasted for nine months. Before it ended, Śrī Rāmakṛishṇa passed away at Kāśipur. She was so smitten with grief that she decided to end her life by severe austerities, but was dissuaded from this extreme step by a vision of Śrī Rāmakṛishṇa. When the Holy Mother went to Vṛindāvan soon after his passing away, she had her searched out and met her in a solitary cave at Rauā. Following the Holy Mother's departure from Vṛindāvan after a year's stay, Gaurī-Mā continued to stay in and near that sacred place, except for a second pilgrimage to the Himalayas. In all, she spent nearly ten years in North India before returning to Calcutta.

Her long and wide travels in the country, her keen sense of observation, her first-hand knowledge of the deplorable condition of Indian women and girls, her deep scholarship and great organizing ability, eminently fitted her for the task assigned to her by Śrī Rāmakṛishṇa himself. In 1895, with the meagre resources at her disposal, she started the Sāradeśwarī Āśrama—named after Sāradā Devī, the Holy Mother—at Kapāleśwar, on the Ganges at Barrackpore, near Calcutta. It grew and developed: in 1911 it was removed to a rented house in Calcutta, and in 1924 to its present home at 26, Mahārānī Hemanta Kumārī Street, Śyāmbazār, Calcutta.

By 1932 her health had begun to decline. She was then nearly seventy-five years of age. She visited the Temple of Jagannāth at Purī for the last time, and two years later she went to Vaidyanāth for a change, and the year after to Navadwīp.

In February, 1938, on the holy Śivarātri which fell on the last day of the month, she said that the play of her life was over. Towards the close of the night she asked for the emblem of Dāmodara to be brought to her. On seeing it she said: "Beautiful. I see Him vividly with my eyes open and with my eyes closed. I see Him all the time." She kept the emblem on her head and then on her bosom, before handing it over to the chief inmate of the Āśrama. The next day she thrice uttered "Guru Rāmakṛishṇa", before repeating the Lord's name, and passed away at 8.15 p.m.

As a *guru* she accepted and guided hundreds of spiritual aspirants.[1]

[1] Materials for this chapter have been drawn from *Sri Ramakrishna, the Great Master* and *Vedanta Kesari* (Holy Mother number), both published by Sri Ramakrishna Math, Mylapore, Madras, as well as issues of *Udbodhan* (Udbodhan Office, Baghbazar, Calcutta) for 1954.

PART II

WOMEN SAINTS OF BUDDHISM AND JAINISM

CHAPTER XV

IMPROVED STATUS OF WOMEN IN BUDDHISM AND JAINISM

INTRODUCTORY

Gifts of Jainism and Buddhism

JAINISM and Buddhism mark a departure from Hinduism in several ways, and are therefore considered to be heterodox by the Hindus. *Social* and *spiritual* equality for men and women of all classes and communities is one of the greatest gifts of these two religions.

The religion of the Vedas and the social structure of Vedic times accepted the system of *varṇa*, which was later known as the caste system. In the post-Vedic period the social and spiritual privileges which were enjoyed by the members of the first two *varṇas* or divisions of society, of which the priestly division was the higher, were denied to the members of the fourth *varṇa* which consisted of labourers, and to the Dāsyus and other low classes who were outside the pale of Aryan society, and even to the Vaiśyas who belonged to the third *varṇa*. Indeed, the Dāsyus and other low classes were given none of the social and spiritual rights which were their due as human beings.

It was Śrī Kṛishṇa, the greatest teacher of the post-Vedic age and author of the *Bhagavad-Gītā*, who first conferred *spiritual* equality on one and all.[1] He also attempted to establish social equality, but was not so successful in this direction.

Centuries later, Mahāvīra and Buddha held that religion was for all castes and classes, and for all men and women alike. The *spiritual* equality of men and women which obtained among the higher classes in Vedic times was extended to all men and all women of the lower classes. The two Teachers also stood for *social* equality amongst the people of all communities and classes, extending it also *to all women* of the country. Mahāvīra (599–527 B.C.), an elder contemporary of Buddha (*circa* 560–480 B.C.), is the first to deserve credit for bringing about a change in the *social and spiritual* status of women in India.

[1] cf. *Bhagavad-Gītā*, IX. 30-32.

Two Contrary Forces

The forces of conservatism and of liberalism have been alternately influencing both the social and the religious life of India from ancient times in a manner that reminds us of the systole and diastole of the human heart. Whenever the spirit of freedom in society and religion was stifled by the encrustations of rigid traditions, liberalizing influences began to operate and conferred equality of social and religious rights on men and women alike. In a similar manner, when the generous tendencies of liberalism outlived their period of usefulness, and the social and religious life of the country was threatened by alien elements, religion and society were preserved by the exercise of the spirit of conservatism. These two tendencies have thus been contributing, each its own share, to the life of the Indian nation.

Buddhism

Freedom from the orthodox spiritual traditions of Hinduism characterized Buddhism as a way of life, and this freedom was reflected in Buddhist society, customs and manners. The Compassionate One declared that Dharma was for one and all, irrespective of distinctions of caste, class or sex. In the order of monks which he established he admitted candidates from all sections, high and low, rich and poor, learned and illiterate; and the order of nuns which he permitted to be started, admitted all women aspirants—married women, unmarried women and widows of all classes.

Spiritual progress alone was counted in the order and no distinction was therefore made amongst the women admitted: even a courtesan or a woman who had lived a low life was admitted to the order and treated in the same way as the other women, without any disrespect being shown to her for her past life. The ordained nuns and women novices were given the same education as the monks and the novices. The women lay devotees also were taught the principles of Buddhism.

Though the status of women in general improved in the Buddhist period, the nuns ranked below the monks. Indeed, Buddha was at first reluctant to admit women into the order, but refusal to admit and ordain them being incompatible with the fundamental principles of his message, he finally had to agree to the establishment of the order of nuns. Nevertheless, he laid down strict rules for its conduct.

HOW THE ORDER OF BUDDHIST NUNS WAS FOUNDED

According to all Buddhist accounts, Mahāprajāpatī Gautamī and five hundred ladies who were her attendants in the palace were the first to renounce the world and form the order of nuns. Gautamī, who was the foster-mother of Buddha and second queen, was the first to cut off her hair and put on the yellow robe. Buddha was then staying in Kapilāvastu, in the Nigrodhārāma. She went there to see him, bowed down before him, and said: "It would be well, O Lord, if women should be allowed to renounce their homes and enter the homeless state and follow the discipline proclaimed by the Tathāgatha." "Enough, O Gautamī! Let it not please thee that women should be allowed to do so!" Gautamī made the same request a second and a third time, but Buddha was unbending and gave the same reply. Then Gautamī became very sad and departed from his presence in tears. After some days Buddha set out on his journey towards Vaiśālī, and when he arrived there he stayed in the Mahādvana Kuṭāgāra Hall. Gautamī went to Vaiśālī where Ānanda happened to see her waiting under the entrance porch of the hall. He enquired of her why she had come "with swollen feet and covered with dust", "dejected and in tears". She replied that the Blessed One did not permit women to become nuns. Then Ānanda went to the Blessed One and informed him about Mahāprajāpatī Gautamī, saying: "It were well, Lord, if women were to have permission granted to them to do as she desires." Buddha, however, said, "Enough Ānanda! Let it not please thee that women should be allowed to do so!" A second and a third time did Ānanda make the same request but received the same answer. Later on Ānanda asked Buddha in another way with the words, "Are women, O Lord, capable—when they have gone forth from the household life and entered the homeless state under the doctrine and discipline proclaimed by the Blessed One—are they capable of realizing the fruit of conversation, or the second Path, or of the third Path or of Arhatship?" Buddha answered, "They are capable, Ānanda!"

"If then, Lord, they are capable thereof, since Mahāprajāpatī Gautamī has proved herself of great service to the Blessed One—when as aunt and nurse she nourished him and gave him milk, and on the death of his mother suckled the Blessed One at her own breast—it were well, Lord, that women should have permission to go forth from the household life and enter the homeless state, under the doctrine and discipline proclaimed by the Tathāgata."

"If then, Ānanda, Mahāprajāpatī Gautamī take upon herself the eight chief rules, let her take that as her initiation."

THE EIGHT CHIEF RULES

The eight chief rules were:—

(i) A nun, even if she is a hundred years old, should bow before a new monk. (This rule was first resented by Mahāprajāpatī Gautamī, but she had to accept it, as it was the will of the Teacher.)

(ii) A nun must not spend the rainy season in a place where there is no monk.

(iii) When the rainy season ends, a nun must ask pardon for any fault, seen, heard or thought of, from both the order of monks and the order of nuns.

(iv) Before fixing the date of the fortnightly assembly (*uposatha*) and exhortation (*ovāda*), a nun must receive the necessary directions from a monk.

(v) A nun should ask pardon from both the orders if any serious offence is committed.

(vi) A nun must ask permission for *upasampadā* (higher ordination) from both the orders after she has learnt six precepts for two years.

(vii) A nun must not admonish any monk, but a monk may admonish a nun.

(viii) A nun must not abuse or speak ill of any monk![1]

The order of nuns had several other rules which they were required to obey. The rules, as will be evident from their character, were very strict. They were calculated to ensure the practice of the ideals of celibacy, austerity and strict mental

[1] *Women in Buddhist Literature* by Dr. B. C. Law, pp. 80-81.

and spiritual disciplines. The restrictions mentioned above were actually meant for the nuns under training.

The existence of the orders of monks and of nuns was naturally a source of great anxiety to Buddha, and hence he made the rules for nuns so rigid. The rules placed the nuns under the monks, association with whom therefore became necessary for the nuns and proved unhealthy later on. In time the orders of Buddhist monks and of nuns became extinct in India. From the fifth century A.D. women ceased to be admitted to the Buddhist order.

Jainism

Mahāvīra was very liberal in his outlook and did not feel any hesitation in admitting women to the order. His followers were grouped into four classes, monks, nuns, laymen and laywomen.

The religion of Jainism was divided into two main sects, known as the Digambaras and the Śwetāmbaras. The Digambaras hold that women cannot attain salvation. They therefore do not admit women to the order. But the Śwetāmbaras make no distinction between the men aspirants and women aspirants, and freely admit them both into the order. Thirty-six thousand women as against fourteen thousand men, renounced the world and became nuns in the days of Mahāvīra. Chandanā, a first cousin of Mahāvīra (according to some, his aunt), was the head of the order of nuns. These nuns, among whom were even queens like Paumāvaī, and wealthy and respectable ladies, were highly esteemed.

CHAPTER XVI

WOMEN SAINTS OF BUDDHISM AND JAINISM

I. Women Saints of Buddhism

THE Buddhist age forms a great period in the history of India, and is known alike for its missionary zeal in other countries and the expansion of life and thought which took place in the mother country itself. A galaxy of great and noble women is also a distinguishing mark of this age. Inspired by the life and teachings of Buddha, many of them renounced home and family and joined the newly established order of nuns—the first of its kind in the world. These *bhikshuṇīs,* like their spiritual brothers, the *bhikshus,* lived in *āśramas* or wandered about as *parivrājikās,* spreading the light of Truth and knowledge to the people of many lands.

To deepen one's own faith and devotion is the easiest way to quicken the spiritual impulse in others. Thus wherever they went the idealism and purity of the lives of these women created a deep impression; many hearts responded to their appeal and, like a mighty ocean wave, the Buddhist way of life swept over the world capturing the imagination of the people.

GOPĀ

Foremost amongst these Buddhist women is Gopā, the wife of the Blessed One. When the Prince Siddhārtha (Buddha to be) left her at dead of night sleeping with her baby son, Gopā, though exceedingly sorrowful, did not lament her loss, nor did she blame him for his desertion. She understood the largeness of his heart that bled in loving pity for the unhappiness of the world. Surrounded by the luxuries of the royal court, henceforth she lived a life of austerity, no less severe and rigid than her husband's wandering life in the forest.

Great was the rejoicing of the people of Kapilāvastu, when, after his Enlightenment, Buddha returned to the home of his father; but shaven-headed and barefooted he came, no longer a prince but a servant, a teacher and saviour of mankind.

Through all the long and lonely years of separation, Gopā had so attuned herself to his thoughts that the idea of renunciation came as spontaneously to her as to him, and on his return to the capital, in loving homage and welcome, she gave to him the precious gift of her only son, Rāhula. She asked Rāhula to go to his father and ask for his patrimony. But Rāhula had grown up a fatherless boy and so he said, "Mother, how shall I recognize my father?" "My son," proudly replied his mother, "know him to be your father who looks like a lion amongst men." The young boy then walked straight to the father he had never known and fearlessly repeated his request several times, till at last, moved by his entreaties, Buddha asked his chief disciple, Ānanda, to present Rāhula with the begging-bowl and yellow cloth. This was the last and greatest sacrifice of Gopā. Like a queen mother, crowned in sorrow but joyful and serene, she stands at the threshold of a great national awakening as if blessing all those who were to follow in the way of her lord. And as a token of the love and gratitude that the people bore for her, she was renamed Yaśodharā—the bearer of glory and renown—by which name she is still spoken of to this day.

Swāmī Vivekānanda,[1] who often spoke of Buddha, said on one occasion, "One of his greatest disciples was his own wife, who became the head of the whole Buddhist movement amongst the women of India".

But according to another version it was his stepmother Gautamī who organized the Buddhist order of nuns.

GAUTAMĪ (MAHĀPRAJĀPATĪ)

Māyā Devī, the mother of Buddha, had a younger sister called Gautamī, who was also married to King Śuddhodana. When Māyā Devī died seven days after the birth of her son Siddhārtha, Gautamī was heart-broken, and the king became anxious for the upbringing of his son and heir. Meanwhile, a few days later a son was also born to Gautamī, but such was her love for the motherless babe and her sense of duty towards her husband the king, that she kept her own son under the care of a nurse and lavished the love of her mother's heart on her dead sister's child. Siddhārtha also loved her as his own

[1] Swāmī Vivekānanda, *Complete Works*, vol. VII. p. 76.

mother. Though we do not wish to deny that even in childhood the prince must have possessed the inborn qualities of the future Buddha, there can be no doubt that the many virtues of his head and heart must have been fostered by Gautamī. She in turn was deeply influenced by him and, when the time came, under her leadership five hundred women of the Śākya clan went to Buddha and took the vows of Buddhist nuns. She attained a very high degree of spirituality and spent her life in preaching the new religion. Addressing Buddha she wrote in the *Therī-gāthā*: "O Sugata, when you were a baby my eyes and ears delighted to see you and hear your sweet lisping talk; but it cannot be compared to the joy that fills my heart when I listen to the words of wisdom that you now speak."

These words show that Gautamī, in addition to being a devoted disciple of Buddha, remained a loving mother to him to the very end. She earned for herself the title of Mahāprajāpatī, and in this way was distinguished from another woman disciple bearing the same name.

KISĀ GAUTAMĪ

The other Gautamī was born of poor parents and was badly treated by her husband's relatives. Thus, thin and miserable, she came to be known as Kisā Gautamī—*kisa* being the Pali equivalent of the Sanskrit word *kṛisha*, emaciated. But things brightened up in the home when Gautamī gave birth to a son: all the affection of her starved heart was centred in him and she was filled with a new hope and courage for the future. Henceforth she lived for the child alone, but her happiness, alas, was short-lived. One day while playing in the garden the boy was bitten by a poisonous snake. He died instantly and Kisā Gautamī was beside herself with grief. With the dead body of the little boy in her arms she went about like a demented woman looking for a herb that would bring back life to the beloved form. Just then Buddha and his disciples happened to pass that way, and seeing his calm and compassionate face, hope revived in her heart. She put the dead body of her son at his feet, knelt before him weeping and said, "The world is dark to me without my son. Please give me light by bringing him back to life." Buddha replied, "O thou blessed one (*Kalyāṇī*), go and fetch one *tola* (two-fifths of an ounce) of mustard seed and I will infuse life into the dead body of your son; but remember, you must get it from a home which has never been visited by death". The deep meaning of the Lord's words did not dawn on the sorrow-stricken and simple-hearted Gautamī. She went from house to house for a handful of mustard seed, but the shadow of death had darkened every home and no family could be found where it had not taken the toll of a loved one. Disappointed and disillusioned, Gautamī returned to Buddha and sadly told him that though many were willing to give her the mustard seed, she could not fulfil his condition of bringing it from a house where death was unknown. Buddha then said in gentle tones, "O thou blessed one (*Kalyāṇī*), birth and death are the law that governs the world. As you have seen for yourself, this sorrow has not fallen on you alone." The words of the Lord fell like balm on her wounded heart, despair gave way to dispassion, and the growing pain that seemed to fill her being turned into a quiet resignation. She performed the last rites of her son and with a new vision of life born of the teachings of the Lord, she surrendered herself at his feet, gave up her home and family, and became a nun. In the course of time wisdom illumined her heart and she attained to the position of an *arhat* (liberated soul).

All teachers of religion have repeatedly emphasized that it is foolish to seek for enduring happiness in external environment. The external at best serves as raw material out of which we must shape our lives, not by succumbing to it but by going beyond it. This moving story, profoundly simple and tragically true to life, would not have been worth recording were it not for the nobility of purpose that filled the heart of Gautamī on the death of her son. Her sayings are also recorded in the *Therī-gāthā*, and her life bears glowing testimony to the abiding peace that comes in the wake of spiritual life; it enables a sincere seeker of Truth to transcend the limitations of pleasure and pain, which are the inevitable accompaniments of the evanescent and fleeting things of the world.

Incidentally this story also throws light on the prevailing misconception regarding the essential features of a holy life. To the average man, physical life is the only reality and he can conceive of no greater boon to mankind than the healing of the sick and bringing the dead back to life. But, though venerated by the world as a veritable incarnation of love and compassion, Buddha, we see, did not on this or any other occasion exercise occult powers or indulge in miraculous healing. On the other hand he looked upon miracles as the greatest stumbling-block in the way of Truth. Once his disciples told him of a man who had taken a bowl from a great height without touching it. Buddha took the bowl and crushed it under his feet and told them never to build their faith on miracles. He was supremely human in everything that he did, as may be seen in his offer to sacrifice his life to save a goat. We therefore find that no supernatural element was allowed to enter into the lives of his followers, and in this lies their great strength and appeal.

SUPRIYĀ

Supriyā was the daughter of a well-known millionaire of Śrāvastī called Anātha Piṇḍada. Her fond parents brought her up in the lap of luxury and bestowed all their love and attention on her upbringing and education. It is said that she had an unusually brilliant mind: even in early childhood she remembered her former birth and often related incidents of her previous life. Mahāprajāpatī Gautamī, the foster-mother and aunt of Buddha, initiated her into Buddhism at the tender age of seven. Supriyā was known for her wisdom and spiritual knowledge, but it is not to be inferred from this that she lived a life of solitude and seclusion. Along with her prayers and meditation she found time to help in the nursing of the sick and in looking after the poor and the destitute. One outstanding incident of her girlhood brings out her moral courage and strength of character vividly to us even at the present day.

At one time, when Lord Buddha was living in the *vihāra* (monastery) of Jeṭa-vana, this prosperous and flourishing town of Śrāvastī was in the grip of a devastating famine. Scarcity of food had reduced men and women to skeletons, and had lowered their physical resistance. Thus they became an easy prey to disease, and death stalked through the town taking its toll of the flower of human lives, leaving broken hearts and desolation in its wake. It is not as if Śrāvastī did not possess sufficient means to buy food for the people and tide over this great crisis, but selfishness and avarice had hardened the hearts of those well-to-do citizens who could have helped with food and money. Unmoved by the suffering of their fellow-men, they neither cared to see their pitiable condition nor hear the sad and lamentable cry that filled the poorer quarter of the town. On the other hand, fearing that the poor, driven to desperation by hunger and starvation would become lawless and would endanger the lives and property of their fortunate neighbours, they began to take measures to strengthen their own security.

One day a child, utterly prostrated, was found lying at the entrance of the *vihāra*. Ānanda, the chief disciple of Buddha, deeply moved to see his miserable condition, went to the Master and said, "The people round about are dying of hunger. What is the duty of our *Saṅgha* (the order of Buddhist monks) under the existing circumstances?" Many rich citizens of Śrāvastī had come to listen to the teachings of the Master and were present there. Buddha addressing them said, "All of you gentlemen are men of wealth and position. If you desire you can easily save the lives of the people who are dying in such large numbers." Hearing these words of the Master each of them brought forward some excuse. Some said, "Our granaries are empty". Others said, "Śrāvastī is a big town and the population is large. It will be impossible to feed them all." Anātha Piṇḍada, who was a close disciple of Buddha, was absent at that time. The Master looked around and said again, "Is there no man here who can save his brothers from the grip of this terrible famine?" No one answered, but after a moment of tense silence a young girl got up from her seat and speaking fearlessly and confidently said, "My Lord, thy handmaiden is ready to obey thy command. To be able to serve man is a great blessing even if it be at the sacrifice of one's life." Needless to say, the girl was none other than the heroine of this story, Supriyā. The audience were amazed, but they thought that she spoke heedlessly with the irresponsibility of her age. The Master, smiling at her, then said, "My child, how wilt thou fill the stomach of this vast multitude?" Supriyā answered, "By thy grace, O Master, my begging-bowl will never remain empty. It will feed the hungry and bring the dying back to life, and the famine of Śrāvastī will be a thing of the past."

Ānanda's heart was filled with joy to hear the sweet nectar-like words of Supriyā and, blessing the girl, he said, "O Mother in the form of a child, may the Lord Amitābha fulfil thy heart's desire". The Master also blessed her, and then the meeting dispersed.

The news that Supriyā, the daughter of Anātha Pinḍada and the beloved disciple of Mahāprajāpatī Gautamī, had taken a vow to remove the famine of Śrāvastī spread like wildfire throughout the city. A wave of enthusiasm arose softening the hearts of the people, and with one accord they said, "Supriyā's begging-bowl shall not remain empty". From house to house Supriyā went begging for food. Her love for humanity had already found an echo in every heart, and every man, woman and child in the town was ready to give her a helping hand. As the dawn of day dispels the horror of a nightmare, so the radiant personality of Supriyā brought renewed faith and hope to every heart. The famine of Śrāvastī thus came to an end, and by this one act of hers she made herself immortal in the annals of Buddhist literature.

PAṬĀCHĀRĀ

Paṭāchārā was born in Śrāvastī in the family of a business man. When she attained maturity her parents selected a young man of good looks and character, and also of the same social standing as themselves, for her husband; but Paṭāchārā did not want to marry him. She married a youth of her own choice. Her parents were displeased with her and she left her parental home and town with her husband to live in a foreign land.

Many years passed by. After the birth of two sons Paṭāchārā had the desire the visit her parents once again. So, accompanied by her husband and children, she left for Śrāvastī. On the way, as they walked through the forest, her husband was bitten by a poisonous snake. No aid was near by and the poor man died. Bearing this unexpected loss as best she could, and weeping pitifully, Paṭāchārā continued her journey; but misfortune pursued her still further. While her children were sleeping under the shade of a tree a wild bird came and carried away the younger child; but this was not all. Her elder boy too was swept away by a strong current while crossing a stream. This filled her cup of sorrow to the brim. Thus, having lost all the members of her small family, Paṭāchārā, demented with grief and not knowing what to do, walked on in a daze. Her heart was so heavy and her mind so distracted that she hardly knew which way she was going. The last hope that she clung to in this moment of sorrow was a reunion with her parents. The chosen ones of God, however, must give up all worldly support and attachment and learn to rely on Him alone. And perhaps to learn this Paṭāchārā had yet another disappointment in store for her.

By this time she had come close to the town of Śrāvastī; but arriving there she could not find the home of her childhood. On making enquiries she learned that during her absence the roof of her parental home had collapsed and both her parents had been buried under the debris. Her endurance gave way under this last strain and she roamed around the town weeping loudly and relating her tale of woe to everyone that she happened to meet.

Lord Buddha was in Śrāvastī at that time. The sorrow-stricken Paṭāchārā went to him, fell at his feet and told him of the death of all her dear ones. Buddha consoled her, saying that life in the world was in any case transient, and his words calmed her mind. She took refuge in the *Saṅgha* and became a nun of the Buddhist Order. Henceforth she spent her life in the service of humanity, in teaching the new religion and in urging her fellow-men to follow the eightfold path of Dharma. Through her lifelong *sādhanā* (spiritual disciplines) she gained so much spiritual strength that she was able to impart peace to the hearts of thousands of men and women. It is said in the *Pīṭaka* that while addressing a gathering of five hundred women, Paṭāchārā's words created such a deep impression on their minds that they all became initiated disciples of Buddha. To influence the hearts of such a large number of people through public speaking only is rare in history, and there can be no doubt that it must have been her life and character that added force and conviction to her words. Paṭāchārā is a shining example of one who through self-effort was able to raise her own life from the level of ordinary mundane existence to spiritual joy and abiding peace, and was also able to influence others to lead good and noble lives.

AMBAPĀLĪ

A beautiful prostitute named Ambapālī lived in the city of Vaiśālī. She was a woman of considerable wealth, but the best known amongst her possessions was a large garden outside the town, known as the *āmra-vana* or mango grove.

During his wanderings Lord Buddha and his disciples once happened to come this way. The cool and quiet of the garden attracted him, and seeing that it would be a suitable place to live in, he decided to camp in the shady grove of mango trees. Hearing of his arrival Ambapālī went to visit him there. Her dress and jewels were ordinary but her beauty was striking, and when Buddha saw her coming from a distance he thought to himself: "With all her beauty, which enslaves even kings and princes, she also possesses great calm and steadfastness. Women of such character are in truth difficult to find in the world!"

Prostrating herself before the Master, Ambapālī sat reverently near him; and seeing her faith the Lord taught her the Dharma. His benign glance destroyed all her worldly desires; Ambapālī's heart was purified and her faith in his words became firm. She then spoke to the Master and said: "Please bless me, O Lord, by accepting alms from me tomorrow with your disciples." The Tathāgata signified his assent by silence. Soon afterwards some rich young merchants attired in costly clothes and jewels came in their chariots and invited the Master to their home for a meal the next day, but Buddha had already accepted the invitation of Ambapālī and so was obliged to refuse them. They tried their best to get Ambapālī's invitation cancelled, and were also ready to give the Master costly jewels and precious stones, but the Master, who had rejected his own kingdom, was the last man to be tempted by mere material wealth; and so the invitation of Ambapālī remained.

The next day, according to plan, Buddha and his disciples went to the house of Ambapālī. In the midst of a spacious compound and a well-kept garden she had an imposing house, no less grand and luxuriously furnished than the palace of a king. The home and garden had been lavishly decorated to welcome the Master and a variety of dishes had been prepared to feed him. After the Master and his disciples had partaken of the good food, Ambapālī, folding her hands, said to him, "O Lord, this house and garden, my clothes and jewels and all my other possessions I offer at the feet of the *Saṅgha*. Please fulfil my heart's desire by accepting this insignificant gift."

The Tathāgata accepted Ambapālī's gift and made her his disciple. The Master left Vaiśālī after a short stay but she remained there to serve the people of her home town. She spent the remainder of her life in serving the poor and miserable, in contemplation of the Dharma, and in trying to achieve purity of thought and conduct. Though she once followed the lowly profession of prostitute, she was now able to reform her life, and to utilize her environment to reveal the greatness of the human spirit, instead of being dominated by it.

SAṄGHAMITRĀ

Saṅghamitrā was the great daughter of the great emperor Aśoka. Western scholars are of opinion that she was his sister, but they do not bring forward any convincing proof for this departure from Indian tradition which holds she was his daughter.

After his conversion to Buddhism Aśoka spent his life in the propagation of the Dharma. Buddhism became the State religion, the killing of animals was prohibited, hospitals for animals and nursing homes for men were established all over the kingdom, and food and cloth were distributed to the poor and needy. A new department for public religious education was opened by the State, monasteries were endowed, and the teaching of religion was carried on zealously. On the walls of temples and monasteries, on rocky hill-tops and pillars, in towns and villages, in places where the crowds moved as well as in secluded corners of India and the outside world, were engraved moral and religious instructions, and the commands of the pious king. Meetings and conferences where learned *bhikshus* and *sannyāsins* discussed religious problems were convened under royal patronage; saintly and capable teachers covered the length and breadth of the country and were sent to foreign lands as well, to preach the new gospel of ethical endeavour and love for every living creature.

The education of Saṅghamitrā and her brother Mahendra received the special attention of their father. At this time the prince was twenty years of age, and the princess about eighteen. Both were handsome, sweet-tempered, intelligent and possessed of great humility. Their close association with *bhikshus,* and the moral and spiritual fervour of their environment, made a deep impression on their young hearts; their enthusiasm was no less than that of their father for the cause that he served and loved so well.

Once, when Aśoka wished to appoint his son as heir to his throne, a teacher came to him and said, "He alone is a true friend of the Dharma who can dedicate his children to it". The king responded to these words, and turning towards his children with a loving look he said: "Are you prepared to take the vow of lifelong poverty, chastity and service to the world?" At this question of the king's, the pure and innocent hearts of Mahendra and Saṅghamitrā were delighted beyond measure. A desire to serve the *Saṅgha* had already been born in their hearts, but they all along imagined that the duties and obligations of their royal descent would not permit them to renounce the world. But now with one voice they replied, "It would be a great destiny for us if we could be instrumental in spreading the message of universal love as taught by the compassionate Lord Buddha. If you will give us permission we will join the order and achieve the end and purpose of human life."

Aśoka's heart was filled with joy to hear these words of renunciation from the lips of his children. He then sent word to the *Saṅgha* that Aśoka had dedicated his children in the service of the Lord Tathāgata. Soon the news spread throughout the town of Pāṭaliputra and the kingdom of Magadha, and the people rejoiced to hear of the high resolve and selflessness of parent and children.

Mahendra was renamed Dharmapāla and Saṅghamitrā was henceforth known as Ayupālī. Both were initiated into the order and began earnestly to follow in the ways of the Lord. At the age of thirty-two Mahendra was sent to Siṅghala-dvīpa, or the island of Ceylon. Tishṭha, who was then the reigning king there, was astonished to see the handsome face of Mahendra illumined with the light of spiritual knowledge. With great devotion and reverence the king welcomed him and treated him as a royal guest. Mahendra began his teachings, and thousands of men and women became his followers.

After some time Princess Anulā of Ceylon and five hundred of her women companions decided to renounce their homes and families and join the order of Buddhist nuns. Thus it became imperative to find a suitable woman to teach and train these novitiates. Mahendra thought that his sister would be eminently fitted for this arduous task, so he wrote to his father asking him if Saṅghamitrā could be sent to the island to work amongst the Singhalese women. When Saṅghamitrā heard of her brother's request, her happiness was unbounded and she left immediately for her new destination.

This was the first time in the history of India that the daughter of a great emperor, well-trained and educated, set out to give the message of peace and love to the women of a foreign land, and the enthusiasm with which this news was greeted by the Indian people can hardly be imagined by us today. It is said that when Saṅghamitrā arrived in Siṅghala, the islanders, seeing her radiant purity, her garb of utter renunciation, and the nobility and peace that were stamped on her brow, were struck with wonder and became as motionless as the figures of a painted picture. She soon established a nunnery and took charge of the training of the nuns. Due to the untiring labours of both brother and sister the whole of Ceylon was converted to Buddhism. A great city called Anurādhapura was built in the centre of the island. Huge *stūpas* and dilapidated stone buildings extending for miles and miles give us an idea of their attainments. Large figures of Buddha in meditation, or preaching the Law, or entering *nirvāṇa*, were built extensively, and these remind us even now of the glory of the Buddhist age.

In a Buddhist book called *Mahāvaṁśa* the author says, "Saṅghamitrā attained complete knowledge. While living on the island she performed many meritorious deeds for the propagation of the Dharma. And when she died the King of Siṅghala performed her last rites with elaborate ceremony as a fitting tribute to her memory."

Two thousand years have passed, but the torch of love and truth lighted by Mahendra and Saṅghamitrā burns to this day in the island of Ceylon.

II. Women Saints of Jainism

The great women of Jainism are mentioned in the literature of both the principal Jaina sects—the Śwetāmbaras and the Digambaras. Though some of them are legendary, the rest were real historical figures. But whether historical or not, they have been a source of inspiration to the followers of Jainism, both monastic and lay, for many generations.

The Jainas paid the highest veneration to the parents, especially to the mothers, of the twenty-four Tīrthaṅkaras. Stone plaques showing these mothers sitting with their infants on their laps are still worshipped in the Jaina temples at Abu, Girnar and other places.

Marudevī was the mother of Ṛishabhanātha, the first Tīrthaṅkara. When she heard that her son had attained *kevala-jñāna* in the city of Purimatāla, she rode on an elephant, followed by the royal retinue, to see him. She was so much struck by the spiritual effulgence of the Tīrthaṅkara that she developed a high state of concentration, entered into *samādhi*, and passed away.

Mallinātha, who was a princess, became the nineteenth Tīrthaṅkara. The Śwetāmbaras hold that she was the daughter of Kumbha, who ruled Mithilā (modern Bihar). As she was very beautiful and learned, her hand was sought in marriage by many kings, but her father refused them. Their anger was roused by this refusal, and they fiercely attacked Mithilā in battle. When Malli's father was about to be defeated, she requested him to invite all the kings to her apartment so that she might meet them. When they entered it, they were taken aback at the sight of the charming figure of Malli standing there. In a short while another figure, just the same as the one standing, entered the room by another door and removed their illusion by telling them that what they had first seen was her lifelike golden statue. She then opened a lid on the statue's head, and an extremely foul smell issued from the statue. It was hollow and had been filled with eatables for some days; these had rotted by the time the kings visited her. Malli then told them that beneath her external charms there was equally foul and filthy matter. She further told them that she was going to renounce worldly pleasures and become an ascetic. On hearing this the kings were filled with remorse. They realized that the way to genuine happiness lay in meditation and the practice of austerities. They therefore left their kingdoms to the care of their successors, followed in her footsteps, and became themselves ascetics.

It was but natural that Jainism, with its characteristic respect for womanhood and for the lofty ideals of the life of renunciation practised and taught by Mahāvīra, should have produced many nuns. The order of Jaina nuns seems to be older than the order of Buddhist nuns. Some of these prominent Jaina nuns are mentioned below:—

(i) Āryā Chandanā was a contemporary of Mahāvīra. She was deeply religious and became his first woman disciple and the head of his Jaina order of nuns.

(ii) Jayantī was the sister of King Śatānīka. She used to listen to the discourses of Mahāvīra and discuss with him the problems of life and death. She ultimately gave up her life in the palace with its royal comforts and joined the order of nuns.

(iii) Mṛigāvatī was a beautiful queen of King Śatānīka. Her name has come to be known as a symbol of chastity and heroism. Tempted by her loveliness, Pradyota, the King of Ujjayinī, attacked the kingdom of Kauśāmbī over which Śatānīka was ruling. Śatānīka was taken ill and died while the battle was still raging. Mṛigāvatī in her wisdom declared that the king was unwell. She led his army herself, drove the enemy back, and then gave out the news of the death of the king. As the army had been overcome by fatigue and was unequal to the task of coping with the overwhelming strength of the enemy, she changed her tactics and offered to go with him if he built a rampart around her kingdom and placed her young son Udayana on the throne as an independent ruler. When this was done, she went to the congregation of Mahāvīra and expressed her desire to become a Jaina nun with the consent of Pradyota. The latter, who had come under the influence of Mahāvīra's teachings, was then sitting with the other members of the congregation. Filled with remorse for his past, he resolved to live a better life. He also readily consented to Mṛigāvatī's becoming a nun; nay more, he gave consent also to some of his own queens to join the order of Jaina nuns and they were fortunate enough to receive their initiation at the hands of Mahāvīra himself.

(iv) The seven sisters of Sthūlabhadra (about a hundred and fifty years after Mahāvīra), Yaksha and others all became Jaina nuns.

(v) Yākinī Mahattarā was a profound and brilliant scholar of the seventh century A.D. She contributed more than any other nun to the dissemination of Jaina scriptures. She defeated the learned Brahmin, Haribhadra Sūri, in argument, who thereupon accepted her as his *guru* and became converted to the Jaina faith. Haribhadra became a great Jaina scholar who wrote books on ethics, Yoga and logic, commentaries on the older books, and stories. He also initiated reform of the Jaina sect. From the fact that this great scholar took special pride in calling himself the son of the Jaina nun Yākinī, one can infer what a great genius she must have been.

(vi) Guṇā Sādhwī was a nun of high spiritual calibre and deep scholarship, who was born in the latter half of the ninth century A.D. In A.D. 905 she prepared the first copy of the *Upamitabhava-prapañcha-kathā,* a monumental allegorical work of Siddharshi.

(vii) In A.D. 1118 two nuns, Mahānandāśrī Mahattarā and Gaṇinī Vīramatī, substantially helped Maladhāri Hemchandra in the composition of a very long commentary on *Viśesh-āvaśyaka-bhāshya* of Jinabhadra.

(viii) In A.D. 1350 Guṇasaṁṛiddhi Mahattarā composed a Prakrit work called *Añjanā-sundarī-charitra.*

Unlike the order of Buddhist nuns which ceased to exist after the fifth century A.D., the order of Jaina nuns has continued until today. They are pious, highly austere and self-sacrificing. They are well known for the practice of the ideals of non-injury to living things. Fasting is considered an act of merit; the longer the period, the more meritorious it is. Many women, especially in Karṇāṭaka, performed the vow of *sallekhana* (death by fasting), as this is considered to be the most meritorious of all.

CHAPTER XVII

MI CAO BU, A HOLY WOMAN OF BURMA

IN the fifteenth century, the land of Rāmañña (Lower Burma) was graced by the living presence of one whose life and period of reign have left to posterity, and particularly so to the womanhood of Burma, a heritage rich beyond measure, at once gentle and tender, and strong and fearless. Though she is the only queen regnant that we have ever had to rule over us, yet she is remembered not so much as a great sovereign but as an ideal mother. To her people she still lives and is always with them, and in their hours of stress and strain their thoughts unconsciously turn towards her.

It is difficult for me to portray one who occupies such a warm corner in the hearts of her people. I can but do my best by presenting a picture of her life as it appears to me. Historical records written on palm leaves in the Mon language found in Tenasserim provide the basis of her life.

To King Rājadhirāt and Queen Suddhamāya of Haṅsāvatoi (Pegu) was born a daughter, on Wednesday, the 12th waxing of the moon, in the month of Māgh 775, which according to the English calendar would correspond approximately to the 25th January of the year 1393.

Named Mi Čao Bu by her grand-aunt, she grew to fulfil the entire meaning of her name—*mi* meaning mother, *čao* meaning grandchild, and *bu* meaning fair. She was, as the fair grandchild, to sweeten the remaining years of her old aunt's life; and she herself in her old years was to be the mother within whose heart souls like weary travellers would find rest and quiet; and whose shining legacy to us her children, in the great pagoda, Kyāk Dguṅ (Shwe Dagon), was to inspire us to heights of imagination, lifting our earth-bound feet above the trivialities of common everyday life.

When she was seven, her father's aunt came on a visit from the neighbouring court of Dguṅ (Rangoon). Seemingly detached, the grand-aunt yet could not escape the charm of this little offspring of her nephew's. She pleaded with Rājadhirāt to allow her to take the child to her own court, where she would with the greatest care nurture the little one on Buddhistic culture. With his consent she carried the little one to her own home, there to install her as heir-presumptive to her principality of Dguṅ. In the court of Dguṅ little Mi Čao Bu made her new home. At so tender an age she was already living and assimilating, though unconsciously, the ideals of the culture of the land. Like soft fertile soil to a young healthy seed, the daily routine of her life nourished her, helping the young mind to develop, and later to unfold, into the rare and fragrant flower of saintliness.

Swiftly the years glided by, and ever a source of happiness, she sweetened the remaining days of her father's aunt, who, when she died, left Mi Čao Bu, at the age of twelve, the principality of Dguṅ. Soon after, Rājadhirāt took his daughter back to his own court of Haṅsāvatoi, and when she came to be twenty years of age, he gave her in marriage to a relation, Smiṅ Sethu, Lord of Mattma (Mataban). To the court of Mattma she went as a young bride, where for five years she lived a happy married life, and during which time three children were born to her. So passed the days till fate struck its blow, when, at the age of twenty-five, Mi Čao Bu found herself a widow with three children. In her anguish her mind turned to Dguṅ to which place she returned. Here for a time she lived with her children, having for protector her younger brother Baññа Rām.

At the time of her return her father was still reigning in Haṅsāvatoi, but soon after he died of a wound which became septic, when her elder brother Baññа Kim ascended the throne. After the death of Rājadhirāt peaceful conditions did not prevail, so she, her children and brother all moved to Haṅsāvatoi, to live under the care and protection of her elder brother the king.

Frequently from there she made pilgrimages to Kyāk Dguṅ, which involved covering a distance of fifty miles.

The King of Ava, Thihathu, was already laying plans for secretly sending an army under the command of four generals. They were to lie in wait in a lonely and secluded spot between Haṅsāvatoi and Dguṅ, and when she passed by that way, were to seize her and her retinue, and bring them to Ava.

Travelling leisurely, almost at a sauntering pace, it occasioned her no little surprise to see men furtively moving in the forest about her. Soon was to be heard the neighing of horses and trumpeting of elephants, filling her with much wonder. Before she had time to realize the position, she found herself surrounded by an army against which her retinue could not possibly defend itself, commanding her to proceed north towards the court of Ava.

According to the Burmese version, this is how she came to the court of Thihathu at Ava. After the death of Rājadhirāt, there arose a dispute between her two brothers. Thihathu came and amicably settled the dispute, for which kind act her two brothers were extremely grateful. To pay the debt they felt they owed him, they gave her in marriage to him.

At the age of twenty-nine, Mi Čao Bu was formally installed as Thihathu's chief queen. Circumstances filled with such perplexities would for any human be difficult to cope with, and she would have found it difficult too. Fortunately for her she had always a leaning towards intellectual occupations, and in this way busied herself with teaching and studying. In day-to-day life she was a teacher and a guide to the women of the palace and during her five years' stay at this court, the level of culture rose.

Within a year or two of her arrival in Ava, one of Thihathu's queens conspired with an enemy of the king's to murder him while he was supervising the digging of a lake. On his death, his eldest son succeeded him; but the same queen poisoned his food and he also succumbed. Great was her happiness to see her plans for putting her own son on the throne materialize, but the unfortunate king ruled only for a short while, for soon the Lord of Mohnyin marched on Ava and, defeating the young king, ascended the throne. It was during this reign that Mi Čao Bu at the age of thirty-four found a means of escape to Rāmañña.

Though she found something worth while to occupy herself with, she could not imagine that she would remain there for any length of time, for her thoughts ever sped southwards towards her home and children. Often her maids would find her standing by the window facing south, gazing far into the distance. Watching the soft fleecy clouds drifting on the horizon, she would silently plead with them to carry a message to her brother, to tell him how she longed to come home.

As if in answer to her prayers, two *brahmachārins* from her country by chance came to visit Ava. With the king's permission she invited them to a meal, when she heard from them that her elder brother had passed away and that her younger brother was now ruling in his stead. She confided to them her great desire to return home and they laid plans for her escape.

On arrival at Haṅsāvatoi her brother greeted her warmly, and installed her and her three children in a house close by his own palace, where for many a long year she lived a quiet undisturbed life, her children growing all the while just as she had grown in her old aunt's palace. It was a long stretch of unbroken domestic happiness when most of the time she was not engaged with her children was spent in seeing to the welfare of the monks and the poor and needy, towards whom she was ever solicitous; so much so, that when her brother died leaving no heir, and she ascended the throne of Haṅsāvatoi at the age of fifty, the people had complete confidence in her.

Her son died early in life. Her elder daughter was married to a prince and her younger to Dhammaśeṭi the scholar. During the period of her reign she had much confidence in Dhammaśeṭi, who helped her a great deal in the management of state affairs.

She sent her daughter and son-in-law the prince to Phasem (Bassein), where they were to build fortifications for the defence of the town, and to be ready with an army should invasion come from the north. Having received all facilities from the queen, the prince was seeking to march on Haṅsāvatoi itself, as Dhammaśeṭi's growing power there proved irksome to him. News leaked through and she planned to nip it in the bud. The queen recalled her daughter, who, when she arrived, was kept virtually a prisoner. The queen's army marched on Phasem, and in a fierce hand-to-hand battle the prince was slain. Great was the sorrow of the princess on hearing of her husband's death. She asked to be allowed to proceed to Kyāk Dguṅ; arriving there, she cut off her hair, and robing herself in white, took the vows and lived as a nun.

One day while Mi Čao Bu was travelling in a palanquin, an aged man was seen to be approaching her from the opposite direction. Her bearers shouted to him to move aside. He was seen not to move away, but unperturbed walked straight towards her, and looking up at her remarked, "Oh, it is the old queen". Having uttered these words he disappeared instantly, and none could tell in which direction he had gone. The queen knew deep within her that some kindly *devatā*, filled with compassion for her, had troubled himself to take on human form, only for the purpose of giving her a friendly reminder that she was ageing, and it was time she retired to a life of quiet and prayer.

After some years had gone by she announced to her ministers her intention to renounce the throne, naming Dhammaśeṭi as her successor. So Dhammaśeṭi (Rāmādhipati) came to be crowned king of Haṅsāvatoi, and his reign was one of long unbroken peace and prosperity. He ruled justly and well, and in the long annals of the kings of Burma, his name stands supreme as the most able administrator, doing away with laws which he found unsuited to the need of the times, and making new ones instead to meet the demands of changing conditions. In any such period of peace and plenty religion and the arts could flourish, and to this period we owe many of the finest monuments standing in Rāmañña today.

On her departure for Dguṅ she bade him farewell with these words: "Rule righteously and with mercy, ever basing your life and actions on the Laws of Dharma as laid down for all ruling monarchs: the doors of Nirvāṇa will open themselves to you." Do these words not reveal to us a deeper truth of life? Is it not that righteousness is a child born of detachment and fearlessness? Detachment lends one vision to see clearly and so to judge correctly: hence from it springs justice. And how may fearlessness come to us? To the measure that the ego is less dominant, to that measure will fearlessness grow; and the easiest way to outgrow the ego is to grow towards an ideal. Hence detachment brings with it clear and correct judgment, and fearlessness the strength and courage to put into execution the judgment arrived at. So from these two parent qualities are born righteousness. And how may mercy grow within us? It comes in larger or smaller measure, to the extent that we learn to identify ourselves one with the other. Let us now ponder over the Laws of Dharma for a monarch: his is the power to ward off oppression and aggression, and give protection to the wronged and oppressed. His privilege as a chosen ruler entails with it countless responsibilities, bringing in its train endless effort.

Mi Čao Bu was leaving the affairs of state in his hands because she felt a call elsewhere. The throne involved him in work heavy with responsibilities, yet it was to be for him a means to an end and not an end in itself. Was she here not stressing the importance of work as a means to attaining Nirvāṇa?

The people awaited her departure with great sorrow, and were inconsolable. The town was thrown into deep gloom. She could not avoid seeing their reaction to her departure and therefore she sent a crier round the town to the effect that those who wished to, could follow her. When she was about to depart, three-fourths of the population were found ready to leave with her. It was a big responsibility, but she allowed them to proceed. On arrival, she housed them and settled them down.

Now began her life of complete dedication, a life of ten years of work and prayer. Personally and with the utmost care, she supervised the building of the Pagoda, pouring into it all her thoughts and emotions, much as an artist would into his picture. Up to this time it was smaller in size and was ungilded, but now she was putting into it all her time and the means at her disposal, to bring it to a size and shape in which alone her mind could find its fulfilment. She might not have realized it at the time, but it seems to us today that the *devatā*, in turning her mind towards a life of dedicated prayer, foresaw that she was to be the chosen architect and builder of the Master's monument for posterity.

In the sublime beauty of its lines and curves, Kyāk Dguṅ ("Shwe Dagon"), as it stands today, portrays to us the soul of Mi Čao Bu, revealing to us all the more truly the strength and beauty of her character, and giving us an insight into the fact that beauty has no other basis than strength.

At the age of seventy-five she passed away peacefully after having fulfilled the work she was inspired to do, and by which, offered as worship to Him, she came to Him. In her last moments she asked those around her to move her bed to the window from where her eyes might rest on His shrine, and with her mind meditating on Him she entered unto Him with her last breath. So came to a close a life happy and carefree to start with, but inevitably passing through the many trials and tribulations all mortals are but heir to, and finally reaping a harvest which becomes a blessing in a growing capacity of the heart to love, and yet not to possess.

Though five centuries have gone by, her name Mi Čao Bu, commonly known to the Burmese as Shin Saw Bu, is affectionately remembered, and gently loved and revered throughout the land of Burma for a grace and charm that is all her own. Even in the place of her captivity, the people still dramatize the many touching incidents of her life, stirring within their hearts profound emotions.

Down the vista of the years we cannot but fully realize that the forced abduction and captivity at Ava, bringing with it untold misery and pain, only served a purpose in her life. Had hers been a happy domestic life, sheltered and protected, she would, I dare to think, have died just an ordinary woman. But as it was, the reverses in her fortunes, with their accompanying pain and grief, served to lay bare before her the stark reality of life; and in grappling with the situation in a most realistic manner to divert her mind through work and service from her own hardships, she was unconsciously though nevertheless surely, paving for herself a road to Nirvāṇa. Seen in this light, Thihathu becomes only a pawn in the hand of Destiny, to reveal to her the hard facts of life, from which she could only find release by occupying herself with the welfare of others. Even so, her many bereavements fulfilled a like purpose.

Under the most difficult and trying circumstances, when an ordinary woman would have lost her bearing, Mi Čao Bu still had faith in herself, and remained firm and unshaken. Her calm and saintly manner in quietly occupying herself with the welfare of others, even at a time when her heart was torn with grief, gives us courage and strength in our own dark moments. In hours lonely and dismal, when pain and sorrow weigh themselves heavily on the heart, she seems to appear as a beacon light, summoning us to gather strength through suffering and restraint, which is the only way to growth.

Neither name nor fame, nor wealth nor progeny, nor anything the world has yet to offer, may be compared to strength. In its absence the most beauteous things of the world lose their beauty. Its presence lends grace and charm to the most common and ordinary things of life.

PART III

WOMEN SAINTS OF CHRISTIANITY

CHAPTER XVIII

WOMAN'S PLACE IN CHRISTIANITY

INTRODUCTORY

IT was the opinion of Pythagoras that "women as a sex are more naturally akin to piety"[1]; he is said, moreover, to have derived the substance of his own ethical doctrine from Themistoclea, a Delphic priestess.[2] Here, then, is clear evidence that the place of women in human religious activity was recognized, in the West, at a very early date. Plato, in his time, is seen to have crystallized his inheritance from Pythagoras in the episode of Diotima and Socrates, in the *Symposium*. Later still, with the advent of Christianity, it was first of all the Platonic tradition in Greek philosophic thought which was found by the early fathers of the Church to furnish just those conceptual vehicles—those old vessels for new wine—which could most readily be accepted for the process of intellectualizing the new religion, with the least degree of detriment to its own essential quality.[3]

This is by no means to suggest, however, that Christianity owes to the Greek modes of its early expression the altogether unparalleled depth of its consciousness as concerns the matter here in question. On the contrary, the exalted place assigned by it to the feminine personality is assured in advance, if by nothing else, by the primary circumstances themselves of its own entrance into the world: namely by the fact that the free consent of a woman was required for the Incarnation in human form of its Divine Founder. While the likewise unparalleled degree of estimation in which it has ever held the state of virginity is sufficiently accounted for by the further fact that the woman in question was herself—*ante et post partum*—a virgin. Thus when philosophic expression had to be found for these, and other, high realities and truths, the body of human

[1] In a letter to the women of Croton; Diog. Laert., *Vita Pyth.*, 8.1.10.

[2] *Ibid.*, v. (See J. E. Harrison: *Prolegomena to the Study of Greek Religion*, p. 647).

[3] Cf. A. J. Festugière: *Contemplation et Vie Contemplative selon Platon*, p. 5: "the movement issuing from Jesus Christ has dowered with a new life a pre-existing organism of which the structure goes back to Plato. When the fathers 'think' their *mystique*, they Platonize".

wisdom shaped in the course of centuries by the Greek Platonic tradition was found to provide a not wholly unfitting vesture for them: as the holy Maiden of Nazareth herself provided, of her own virginal substance, a fitting bodily vesture for their Divine Author. Moreover, as the Scriptural narratives bear witness, certain women came to play a very definite part in His earthly life and work, towards its close.

Given such beginnings, therefore, it is only to be expected that the history of the Christian Church should be everywhere lighted up by the luminous figures of holy women; and that of these, the great majority should be invested with that peculiarly incandescent glory which arises from their virgin status. And it is little wonder that the Church continues, as she has ever done, to exalt and venerate these shining figures, and to propose them unceasingly as high examples, for the love and imitation of her children.

The unique and particular quality of this veneration itself arises, in the first place, out of the Church's recognition of the Divine reverence for the free and independent being of His own creation—for the "personality" of each single individual. This Divine reverence, too, is such as to override completely the conditions and limitations—products of the biologic laws and necessities—attendant upon human life as we know it: in other words, it is entirely without regard to sex. More than this indeed, it would even seem, if only by the high initial circumstances above mentioned, to attach itself with a certain predilection, as between the two sexes, rather to the feminine; for it was a woman who was chosen as that "fiery point" by which the Divine was to find first entrance into the terms and conditions of the human: by which God was to become man.

It was inevitable, then, at an early date, that provision should come to be made by the Christian Church, for the benefit of those women who desired, by a full use of their already conceded prerogative, to engage themselves by special vows in a deeper practice of the religious life. Hence arose, roughly coeval with the monastic orders, the first convents for women. While, for the far greater proportion of Christian womanhood, "the way of nature"—marriage and maternity—still remained, even as with the pagan peoples, the generally accepted way of fulfilment, there were those, in ever-increasing numbers (though still, and ever to remain, a minority), who were aware of another. It was for such as these that the Church instituted first of all, at a very early date, a special vow for the consecration of their virginity, to be observed by girls of marriageable age (in those times of violence and persecution) while continuing to live in the midst of their own families.[1] At a later period, with the cessation of persecution, and the emergence into open recognition of the Church, more far-reaching measures became possible, and this practice was largely superseded by the setting up of religious foundations for women—even as for men—which were designed to provide those conditions of seclusion and quietude in which the life of the spirit might be followed with a greater degree of fullness.

It is not certainly known where, when and by whom the first of these foundations was made: opinion appears to vary between (*a*) Middle Egypt, about A.D. 271, by the sister (her name is unknown) of St. Antony the Hermit; (*b*) Alexandria, towards the mid-fourth century, by St. Syncletica; (*c*) Annesi (in Anatolia), before 379, by St. Macrina; or (*d*) at Bethlehem, in 388–390, by Sts. Paula and Eustochium, the friends and protegées of St. Jerome.

From the time of the first foundation, the number of convents for women has ever continued to increase with the growth of the Church itself, on an even footing and at an even pace with those intended for men; and the processes of canonization, the necrologies and biographical archives of individual foundations, and many other documents are open testimony to the spiritual altitudes sometimes attained therein. In addition to the very small number of holy Christian women of whom it has been found possible to give some account in the succeeding pages, mention may here be made (apart from St. Teresa) of such famous foundresses as the following: In the sixth century, St. Radegund of Poitiers; seventh century, St. Werburg, St.

[1] Among the early Christian writers and Fathers who produced special treatises, or wrote otherwise in praise of virginity, the following may be mentioned: Athenagoras (second century); Tertullian, Minucius Felix and St. Cyprian (third century); St. Methodius of Olympus, St. Athanasius, Basil of Ancyra, St. Gregory of Nyssa, St. Jerome and St. Ambrose (fourth century); and in the fifth century, St. Augustine. The two last-named in particular were especially zealous in promoting the practice of consecration with special vows, for those among the younger women who did not desire to enter the married state.

Etheldreda, St. Ethelburga, St. Hilda; twelfth century, St. Hildegarde of Bingen; thirteenth century, St. Clare (companion of St. Francis); fourteenth century, St. Brigid of Sweden; fifteenth century, St. Frances of Rome, Ste. Colette, Bl. Frances of Brittany, St. Catherine of Bologna; seventeenth century, St. Mary Magdalen dei Pazzi, Ste. Jeanne-Françoise de Chantal and Bl. Marie de l'Incarnation (Madame Acarie). Many of these (e.g. Ste. Colette, St. Catherine of Bologna, and the three last-mentioned) are known to have attained the highest level of mystical spirituality.

Of more isolated figures, only a few of the most illustrious can be named: e.g. Ste. Geneviève (of Paris), St. Catherine of Genoa, St. Rose of Lima, and that amazing spiritual phenomenon who was Ste. Jeanne d'Arc (in whom the virginal condition glowed with so great an intensity that she was known throughout the armies under her command as "the Maid").

It is by no means, of course, solely in a life of isolation, or in the vowed life of the cloister, that women have attained to sanctity; the Christian Church, in its constant maintenance of the rights of the individual soul, has provided, in declaring the sacramentality of marriage, another though more universal and well-trodden way by which that same goal may still be reached. In marriage, accepted as a sacramental state, the woman may no longer be regarded as the property, the instrument, or even as a part of her husband. In entering as a free partner upon this state, she undertakes, it is true, certain very real responsibilities, the precise extent and weight of which she is unable at the outset to foresee. Her problem as a soul aspiring towards perfection in the married state is considerably less simple than that of her sister entering upon a life of consecrated virginity. Nevertheless, the annals of the Church are very rich, even here, in illustrious examples. Among the more famous saints of the wedded state may be mentioned: St. Mechtildis, Empress of Germany; St. Margaret, Queen of Scotland; Ste. Blanche of Castile, Queen of France (Mother of St. Louis); St. Elizabeth (or Isabel), Queen of Portugal; St. Elizabeth, Queen of Hungary; St. Hedwig (or Jadwiga) of Poland and in humbler life Bl. Anna-Maria Taigi. Ste. Jeanne de Chantal was a devoted wife and mother until widowed at an early age, as also was Bl. Barbe Acarie, and both did but carry on in the cloister a work already well begun in the world. St. Catherine of Genoa, one of the greatest mystical souls of her own, or of any century, was unhappily married, but lived to see the complete reformation of her husband.

There are, however, certain rarer cases which demand a brief consideration of the Church's doctrine and practice with regard to the sacrament of matrimony. It is her teaching that the sacramental grace extends to every aspect of the bond in its entirety. Procreation, and the act of procreation, are therefore included under the action of grace and—for the great majority of her children—the Church enjoins the fullest physical realization of the bond. Yet, this notwithstanding, it is also the teaching of the Church that the essence of the sacrament does not inhere in the physical aspect, but solely in the fact that two human souls of opposite sex have freely chosen to abide together in lifelong companionship and mutual love, within the terms of which association the physical realization may, or may not, be included. The Church has therefore, on several occasions, solemnly condemned the opinion that the state of marriage requires for its full perfection the act of physical consummation. She has recognized, with St. Thomas Aquinas, the concept, in certain cases, of a marriage *ratum sed non consummatum*. Indeed, how should this be otherwise? Holding, as she does, the birth of Jesus Christ to have been completely virginal, she must necessarily hold that the essence of the bond subsisting between His holy Mother and her consort St. Joseph must be sought elsewhere than in a physical concourse which she recognizes to have been, in their case, non-existent. Thus, then, there have not been wanting, in the roll of Christian sanctity, the names of certain married pairs who have been moved by the Spirit to interpret their own bond after a similar fashion; and, having chosen from the outset to abide together in perpetual virginity, have sealed their choice by solemn vows. A few historical examples must suffice: in the eleventh century, St. Cunegunda, Empress, and the Emperor St. Henry II, of the Holy Roman Empire; in the thirteenth century, St. Cunegund, Queen, and Boleslaw (surnamed "the Chaste"), King of Poland; in the fourteenth century, St. Elzéar de Sabran, Count of Ariano, and Bl. Delphine de Glandève de Puy-Michel; also St. Catherine, Princess of Sweden (daughter of St. Brigid of Sweden), and Eggard Lyderssen de Kyren; and, in the fifteenth century, Bl. Angelina of Corbara and the Count of Civitella.

It is hoped that this brief sketch may help to convey some idea of the high place held by women in the life and annals of the Christian Church.

CHAPTER XIX

MACRINA

IN Western civilization the emergence of the saint, in the sense of a person of recognized and venerated holiness, dates from the spread of Christianity. Greek and Roman domestic life, enlightened though it was in many respects, did not afford scope for a woman so to develop her personality and widen her influence that she could achieve a full life in the public eye. To this there were certain marked exceptions, as for instance Aspasia the mistress of Pericles, who by her wit and intelligence was a dominating figure in the aristocratic society of Athens in the middle of the fifth century B.C. But Aspasia, though what we should call a completely integrated and fully developed personality, was no saint. The Athenians kept their women at home, and Pericles himself once said that the best thing for a woman was not to have her fame bruited abroad. In Sparta women were treated on a footing of equality with men, but were required above all to develop strictness and even savagery of discipline among their children, so that their ideal was the matron who told her son to return from a battle either with his shield or upon it. The typical Roman lady was a fainter counterpart of the Spartan matron, and women tended to be either dominating martinets like Cornelia the mother of the Gracchi, or colourless lay figures, or slaves, or smart and abandoned society women like Clodia, the sister of Cicero's enemy Clodius (the Lesbia of Catullus's lyrics).

Yet here and there in Greek and Roman literature we come across women who had many of the qualities of sainthood; who lived quiet, devoted lives, enduring many things and expecting no fame. There is a brief Roman epitaph of the second century B.C., which describes with pathetic brevity the qualities of a good wife. It ends: *Domum servavit lanam fecit. Dixi. Abei.* ("She kept the home, she spun wool. I have spoken. Farewell.") Glimpses of this ideal of quiet devotion speak to us from the centuries: there is something of it in Homer's Penelope, in Ismene the sister of Antigone, and it emerges with startling clearness in a Latin inscription of the time of Augustus, a long epitaph by a widower named Vespillo on his wife Turia. She was unable to have children and had begged her husband to take another woman so as not to be bereft of offspring; she would regard any children of such a union with the same love as if they had been her own; she would yield her place in the household to the newcomer and would not even make any separation in the joint patrimony which she enjoyed with her husband. He recounts his horrified repudiation of this suggestion and heart-brokenly wishes he had died first so that she could have paid him the last rites. Now he is alone.

The life of St. Macrina shows devotion and sainthood of this same order, but directed into different channels through the spreading ideal of monasticism which had taken hold of the Christian world. Her name means "blessed" in Greek and had been given to her after her grandmother, according to accepted Greek custom. The only source of our information about her comes from her younger brother Gregory of Nyssa, who embodied a short life of his sister in a letter to a monk of Antioch named Olympius. This biography resembles many of its kind in its unevenness; it gives us exasperatingly scanty information about the life of Macrina and describes her death and burial in minute detail, just as the trial and death of Jesus occupy a large proportion of every Gospel, to the exclusion of other facts about Him which we would give a great deal to possess. Gregory's life of his sister has been translated by W. K. Lowther Clarke, B.D., and was published by the S.P.C.K. in 1916.

Gregory of Nyssa was born about A.D. 335, probably at Caesarea in Cappadocia. Macrina was the eldest of ten children, and Gregory one of the two youngest, so that she was born probably about 325. The eldest brother was St. Basil the Great, and the youngest brother, Peter, became Bishop of Sebaste—a remarkable record for one family. The family was wealthy and lived on their estates, and had been Christian for at least two generations, for there is a hint that the grandmother Macrina may have suffered for her faith—she had "confessed Christ like a good 'athlete' in the time of the persecutions".[1] Gregory's mother, herself an exceptionally beautiful woman, was attracted to the celibate life but married in order

[1] 962A (the reference is to the text of Gregory of Nyssa in Migne's *Patrologia Graecia*, XLVI. p. 960 ff.)

to secure herself from the many suitors who were ready to abduct her.

To understand the appeal of monasticism in the Christian world of the period one must take into account many factors. There was of course the powerful example of celibacy in the life of Jesus, which may have been influenced by Buddhism through the doctrines of the Essenes.[1] Then of course the other-worldliness of Christianity led to a scorn of this world. But deeper still is the rooted conviction in man that the true life of the soul is uncovered only when the body and its desires, and indeed all the dance and play of the outward world, are subdued or in abeyance. This is the inner doctrine of the Upanishads and of Buddha. Plato finds the true happiness of the soul to emerge when the passions are allayed and at rest, in other words when the body is at its quietest. Something of this sanity always remained in Western monasticism. The centre and inspiration of Christian monastic life was Egypt, where the discovery of a fragment of St. John's Gospel dating to the beginning of the second century attests a remarkably early date for the settlement of Christians there.[2]

The formation of monasticism was in two stages: first came the solitaries or "desert men", of whom the first was Paul of Thebes, and then the formation of communities or *coenobia*, the first to gather disciples round him being St. Antony (*c.* A.D. 250–356).[3] The full organization of the monkish community life is due to St. Pakhom or Pachomius (d.*c.* A.D. 349) who made his monks a self-contained society under strict discipline, its members all engaged in various crafts in order to earn a livelihood. This, the highest of all ideals of monasticism, has achieved a vast amount of good in the world and its ideal of manual labour and meditation has found adherents in the East. The Buddha's ideal was not quite so practical since he preached absolute poverty, but the Zen Buddhists of Japan have unwittingly captured the very spirit of Pakhom in their insistence on balancing work and meditation. "At all the Meditation Halls", says Professor D. T. Suzuki, "work is

[1] For a discussion of this possibility see Albert Schweitzer, *The Quest of the Historical Jesus*, Chapter XVII (1906 edition).

[2] This fragment is in the Rylands Library at Manchester (Ryl. Pap. 457) and is the earliest fragment of the New Testament in existence.

[3] See the article *The Coptic Church and Egyptian Monasticism*, by De Lacy O'Leary, in *The Legacy of Egypt* (ed. S. R. K. Glanville), pp. 317–31.

considered a vital element in the life of a monk. It is altogether a practical one and chiefly consists in manual labour, such as sweeping, cleaning, cooking, fuel-gathering, tilling the farm or going about begging in villages far and near. No work is considered beneath their dignity, and a perfect feeling of brotherhood and democracy prevails among them. How hard, or how mean from the ordinary point of view a work may be, they will not shun it."[1]

One of their favourite sayings is, "A day of no work is a day of no eating", and Professor Suzuki adds these eminently sane reflections: "Unless the hands are habitually trained to do the work of the brain, the blood ceases to circulate evenly over the body, it grows congested somewhere, especially in the brain. The result will be not only an unsound condition of the body in general but a state of mental torpidity or drowsiness, in which ideas are presented as if they were wafting clouds. One is wide awake and yet the mind is filled with the wildest dreams and visions which are not at all related to the realities of life."[2] This danger has been clearly seen by such monks as Brother Lawrence, and even the great scholastic Eckhart said, "What a man takes in by contemplation he must pour out in love".

For a long time Egypt was regarded as the Holy Land in preference to Palestine, because of the multitudes of ascetic saints there, who were visited by Christian pilgrims from all parts of the Mediterranean world. Among these visitors was St. Basil, the elder brother of Gregory of Nyssa and the younger brother of Macrina. He was much impressed by the mode of life instituted by Pakhom and resolved to inaugurate a small community near his own family estates in Pontus. To this he summoned his friend Gregory of Nazianzus, and thus Greek monasticism was begun. Basil's mother Emmelia and sister Macrina on their estate on the opposite bank of the river Iris had already been much drawn to the ascetic life, and very soon there was a double monastery at Annesi, the men being presided over by Peter, a younger brother of Macrina, and the women by Macrina herself. Brother Gregory spent some years in studious seclusion here before being summoned by Basil to the bishopric of Nyssa. Basil died on January 1, 379, and

[1] D. T. Suzuki, *Essays in Zen Buddhism*, vol. I, p. 302.
[2] *Op. cit.*, p. 304.

Gregory soon afterwards attended a Council at Antioch, after which he visited Macrina at the monastery. While he was there Macrina died, and he wrote a sketch of her life as a letter to the monk Olympius.

Like many biographies of ancient times this short account by Gregory breaks all the rules of art: it gives a disproportionate space to the death of Macrina (death-bed scenes have always tempted the Christian apologist to linger unduly), and instead of early detail we are put off with rhetorical commonplaces; but in spite of this we receive the impression of a strong yet gentle character, firm without hardness, keenly intelligent—in fact the highest type of womanhood. We gather this from indirect hints: for instance Gregory speaks of her as having raised herself by "philosophy" to the greatest height of human virtue.[1] The use of this word "philosophy" is highly instructive to a student of Vedānta. It is common in the fourth century to denote Christianity, largely owing to Origen's synthesis of the Gospel and philosophy, and in particular it seems to have denoted the practice of asceticism—a very striking parallel to the cardinal principle of Hindu thought, that truth is to be achieved not by the intellect alone but by the *ascesis* or discipline of quiet meditation which leads to the intuition of truths far vaster than the reason can compass. This preliminary *ascesis* as an introduction to the study of philosophy might be termed India's special contribution to the art of living, and here in the Greek world of the fourth century A.D. we find the term philosophy used in exactly this sense.

Macrina's birth was attended by visions in which an angel appeared and addressed the baby as Thecla, the virgin whom legend made to be a contemporary of St. Paul (the *Acts of Paul and Thecla* has a stronger claim to authenticity than many books of its kind). This was taken to indicate that the baby was destined to the celibate life, and indeed her mother, a woman of exceptional beauty, had "loved the pure and unstained mode of life so much that she was unwilling to be married".[2] The young Macrina was carefully trained from infancy by her mother, who considered the normal curriculum "disgraceful and unsuitable" for a delicately nurtured girl. This curriculum consisted largely, as all Greek education did, in the learning of poetry, chiefly of Homer and the tragedians, whose

[1] 960 C

[2] 962 A

depiction of naked human passions was more suited to the training of a man than of a woman. Instead, Macrina was taught the Old Testament scriptures, in particular the Psalter, which was her constant companion "when she rose from bed, or engaged in household duties, or rested, or partook of food, or retired from table, when she went to bed or rose in the night for prayer".[1]

Macrina was betrothed to a young man of remarkable promise, who died before the marriage could take place, and her steadfast devotion to his memory reminds us of the equally steadfast loyalty of Sāradā Devī to Rāmakṛishṇa, though in the latter case it was loyalty to an ideal embodied in human form rather than to an imperishable memory. "Macrina persisted that the man who had been linked to her through betrothal was not dead, but that she considered him who lived to God, thanks to the hope of the resurrection, to be absent only, not dead; it was wrong not to keep faith with the bridegroom who was away."[2] After the young man's death Macrina scarcely left her mother's side, but devoted herself to the living of a quiet, regulated life of working to govern her mother's household; and "by her own life she instructed her mother greatly, leading her to the same mark, that of philosophy, and gradually drawing her on to the more immaterial and more perfect life".[3] She cooked meals for her mother with her own hands—not, Gregory hastens to add, that she made this her chief business, but after she had "anointed her hands by the performance of religious duties—for she deemed that zeal for these was consistent with the principles of her life—in the time that was left she prepared food for her mother by her own toil".[4]

When her brother Basil arrived, arrogant with the rhetoric of the universities and excelling in his own estimation all the local men of leading and position, the influence upon him of Macrina was such as to make him "forsake the glories of this world and despise the fame of rhetoric, deserting it for this busy life where one toils with one's hands".[5] This is perhaps the greatest single tribute ever paid to her influence, that it transformed and beautified the life of her own brother, irradiating it from within. She, like Sāradā Devī, was a golden example of that influence of which Albert Schweitzer has written these

[1] 964 A [2] 964 D [3] 966 B [4] 966 A [5] 966 C

memorable words: "We all live, spiritually, by what others have given us in the significant hours of our life. These significant hours do not announce themselves as coming, but arrive unexpected. Nor do they make a great show of themselves; they pass almost unperceived. Often, indeed, their significance comes home to us first as we look back, just as the beauty of a piece of music or of a landscape often strikes us first in our recollection of it. Much that has become our own in gentleness, modesty, kindness, willingness to forgive, in veracity, loyalty, resignation under suffering, we owe to people in whom we have seen or experienced these virtues at work, sometimes in a great matter, sometimes in a small. A thought which had become act sprang into us like a spark, and lighted a new flame within us."[1]

The next incident in which the strength of Macrina's spirit was made manifest was the death of her younger brother Naucratius. He had excelled all the family in physical prowess, beauty, strength and "the ability to turn his hand to anything". He had aspired after the life of an eremite and had gone off, accompanied only by his servant Chrysapius, to a delightful and lovely spot in the mountains by the river Iris (reminding us of the ascetics of India who have always chosen the most lovely places for their contemplation of Being). He and Chrysapius met their deaths "on one of the expeditions by which he provided necessaries for the old men under his care". This may refer to a kind of begging expedition like those of the Buddha and of the early *sannyāsins*, and it is noteworthy that even in his solitude Naucratius had deemed it obligatory to look after some old people living in poverty and feebleness. The ideal of *bhakti* or devotion through service is never completely absent from the highest mysticism. Macrina, though suffering acutely the pangs of bereavement, sustained and uplifted the spirit of her mother till it rose completely above all sorrow.[2]

There now follows in Gregory's letter a picture of the progress made by Macrina and her mother in the ascetic life.[3] They adopted the same dress, ate the same food, wore the same rough clothing and slept in the same kind of bed as their own maids. "Continence was their luxury, and obscurity their glory.

[1] *Memoirs of Childhood and Youth*, pp. 89–90.
[2] 970 B
[3] 970 C–972 A

Poverty, and the casting away of all material superfluities like dust from their bodies, was their wealth. In fact, of all things after which men eagerly pursue in this life, there were none with which they could not easily dispense." They seem at times to have experienced something much akin to the Hindu *samādhi*, for we read that "Since living in the body and yet after the likeness of the immaterial beings, they were not bowed down by the weight of the body, but their life was exalted to the skies and they walked on high in company with the powers of heaven".[1]

In fairly quick succession are recounted the deaths of the youngest of the family, Peter, of the mother and of Basil, and we are permitted to see Macrina rising superior to all her grief of heart and remaining a steadfast example to all. For a while after the death of their mother the children seem to have had recourse to self-mortification, and we read, "But they, having fulfilled the command, clave to philosophy with even loftier resolve, even striving against their own life and eclipsing their previous record by their subsequent successes".[2]

It was after the death of Basil that Gregory visited his sister. He seems to have had some foreboding that all was not well with her health, for he recounts visions that came to him on his journey; and though we are not told so, it may well be that Macrina's illness was a direct result of her mortifications, for when he greets her he finds her "already terribly afflicted with weakness. She was lying, not on a bed or couch, but on the floor; a sack had been spread on a board, and another board propped up her head, so contrived to act as a pillow, supporting the sinews of the neck in slanting fashion, and holding up the neck comfortably. Now when she saw me near the door she raised herself on her elbow but could not come to meet me, her strength being already drained by fever. But by putting her hands on the floor and leaning over from the pallet as far as she could, she showed the respect due to my rank."[3] This is the most circumstantial picture Gregory has of his sister; most of his account is regrettably sketchy and imprecise, so that we have to make the best of conventional description and vague generality. Obviously he was better at homiletic rhetoric than at thumb-nail sketches.

Macrina stilled her groans and tried to hide the difficulty

[1] 972 A [2] 974 B [3] 976 D

of her breathing. She took the lead in conversation, cheered her brother who was disconsolate at the death of Basil, and discoursed of holy things in a way that amazed him. "Fever was drying up her strength and driving her on to death, yet she refreshed her body as it were with dew, and thus kept her mind unimpeded in the contemplation of heavenly things, in no way injured by her terrible weakness. . . . She was uplifted as she discoursed to us on the nature of the soul and explained the reason of life in the flesh, and why man was made, and how he was mortal, and the origin of death, and the nature of the journey from death to life again."[1] Even in her extremity her first thought was for the comfort of her brother and his attendants, and she dismissed them for rest and refreshment. Later she spoke to them of her childhood, and, Gregory adds, "Never did she even look for help to any human being, nor did human charity give her the opportunity of a comfortable existence. Never were petitioners turned away, yet never did she appeal for help, but God secretly blessed the little seeds of her good works till they grew into a mighty fruit."[2] The rest of the letter, more than a third of it, is given over to an account of Macrina's death and burial, which were attended by many to whom she had been a benefactress.

To us her lasting memorial is in the lives of her famous brothers St. Basil and St. Gregory of Nyssa, both of whom owed the direction of their Christian lives entirely to her and both of whom were figures of great importance in the history of the Eastern Church. It is in these ways that influence works. In the words of Schweitzer, "Not one of us knows what effect his life produces, and what he gives to others; that is hidden from us and must remain so, though we are often allowed to see some little fraction of it, so that we may not lose courage. The way in which power works is a mystery."[3]

[1] 978 C [2] 982 A [3] *Memoirs of Childhood and Youth*, p. 91.

CHAPTER XX

BRIGIT OF KILDARE

IN the early centuries of the Christian era, Ireland was the cultural centre of the Western world and was considered the most learned country in Europe: *Insula sanctorum et doctorum.* Religion and education went hand in hand and were directly under the supervision of priests and monks. Students in "fleet-loads" came to the island for education—Romans, Gauls, Germans, Egyptians, a king of England and a king of France. The Venerable Bede records that when the English fled to Ireland to escape the yellow plague, "The Irish willingly received them all, gave them food, also furnished them with books to read, and their teaching, all gratis". Schooling was given not only in ecclesiastical subjects, but in poetry, literature, law and medicine. A training of twelve years was necessary to attain the highest degree of scholarship, and learning was held in such esteem that those holding degrees sat next to the king at table. Learned Irishmen travelled extensively on the Continent, not only as missionaries, but were eagerly sought after as professors and teachers in the cultural centres of Europe.

It has been said that with the advent of Christianity in the fifth century, Ireland passed from the Iron Age to the "golden age": the rich pagan culture was enhanced by integration of thought and guidance, and the people changed from paganism to the worship of the one true God; men turned from the shaking sod of war to peaceful pursuits. With the introduction of Latin, literature developed, and, with the invention of a new and beautiful calligraphy based on the Latin alphabet with strong Celtic influence, those histories and traditions which had heretofore been handed down by word of mouth by the hereditary and itinerant *fill-ee* (poets and lovers of wisdom) were recorded in manuscript. Thus, in this "golden age" of Ireland some of the most exquisite illuminated manuscript books in the world were written, a few of which are extant. Craftsmen in gold, silver, bronze and enamel were known for the skill and mastery of precision in their ornamental work, musicians were given an honoured place in society, and as Christianity spread throughout the land, the kings and petty chiefs, who had torn the country asunder with internecine warfare, became gradually less belligerent, and man and beast lived an idyllic existence where the peasantry tilled the land in peace, warriors reared cattle, and the arts and learning were fostered and encouraged.

To assess the true substance of the people at this time of transition, something must also be known of the pre-Christian period. Who were the Irish? And what was their culture? The fifth-century Irish were Celts. They were a people probably originating in Central Europe, who, driven westwards, had crossed to Ireland and there intermixed with the population which by tradition was of Greek, Scythian and Iberian descent. These Celtic people had their own language, culture and lettering, and their history was recorded by the *fill-ee*. They worshipped pillar-stone images overlaid with gold and they had their magicians, their *she-ee* (local deities and fairies) and leprechauns.

Various kings and numerous chiefs and princes arose in Celtic Ireland, some deified, some legendary and some existent. They partitioned the island and all, at some time or other, pursued on their own soil and abroad ceaseless warfare in attempts to preserve the balance of power amongst the numerous petty kingdoms.

Society was graded into five main classes, which cannot be termed castes as it was possible to move from one grade to another. There were the kings, who numbered more than a hundred, the nobles, landed freemen, freemen without property, and bondmen. Slavery was recognized, the English selling their children as slaves to the Irish. The people lived in round houses made of wattle and clay, grouped around the dwelling of a chief, within a circular stronghold surrounded by a dike. These scattered homesteads were connected by roads constructed for chariots. The world of women lay entirely within the precincts of the family, but women within the first four grades of society were not in subjection, they suffered no injustices and had legal status equal to the husband, who incidentally had to give a dowry to the father to obtain the daughter as wife. Although women were concerned only with pursuits in the home and did not participate in outside events, every freewoman attained to a standard whereby she became expert in all types of crafts and the owner of a loom, distaff, spindles, quern and sieve; a woman possessing these appliances was styled "a greater worker" and her prospects of marriage were greatly increased. But among the non-free classes, the enslaved women had no rights and were considered the property of their masters. They toiled ceaselessly at menial tasks: watching the flocks, grinding corn, washing the feet of guests and holding lights at the banquet tables.

Now, at this transitional period of Irish history, some twenty years after the diffusion of Christianity by St. Patrick, there was born in the kingdom of Leinster, about the year A.D. 453 to one of the minor pagan princes, Dubthach, a daughter, whose mother was a Christian bondwoman, and she became St. Brigit of Kildare, a patron saint of Ireland and the foremost woman of her day.

It has been said of this rare and gifted woman, who dedicated her life to God: "Though she spoke words of human and angelic wisdom, she deemed herself as nothing, or not better than sounding brass or tinkling cymbal, if not possessing compassion, the queen of all virtues. In the distribution of temporal goods she was liberal indeed, almost to prodigality, especially when poor and distressed individuals claimed her protection. This was done through no motive of ostentation nor through any pride of soul, through no indirect self-seeking or ambition. She was induced neither to think evil nor to feel indignant even when unworthy persons approached to obtain her alms. She envied not others when fortune dealt adversely with herself; she was humble as the lowliest of her religious, when placed over them as a superior. She bore kindly and patiently with the perverseness and ingratitude of some, while being a lover of what was deemed upright and just, she laboured indefatigably in the cause of religion and divine truth."[1]

Legend gives a romantic touch to historic facts, and emotion, born of devotion, will envelop the life and character of a saint in myth, and when that saint is born, as it were, on the threshold of an epoch in the history of a race, past beliefs and traditions are transfused into the future to present a remarkable tale of superstitions, miracles and folk-lore through which the saint's spiritual transcendence alone shines as a beacon of light to guide devotees and draw aspirants to the sublime.

In the case of St. Brigit of Kildare, manifold are the tradi-

[1] *Lives of the Irish Saints*, by John O'Hanlon, 1875.

tions, the superstitions, the miracles and the folk-tales told by the hereditary *fill-ee* and handed on to the monastic scribes, and it has been difficult for scholars through the ages to know where, with regard to this early Irish saint, tradition ends and reality is born, because the advent of Christianity in Ireland did not mean a ruthless sweeping away of the pre-Christian religion, nor an antagonism towards the new belief, but rather a reasoning and a confluence of the old with the new. Thus, Patrick, the Roman Christian who taught the new faith in Ireland before Brigit was born, met with a willingness for conversion not only amongst the peasantry, but amongst the rulers, and he acknowledged what could be accepted of the old religion and incorporated it with Christianity. Accordingly, although Patrick would not accept the worship of gilded stone images, he recognized the lighting of the festal fire on the Hill of Tara, an ancient pagan ceremony, and propagated this as the light of the Paschal fire. Therefore, with this overlapping of Christian and pre-Christian ceremonies and rites, it is not surprising to find Brigit, the daughter of a pagan prince and Christian bondwoman, being confused with the pre-Christian Brigit, daughter of the sun-god, the goddess of wisdom and knowledge, the arts and fertility, and patroness of the crops. Thus, the flame of fire kindled on the altar of the church at Kildare when St. Brigit died and kept burning continuously until the Reformation, carried within it a more ancient symbol of the daughter of the sun-god and was invoked to secure a bountiful harvest.

It may be seen, therefore, how difficult it is to determine where reality begins and tradition recedes into the past when writing about St. Brigit. Although it has been said many legends about Brigit are false, they embody an incidental truth because they have served through the ages to convey some inkling of her character and the effect of her actions upon the people of her day, so it may not be amiss to relate some of these tales.

Now, Brigit was born into slavery, for her mother was sold to another master before the birth of her child. As she grew up, Brigit performed the usual tasks of bondwomen: tending the flock, grinding the corn and washing the feet of guests. As was customary when she reached an age to be of service, her father claimed her and she returned as a menial to his household. Although her work was lowly, as she matured it became apparent that Brigit had a noble and intelligent mind; she regarded the humblest slave-girl as a sister, but was equally at ease with her father's guests. This quality was a great advantage to Brigit in her work later in life as her deep compassion enabled her to touch the hearts of those with whom she was dealing, be they bishop, king or slave.

At an early age Brigit developed a trait in her character which, throughout her life, disconcerted others who were less open-hearted; this was her excessive generosity. As a young girl she was always giving away her father's possessions: if, whilst tending the flock, she saw a beggar, she would give him one of the sheep. Such liberality became an embarrassment to her father, who, it is said, was only prevented from punishing Brigit by divine intervention, and so expensive did her father find her generosity, he finally decided to sell her to the Christian King of Leinster. Early records say: one morning Dubthach summoned Brigit from her household tasks and put her into his chariot; the young girl smiled with pleasure at her stern father, delighted with anticipation at this unexpected favour, only to be told: "It is not to honour you I am taking you out, but to sell you to the king."

When they reached the fortress, her father went to the king to bargain a price for the new slave, and whilst Brigit was left waiting in the chariot a leper approached her. Now, in those days in Ireland, it was customary for lepers to be treated as privileged people because of their affliction, and they were permitted to roam at will within the king's fortress, so the leper approached Brigit to ask for help. But the slave-girl, sitting in the prince's chariot, in spite of her apparently lofty status, possessed nothing she could give, and turning pitifully away from the leper's beseeching eyes Brigit suddenly noticed in the chariot her father's bejewelled sword, which, without hesitation, she presented to the leper who gladly took it and hastened away. In audience with the king, Dubthach was explaining the reason he had to get rid of Brigit was because of her unrestrained generosity which made her too expensive for him to keep, and, returning to his chariot to fetch Brigit, immediately he noticed his sword, his most valuable possession, was gone. Dubthach, according to the annals "was mightily enraged", as well he might be, and was even more infuriated when, telling Brigit how valuable it was, she responded that

that was the reason why she had given it to one of "God's children".

This episode of disposing of her father's sword is said to have been the turning-point in Brigit's life, because when the King of Leinster heard of her action, he championed the cause of the slave-girl who had fearlessly bestowed her father's valued possession on a leper, whose need she believed was the greater, and he asked her father to free her from bondage, saying "Leave her alone, for her merit before God is greater than ours".

This legend has been variously interpreted to mean that as the saint gave away the sword of a warrior, considering it of no great value, so she was setting an example to her fellow-countrymen to fulfil their lives in ways other than by continuous bloodshed, exhorting them to forsake strife and to live more charitable lives.

This first public action of Brigit in disposing of the sword had its counterpart in later life when she was famed throughout Ireland. It is said there came to her one day a warrior about to lead his men to invade and defeat a neighbouring chief, and, in reply to a request for a blessing on his enterprise, Brigit, who according to her chroniclers "bestowed peace in her blessing", said: "I entreat the omnipotent Lord my God that in this instance you neither inflict injury on anyone nor suffer it yourselves: wherefore lay aside your diabolical emblems of warfare." Thus, in an age when prowess in battle was highly regarded, Brigit stood alone not only in her spiritual desire for peace, but by actively pursuing an end to strife and warfare.

After Brigit had received her manumission, her father had her well educated and ultimately arranged for her to marry a poet, one of the most revered members of society in ancient Ireland. But Brigit insisted on dedicating herself to monasticism and, prevailing against great opposition, finally took her vows as a nun. For Brigit this did not mean entering on a life of dedicated retreat and isolation, but a life of spiritual retreat in the midst of great activity; in an age when women took no part in society, she became the pioneer, drawing her country-women of all classes from the sheltered life of the family into a life of service to the community.

Brigit personally founded convent settlements throughout the country, travelling by chariot from one to the other, supervising their building and exhorting others to dedicate their lives to God and to dispense goodness and kindliness to their fellow beings. These foundations were extensive, self-supporting settlements provided for the nuns, monks and laity. They were centres of religious and secular learning, giving instruction in craftsmanship and practical experience in farming, harvesting, milling, dyeing, weaving and in the care of the sick. Much may be attributed to the spiritual basis on which Brigit founded her centres, because it is recorded they were free from internal discord and were abodes of brotherly love, asylums for the poor, a refuge for the sorrowful, where the stranger and the afflicted went for solace to find themselves greeted by Brigit, who was famed for the warmth of her welcome and personal solicitude after the care-worn. She had consecrated her life to the Divine and desired nothing of the comforts of the world for herself, but she understood the need in others to be helped as pleasantly as possible along life's pathway by comfort and care for well-being. Brigit loved gaiety and good humour, festive gatherings and music, and encouraged them as an essential to good comradeship in her communities.

"The greatest in the land, the humblest pagan and Christian, went to her for sweet counsel", because they recognized in Brigit her amazing wisdom and profited from her guidance, derived, as she simply put it, "because my mind is never detached from God"; and Brigit, the unostentatious, when visited by the famous was often found tending her sheep. It is written in the tenth century manuscript the *Leabhar Breac* (The Speckled Book), ". . . she came from her sheep to welcome them".

Brigit was a prophet honoured in her own country in her own time, but she was not wholly free from censure; her indiscriminate liberality often caused consternation to others. She recognized human failings and if dishonest and insincere people imposed upon her, she had faith in the divine purpose that it was to soften the sinner's heart or, in some way, to fit into the divine order of life.

Brigit—her name means "strength"—was admired for her courage and steadfastness in truth, her tranquillity of mind in adversity, her brevity of speech and her sound common sense. It is interesting to note that in achieving her fame she is not accredited with performing great miracles, but with pursuing a practical course. She was, for instance, in an age when it was regarded as a luxury rather than a necessity to wash, a great advocate of personal cleanliness as a means of preventing illness, and often her cures were preceded by an order to cleanse the sick person.

In Ireland St. Brigit is regarded as the saint of agricultural life, because, did she not secure for all times for her people free grazing for the sheep by her gentle persuasion of the landowners? From childhood she had tended the sheep, milked the cows, made the butter and cheese, ground the wheat and made the bread, and, as Mother Abbess, she personally supervised the farmsteads at her convents and helped the reapers at harvest time. It is said that every mountain-farm and dairy is her wayside shrine, the brooks and glens and villages in her native island are called after her, and in Europe churches, monasteries and wells bear the name of Brigit, Brigid or Bride.

The most famous of Brigit's foundations was in Leinster, where she built for herself a cell of wattle and clay in the shade of an oak tree, *kill-dara* (the church of the oak), around which grew up one of the most famous centres of learning in Ireland, now known as Kildare. In Kildare Brigit spent most of the seventy years of her life, and in the year A.D. 525 it is recorded in *The Annals of the Four Masters*: "On February 1 Brigit died, and was interred in Dun (Downpatrick) in the same tomb with St. Patrick, with great honour and veneration."

But the spirit of Brigit has continued down the ages to inspire the people of her country by her acts of kindness and devotion to duty, however lowly it might be. Her namesakes are the many Brigits, the Brides and Bridies who follow a calling of service to their fellow-men either in the home, in convents or in hospitals. And Brigit, the slave-girl, the dairymaid, the Mother Abbess, the counsellor of the learned and friend of humanity, whose mind was "never detached from God", shone in that "golden age" of Ireland, steadfast in devotion and strengthened by her contact with the Divine.

CHAPTER XXI

MECHTHILD OF MAGDEBURG

THE history of the German mystics begins with religious and ecstatic reports of women of remarkable apprehension and burning love for God. At a time when the Christian faith in its ecclesiastical system was more and more covered by daily growing intellectualism, which found its zenith in the scholastic doctrine, the highest expression of theologically inspired thought, those women appeared out of an unpromising background, driven by the amazing power of religious intuition to give witness to the world about mystical experiences, which still stir every God-seeking man.

Hildegard of Bingen (1098–1179) tells us about her visions of God, which came of her inner fullness and seemed to her fellow creatures like a living light. She herself says that often her soul has seen the light in the light; that means the Light through which all light is shining. And each time all her grief and sorrow, all the burdens of her years, have fallen off.

Similar experiences we find in Gertrud of Hackborn (1251–1291), abbess of the Helfta convent near Eisleben; in her sister Mechthild of Hackborn (1260–1310), famous for her symbolic visions; in the poet in this group of women, Mechthild of Magdeburg (1209–1299), who came to Helfta in 1268; and finally in Gertrud the Great (1256–1311), who in strange subjective dream-occurrences had wonderful talks with Jesus and Mary.

We are primarily interested in Mechthild of Magdeburg as a God-lover who, without the mediation of the Church and its remedies, realized the *Unio Mystica*, and whose reports never trespass on those of previous religious writers or visionaries, but rather give a description of the union with God in such moving language that God-lovers of all times are deeply impressed and feel not in the least shocked by the erotic nature of her symbols, which she took from the inspiring and influential German minnesong.

Minnesong and mysticism are, in the poetical expression and spirit of the Middle Ages, intimately related. It is natural that the metaphorical language of the German minnesong influenced the descriptions of visionary ecstatic experiences of the *Unio Mystica*, and that it lent the means for a distinctive development which survived all philosophical rationalization of God-experience. Even today these accounts are vivid and real to us, for we learn from the life of Śrī Rāmakṛishṇa that always human beings will be able to see God and realize Him. This realization of God, which is the purpose and aim of human life, was gained by Mechthild at a time when intellectual and abstract speculations, and a physical analysis of the universe, prevailed in contemporary thought. Her experiences were the fruition of an incomprehensible, irresistible love for God. We know from the history of mysticism that women, fitted by their intuitive endowment and their capacity for devotion, attained the highest experiences. And now, again, they have a very important part to play. It is up to them to counteract barren intellectualism, developed in men by their daily struggle, with a spiritually and philosophically trained strength of emotion and intuition, and so, consciously to re-introduce deeper values into family and social life. Mechthild of Magdeburg gives eloquent witness of this strength in women which is often aroused in them by mystical experience.

Historical details about her life are few in number. She was born in Magdeburg, the daughter of a rich, perhaps aristocratic, family. Even in early youth she turned towards God, and it is said that at the age of twelve the grace of enlightenment was bestowed on her. Out of love for God arose the desire to serve Him and to live for Him alone. About 1235 she entered the house of Beguines in Magdeburg. These Beguine-houses were religious sisterhoods, not bound by perpetual vows and not dependent on any church or its institution. They were founded with the idea of establishing a community of women where, in simple and common living in upright faith, God could be realized and the teaching of Christ be practised in everyday life. Their main task was dedicated to charity, sick-nursing and devotion. We can be sure that Mechthild in her duty as a Beguine travelled round the country a good deal, and got to know sides of life which forced her the more towards God.

She submitted herself to self-torture and stern exercises of penance. There are many examples in mysticism where the body was tortured in such a way that at last it became a vessel of revelation, the inner mental world making the body an instrument of vision. All these endeavours of the mystics to bring the body under control are in alignment with the Indian practices of *brahmacharya*, namely to direct the strong sex-impulse to a higher level where it is transformed and used for spiritual purposes.

What dawned in Mechthild were worlds of light and love. Every day she found new symbols and parables to express the wonder of enlightenment and the wonder of God-love. An inner voice ordered her to record her revelations. She said that God Himself had shown her how the Godhead reveals Itself in the unceasing transformation and the multifarious colour and beauty of the world. But the mightiest revelation and the most comprehensive is love. We can imagine why she could not withstand this inner voice, why she had to record all these manifestations, and how she arrived at the conception that it was the floating light of the Godhead. Needing to give evidence of her wonderful experiences, she found no other alternative but to describe them in terms of human love. The soul becomes a bride and the Lord the Bridegroom, and in the heavenly marriage love overcomes death.

It is the mystical death, where all downward tendencies are thrown off and the soul enters the realm of pure selfless love, and where she is resurrected in the spirit of God. It is due to the body-bound nature of man's mind that not only Christian mystics, but mystics of all times and all religions depict the *Unio Mystica* in terms of the phenomenal emanation, that is, as earthly love. From the *liebfrauenminne* (love for women), about which the minnesingers of her time sing the most beautiful verses, to the overpowering *Gottesminne* (love for God), was for Mechthild only a short step. Beside the conception of an absolute union with God she expands much on her soul's intoxication with the light and love of God.

He who drinks light and is nourished by light grows a body of holy light, which shines for all people in the darkness. This intoxication from love and light creates an upheaval of the senses, a purification, which leads to enlightenment and finally to liberation.

For fourteen years she kept notes on her experiences and visions. She was not versed in Latin, and so she had to write in Low German. These pages were collected by the monk Heinrich of Halle, but no longer exist. Some time later they were translated by Heinrich of Nördlingen into Alemannic and made available to the public. This text can still be found in the monastery of Einsiedeln. Very early a translation into Latin was prepared, and we are told that Dante was much inspired by this work.

Mechthild not only made notes about her visions and realizations, which were very important for her contemporaries, but also took the liberty of criticizing in a sharp manner her contemporaries, whose vice and corruption had gained entrance even into the churches and cloisters. She preached reform, gave words of consolation and advice, and lived up to what she taught, setting by her life a shining example to her time. Her last years she spent in the convent of Helfta, where in the sisters Gertrud and Mechthild of Hackborn she found spiritual relatives. Here she died in 1299, in her last minutes proving to the nuns who were nursing her, that after a life of glowing love for God the process of passing away is nothing less than the attainment of highest bliss, which is experienced in the absolute union with the Lord.

If we study the written work she left behind we find that Mechthild of Magdeburg realized God through a burning love for Him, and a longing which expressed itself in steadfast and sincere spiritual practice. This brought her to the mystical experience of the *Visio Dei*. After having seen God face to face, her thirst was not stilled, and she strove to be united with Him in an undivided condition. Such bold longing knows no barriers, and finally she experienced the *Unio Mystica*, a state in which absolute peace and harmony reign, and which can only be described as *Sachchidānanda*, Existence-Knowledge-Bliss Absolute. In this condition God was her All in all. She saw Him in everything and understood His grand play in the universe, which is comprehensible only by discrimination between the real and the ego-inspired delusion of the phenomenal emanation. Śrī Rāmakṛishṇa says that for our age *bhakti* (devotion) is the easiest and most suitable way. Mechthild of Magdeburg trod this path with burning fervour to reach *prema*, ecstatic adoration, in which the divine love falls back on the lover in all-forgiving, all-embracing selfless vehemence.

She entitles her work *The Floating Light of the Godhead*, and says in the introduction:

This book should be received with joy. For the Lord Himself is speaking these words. This book is sent as a messenger to all spiritual people, to the bad as well as to the good. When the pillars fall, the work cannot stand any longer. It points to me and lays open my secrets. Everybody who wants to hear this message must read it nine times. This book is named a floating light of the Godhead. Who made it? I made it in spite of all my shortcomings because I could not withhold my endowment. O Lord, what name shall be given to this book to sing Your glory? It shall bear the name "The Light of the Godhead floating into the hearts of all who live without falsehood".

Conceptions of a union with God can be found in all times and all religions. Mechthild of Magdeburg saw the necessity for her time, when the rational forces of theological dogmatism veiled the true teachings of Christ, of giving her contemporaries the description of a condition which in reality is indescribable, and which no words can reach; but nevertheless she describes the wonder of the *Unio* in a vivid and stirring manner. This was a great help to the ordinary man who had only his mechanical, shallow faith, which depended on the intervention of the Church. For Mechthild the *Unio Mystica* was an attainable, living relation between God and the human soul. For the sake of expression her emotions seize on comprehensible objects. She personifies God and soul, and uses for the purpose an outspoken metaphorical language. In the soul she herself is speaking. God creates this soul to make love with her as His bride, and unceasingly He offers her His divine love.

All her ideas turn round the union which, beginning with the vision of God, leads in an exalted mood to God-intoxication wherein the soul unites with God. Sometimes Mechthild uses examples pertaining to the physical plane: she speaks of the tired soul resting at the breast of God, of the mingling of God and soul like wine and water, and even of a yearning God who hurries to meet a loving soul.

In her love for God she wants only the highest. Once she had a vision of the paradise where all souls meet, united with God day and night. The saints were calling her to dance, and God asked the soul to join them, but she refused. She only wanted to dance with the Lord and said:

> I don't like to dance unless You lead me.
> If You want me to dance,
> You must sing Yourself.

Then I will jump into love,
From love into devotion,
From devotion into realization,
From realization into all human hearts.

This verse is difficult to understand, but original dance is a mystical exercise used to purify the different planes of consciousness, making them fit to receive the cosmic forces. The soul dances round her centre and ascends in a spiral through all states of consciousness, until the divine consciousness—Absolute Consciousness—is reached.

Through pure and selfless love Mechthild of Magdeburg was already able, while still in the body, to unite her soul with God, and she was convinced that even in death she was inseparable from Him. What miraculous power could accomplish this? Was it only emotion-inspired, ecstatic love, which in uncontrollable imagination created body-influenced conceptions? Or was it a divine power in man, which, ego-covered and latent, had in this case been freed in a purified heart to strive with overwhelming impulse towards its heavenly source, just as a piece of iron is irresistibly drawn to a magnet?

Such love as manifested in Mechthild is an inscrutable force, the strongest force in the universe. We know three kinds of love. First the love which always asks and never gives, the sensual lower love, created mostly by the impetus for self-preservation. Secondly, there is the trading love which always considers its own profit, and whether the risk is balanced by the gain. All human passions are moving on this plane. Whether you take envy, jealousy, hatred or greed—all originate from this self-centred bartering love. And lastly we know that overflowing all-embracing love which never asks, reasons or demands, which in Jesus Christ endures the crucifixion, in a mother goes through fire for her child, and in Mechthild of Magdeburg falls self-forgotten at the breast of God. This is heavenly love, divine love. Only if we come to know this power can we understand Mechthild's intimate relation with God. The individual strength this created claimed the right to go alone into the battle, and to strive for union with God even without the mediation of Church and confession.

In the I-consciousness the soul becomes the point of intersection. Here God speaks with the soul, and the soul with the senses. In this mysterious point body and spirit meet and mingle. God and senses meet in the soul, and if men are established in their Self and in harmony with the cosmos, here the union is achieved.

Why the soul, which by her nature is omniscient, omnipotent and eternal, entered this prison of the body to become a slave of the pairs of opposites, cannot be reasoned out. In body-consciousness we cannot know what the soul in her real, pure and absolute state is, just as in the waking state we do not know what deep sleep is. When a house burns we try to extinguish the fire without first asking the cause. When a soul comes to know what she really is, she hurries home to her divine source. But this home-coming is possible only in the vehicle of the body. Knowledge and discrimination are the means which can only be learnt in the body with its apparatus of senses, mind and intellect. The body is therefore our precious and most valuable instrument. In it we have to attain knowledge of the essence of our being and to realize the Self. There is no other way, and as Omar Khayyám says:

What you could not grasp here,
How will you grasp it in a sphere,
Where neither sense nor body adhere?

Thought is the mighty force which leads us to the knowledge of our indestructible Self. But the same thought is the barrier which, iron-like, blocks our way when individuality is threatened with dissolution. Thought warns us against adventures on those planes of consciousness where neither reason nor sense can follow. The same happened with Mechthild of Magdeburg. After the Lord had promised her that her soul would achieve union with God, all her longings and endeavours were directed towards the realization of the *Unio Mystica* where reason is transcended and all problems are solved. But the senses protested, telling her to avoid any meeting with God because the soul could not stand the scorching glow, and the fiery light of the Godhead would absorb her as sunlight melts the March snow. Doubts arose in her, and God tested the soul. Her mind must have reasoned about what is Real and what is unreal, and all the controversial questions of her time must have assailed her, questions which could be solved only by God. It belongs to the wonders of mysticism that sometimes human beings attain the grace to hear and understand the voice of God.

The soul of Mechthild became fully aware of her God-like nature, and after shaking off all doubts she wrote:

The fish cannot drown in water,
The bird cannot fall in the air.
God cannot vanish in the fire,
It will only the brighter appear.
God created every creature
To live according to its nature.
And how could I withstand my nature
Which wants to be united with God?
He is my father from the beginning,
My brother in all mankind,
My bridegroom in love,
And I am His in eternity.

So the love of God finds fulfilment in the union of the soul with Him. Mechthild gives us in the records of her revelations a clear and tangible conception of the *Unio*, which is woven into the web of German mysticism. Let us conclude with some of her lyrical verses, which contain not only poetical thoughts, but also a good deal of spiritual experience.

In overcoming the world
Renouncing all desires
And defeating the ego
The soul comes to God.
If the world gives a blow
It causes no sorrow;
If the flesh gives her a kick,
The spirit does not fall sick.
Though the devil may dare
The soul does not care.
She loveth and loveth
And knows nothing other.

And again:

You will only feel free
If love possess you;
All your teaching is useless,
For I cannot be loveless.
I want to be imprisoned by love;
I cannot live without love;
Where it is, there I must go,
In life or death I don't know.
It is the foolishness of the fools
Who live without sorrow and heartache.

To some readers it may appear as if the emotions often overpower the intellect, and that in the mystical poetry of Mechthild of Magdeburg the philosophical treatment falls short: but the following verse shows how she is able to convey the essence of realization with aphoristic pregnancy:

Love without knowledge
Is for the soul real darkness.
Knowledge without realization
Seems to her like torments of hell.

CHAPTER XXII

JULIAN OF NORWICH

IN the person of Julian, Ankress of Norwich, the English religious genius finds its sole representative feminine figure of a stature comparable with that of the great women saints of the European mainland. The strong current of mystical influence which emerged upon the religious life of the more northerly countries during the fourteenth century—producing, in Germany an Eckhart, a Tauler, a Suso, in the Low Countries a Ruysbroeck—extended even to our own island shores, and left its monuments in the writings of Richard Rolle, the Hermit of Hampole; in those of Walter Hilton, author of *The Scale of Perfection*; in the famous anonymous *Cloud of Unknowing*; and in the single small book, *The Revelations of Divine Love*, of Julian of Norwich.

There is no evidence of any intercourse, of any kind of direct influence, even as between the members of this small group of mystical writers; still less is there question of interchange, in any shape or form, with their great contemporaries across the sea. Wholly obscure, in those days of difficult and limited communication, all were unknown beyond their native shores: even as each, most likely, was unknown to the others. Their fame, still but of this last half-century's growth, is wholly posthumous and arises entirely from their rediscovered writings. And of so small and obscure a group, perhaps the most obscure of all was the humble Ankress of Norwich.

To write of her at all is necessarily to describe her book, since this is itself the sole source for the few facts known about her. At the same time its own quality is such that, in its pages, the author stands clearly revealed to us; there exist, in fact, few books of such crystalline simplicity and limpidity of texture, radiating at once a humanity so tender and persuasive and a spirituality so purified and translucent.

At the time of her visions, Julian had been already for many years an "Ankress" or Recluse (a recognized status in the ecclesiastical life of medieval England), inhabiting, by virtue of an act of canonical enclosure, a cell (the foundations of which may still be seen) on the south side of the chancel of

St. Julian's Church, at Norwich. Here, in daily witness of the Church's Sacrificial Liturgy, she passed her life in continuous contemplation of the Christian Mysteries; and it was in this cell that she received those "Revelations" (or "Showings", as she prefers to call them), which form the basis of her book. Of her family nothing is known: it can only be conjectured that it was sufficiently endowed with worldly substance to maintain her in this, her own chosen manner of living. At the time of the revelations, which she dates with precision, she was, as she tells us, "of thirty years old and a half"; and since the scribe of one MS. records that she was "yet on lyfe *anno domini* 1413", it seems clear that she lived beyond the age of seventy. Since she describes herself as illiterate, it would appear also that her book was dictated, not written by her own hand. The circumstances to which it owes its being are best given, as nearly as possible, in her own words.[1]

(Chap. II): "These Revelations were shewed to a simple creature that could no letter the year of our Lord 1373, the eighth day of May. Which creature desired afore three gifts of God. The First was mind of his Passion; the Second was bodily sickness in youth, at thirty years of age; the Third was to have of God's gift three wounds.

"As in the First, methought I had some feeling in the Passion of Christ, but yet I desired more by the grace of God. . . . and therefore I desired a bodily sight. . . .

"The Second came to my mind with contrition, freely desiring that sickness so hard as to death, that I might . . . receive all my rites of Holy Church, myself weening that I should die, and that all creatures might suppose the same that saw me . . . I desired to have all manner pains bodily and ghostly (as) if I should die, with all the dreads and tempests of the fiends, except outpassing of the soul. These two desires . . . I desired with a condition, saying thus: 'Lord, thou wottest what I would—if it be thy will . . .: for I will nought but as thou wilt.'

"For the Third gift . . . I conceived a mighty desire to receive three wounds in my life; that is to say the wound of very contrition, the wound of kind compassion, and the wound of wilful longing towards God. And all this last petition I

[1] All the available printed editions are more or less modernized; that of Dom Roger Hudleston, O.S.B., the most recent, is here followed.

asked without any condition. These two desires aforesaid passed from my mind, but the third dwelled with me continually."

(Chap. III): "And when I was thirty years old and a half, God sent me a bodily sickness, in which I lay three days and three nights; and on the fourth night I took all my rites of Holy Church, and weened not to have lived till day."

She lingered thus for three days further, "and by then my body was dead from the middle downwards, as to me feeling. . . . My Curate was sent for to be at my ending, and by then he came I had set my eyes and might not speak. He set the Cross before my face and said: 'I have brought thee the Image of thy Master and Saviour' ". It was while dwelling with all her failing sight upon this Image that she perceived it take on the semblance of life, so that (Chap. IV) "suddenly I saw the red blood trickling down from under the Garland (of Thorns) hot and fresh and right plenteously".

This, the first of the "showings", was evidently what is termed a corporeal vision, since the Image on the Crucifix appeared to come to life before her eyes; and it establishes the Presence, so to say, in which the ensuing revelations took place. The first fifteen of these occurred between four and nine in the morning, during which time she felt no pain or trouble of her sickness. There seems to have been, however, a constant shifting of plane between the bodily (or outward visual), the imaginative (or inward visual) and the purely intellectual; for she herself tells us of the first revelation: "All this was shewed by three ways: that is to say, by bodily sight, and by words formed in mine understanding, and by ghostly sight." She kept her eyes fixed upon the Image throughout the first fifteen showings; for as she says (Chap. XIX): "In this time I would have looked up from the Cross, but I durst not. For I wist well that while I beheld the Cross I was sure and safe. . . ."

At the end of the fifteenth showing, "all was close and I saw no more. And soon I felt that I should live and languish; and anon my sickness came again . . . like as it was afore. And I was as barren and as dry as I never had comfort but little. And as a wretch I moaned and cried for my bodily pains and for failing of comfort, ghostly and bodily" (Chap. LXVI). With the return of her physical sufferings came an agonizing phase of doubt as to the validity—even as to the actuality—of what she had seen: "Here may you see", she says, "what I am of myself." "But herein would our Courteous Lord not leave me. And I lay till night, trusting in his mercy, and then I began to sleep." She was beset in a dream-vision by the Spirit of Evil: "methought the Fiend set him on my throat, putting forth a visage full near my face . . . I saw never such. . . . This ugly Shewing was made whilst I was sleeping, and so was none other. But . . . our Courteous Lord gave me grace to waken; and scarcely had I my life."

There followed then the final revelation; "which Sixteenth was conclusion and confirmation of all Fifteen". (Chap. LXVII): "And then our Lord opened my ghostly eye and shewed me my soul in midst of my heart. I saw the Soul as it were an endless world, and as it were a blissful kingdom. And . . . I understood that it is a worshipful City, in the midst (whereof) sitteth our Lord Jesus, God and Man. . . . And worshipfully he sitteth in the Soul, even-right in peace and rest . . . and the place that Jesus taketh in our Soul he shall never remove it without end, as to my sight: for in us is his homeliest home and his endless dwelling. And in this sight he shewed the satisfying that he hath of the making of Man's Soul. For as well as the Father might make a creature, and as well as the Son could make a creature, so well would the Holy Ghost that Man's Soul were made; and so it was done. And therefore the Blessed Trinity enjoyeth without end in the making of Man's Soul: for he saw from without beginning what should liken him without end."

In these words Julian delivers to us the essence of her little book. Written as it was, after twenty years of meditation on the actual revelations, it is seen to be the considered testament of a mature and lucid intelligence, aided at frequent intervals throughout those years by direct spiritual illuminations as to the particular bearing of this or that part of the original matter of the showings. It has been customary hitherto, to look rather for the points by which this work may be compared and classified together with the other mystical writings of its period; yet in actual fact the similarities are strikingly few. Unique already as the one woman in the great European spiritual movement of her time to have left a written memorial of any magnitude, Julian is unique also in the independence of her mind, and in the intensely personal manner of that mind's approach to the things set before it. "A simple creature that could no letter", she is entirely without the philosophic background of her contemporaries and peers in the mystical life: there is hardly a trace with her of that prevailing and strongly-marked neo-Platonizing tendency which can impart at times almost a "monistic" flavour to the writings of an Eckhart, of a Ruysbroeck, or to the anonymous *Cloud of Unknowing*. One gains the impression rather, that Julian is everywhere resolutely *dualistic* in the entire attitude of her mind. Dualistic, that is, not in the usually accepted sense, as postulating a so-called "principle" of evil on an equal and co-eternal basis with the Principle of Good; but in the more radical and fundamental sense which involves complete recognition and acceptance of her own creatural condition. It is from the "ground" of her own creaturehood that she looks forth with the eye of the soul upon the "Image" of her Saviour; and if she speaks in places of her desire to unite herself with Him in a participation of His Passion, there is never question of any self-identification therein; just as there is nowhere to be seen the least trace of any seeking (least of all of any claim) towards an ecstatic dissolution of her own personality in a transcendent and supra-personal Being. We find instead, everywhere, the clear witness of a fundamentally humble and deeply reverent soul, keenly (one had almost said, shrewdly!) aware of her own inescapable and irrevocable human status, and aware too, still more clearly, of the pain, the blindness, the confusion, attaching to that status in the conditions of its fallen life. Thus it is ever in terms of the relationship "creature-Creator" that her mind is seen to work; and there mingles everywhere the note of a deep and ever-present wonder with the love and gratitude of the voice which speaks to us so often of "our homely and Courteous Lord". Of her complete independence of mind there is no doubt whatever, since she stood perforce, by the very fact of her illiteracy, apart from the philosophic and speculative currents of her time. Of her overwhelming sense of complete and absolute dependence upon the Love and Compassion of the Living God who made and kept her, there is even less doubt still. Yet this profound consciousness of herself as creature never at any point descends into abjectness and servility; her sturdy and ineradicable "dualism" (the fundamental acceptance of her own creaturehood) preserves her everywhere from those protestations, common to so many mystical souls, of her own "nothingness".

The actual content of Julian's book has never yet been sufficiently studied on its own merits. Primarily of an almost "anthropological" nature, it is mystical only secondarily: in the sense that its communication and development take place upon the supraratational levels of the consciousness. She is never in any doubt about the true status and value of the human soul as God created it (as witness her words in speaking of the sixteenth revelation, quoted above). She says again (Chap. XLIV): "Man's Soul is a creature in God which hath the same properties made, and evermore it doeth that it was made for: it seeth God, it beholdeth God, and it loveth God. Whereof God enjoyeth in the creature and the creature in God, endlessly marvelling." Thus it was first of all intended, and thus it shall be *in aeternum*. But "our passing life that we have here in our sensuality knoweth not what our Self is, but then shall we verily and clearly see and know our Lord God in fulness of joy. . . . It belongeth properly to us, both by kind and by grace, to long and desire with all our mights to know our Self in the fulness of endless joy" (Chap. XLVI).

So strong a soul, a mind so robust and profound, as Julian's could not but be clearly aware of the actuality of evil in the world, if only through the process of her own self-exploration. Thus, she is troubled and puzzled—things being as she sees them to be—at her Lord's express declaration that, despite all appearances, beyond all human vision of possibilities, "all shall be well, and all shall be well, and all manner of thing shall be well" (Chap. XXVII). Yet "we know in our Faith . . . that the Blessed Trinity made Mankind to his image and likeness. In the same manner-wise we know that, when man fell so deep and so wretchedly by sin, there was none other help to restore man but through him that made man. . . . And like as we were like-made to the Trinity in our first making, our Maker would that we should be like Jesus Christ, our Saviour, in heaven without end, by the virtue of our again-making" (Chap. X). Therefore "he willeth not that we dread to know the things that he sheweth. He sheweth them because he would have us know them. By which knowing he would have us love him and liken, and endlessly enjoy in him" (Chap. XXXVI).

It is to be seen, then, that Julian is in no doubt about the real nature of the relationship—at once privileged and responsible—of the human soul with its Creator. Profound and lucid as it is sane and balanced, her mind reaches down also to a fairly clear perception of what it is that lies really at the roots of the problem. For she says (Chap. XXIX): "I stood beholding generally, troubling and mourning, saying this to our Lord, in my meaning with full great dread: 'Ah! good Lord, how might all be well, for the great hurt that is come by sin to thy creatures?' And here I desired, as far as I durst, to have some more open declaring wherewith I might be eased in this matter. And to this our blessed Lord answered full meekly and with full lovely cheer, and shewed that Adam's sin was the most harm that ever was done, or ever shall be, to the world's end. . . . Furthermore he taught that I should behold the glorious Satisfaction; for this Amends-making is more pleasing to God and more worshipful without comparison than ever was Adam's sin harmful. Then meaneth he thus in this teaching, that we should take heed to this: 'For since I have made well the most harm, then it is my will that thou know thereby that I shall make well all that is less.' " And again, in the beautiful fifty-first chapter with its parable of the "Servant": "When Adam fell, God's Son fell: because of the rightful oneing which had been made in heaven God's Son might not be apart from Adam. (For by Adam I understand All-Man.) Adam fell from life to death, into the deep of this wretched world, and after that into hell: God's Son fell with Adam, into the deep of the Maiden's womb, who was the fairest daughter of Adam; and for this end: to excuse Adam from blame in heaven and in earth; and mightily he fetched him out of hell. . . . And thus hath our good Lord Jesus taken upon him all our blame, and therefore our Father nor may nor will more blame assign to us than to his own Son, dearworthy Christ."

In the book of the *Revelations of Divine Love*, we may experience the privilege of contact with a personality of singular and most lovable fragrance, burning with the steady glow of an intense concern for her "even-Christian"—of whatsoever time, her own or the far future—for whose sake alone it is that she writes. It is but fitting, therefore, to end with her own final words: "And from that time it was shewn I desired oftentimes to witten what was our Lord's meaning. And fifteen years after, and more, I was answered in ghostly understanding, saying thus: 'Wouldst thou witten thy Lord's meaning in this thing? Wit it well: Love was his meaning. Who shewed it thee? Love. What shewed he thee? Love. Wherefore shewed it he? For Love. Hold thee therein and thou shalt witten and know more in the same. But thou shalt never know nor witten therein other thing without end.' Thus was I learned that Love was our Lord's meaning. And I saw full surely in this and in all, that ere God made us he loved us; which love was never slacked nor ever shall be. And in this love he hath done all his works . . . and in this love our life is everlasting. In our making we had beginning: but the love wherein he made us was in him from without beginning; in which love we have our beginning. And all this shall we see in God, without end. Which may Jesus grant us. Amen."

In all the fullness of its implications the message of Julian of Norwich had few echoes in her own day: perhaps it has had even fewer since. It belongs rather to a time and a tradition far more ancient; for its first and only real foreshadowings are with certain of the great Eastern Fathers[1] of the as yet undivided Christian Church.

[1] For instance, St. Gregory of Nyssa.

CHAPTER XXIII

CATHERINE OF SIENA

EVEN among the hierarchy of saints there are a few rare souls who seem set apart from the world at an early age. They are the pre-elect, the chosen ones of God, whose sanctity manifests almost in childhood. Of these, Catherine of Siena, who saw her first vision at the tender age of six years, and subsequently experienced innumerable ecstasies and heavenly visitations, undoubtedly holds a high place.

Caterina Benincasa was born at Fontebranda in Siena on March 25, 1347, the twenty-third child of her parents Giacomo Benincasa and his wife Lapa. Her father, a prosperous dyer, was a loving and gentle creature of great piety, whilst it was told of Lapa, a capable and energetic housewife, that it was wellnigh impossible for her to tell a lie. On one matter alone was the dyer adamant; he would not permit any godless or frivolous talk in *his* house. From her mother Catherine inherited her energy, but it was from her father she drew her legacy of gentleness and piety.

Looking back across the vista of five and a half centuries, we can dimly discern two small figures, Caterina aged six, and her brother Stefano a year or so older, returning home hand in hand from a visit to their elder sister Bonaventura. As they near the church of the Dominican friars, set upon the hill of Camporeggi, little Caterina looks up, and lo! there before her very eyes, set in the afterglow of the sunset, is a wonderful throne, with Jesus seated upon it, clad in pontifical splendour, and attended by Saints Peter, Paul and John. As the child gazes in awed wonder, Jesus smiles at her and raises two fingers in blessing.

Pulled back to things of the world by her impatient brother tugging at her sleeve, the small girl left the blaze of glory in which she seemed to have been surrounded and went silently home, telling no one of her vision. Henceforward, the little girl was careful in all her actions, and she would often play at being a hermit in some dark corner of the large house at Fontebranda, which served as a cave, fasting and praying and scourging herself according to her own discipline.

At seven years of age, she seriously decided to become a hermit, there being a settlement of hermits in the forest of Lecceto only three miles from her home. Taking a loaf of bread, she passed through the gates of the city and out into the countryside where she soon, to her delight, found a little cave. Time passed, but after some hours spent in prayer little Caterina's heart seems to have failed her. Loneliness overtook her with the setting sun, and home seemed far away. A strange weakness seized her legs; a giddiness came over her; then it was as if she were floating on a cloud, and lo! she found herself safely back within the city walls, whence she hurried home, never again attempting to become a hermit! The outcome, however, of her hours of prayer in the cave was that she dedicated herself to Jesus Christ as His bride. "I promise Him and Thee that never will I have any other bridegroom", she prayed before a statue of Our Lady. It was at this time that the young Catherine, in addition to giving much time to her prayers, now imposed upon herself a real discipline: she gave up eating meat and lived upon a diet of bread and herbs.

At the age of twelve years, her parents began to consider a suitable marriage partner for her. Catherine would not hear of such a plan, and the repeated remonstrances of her parents having failed, they called to their aid Tommasso della Fonte, who had been adopted as a foster-child by her parents. He had now become a Dominican priest and was later to be appointed Catherine's first confessor.

"If your purpose is serious, my daughter," he said, "prove it by cutting off your hair." Although of great beauty, the girl unhesitatingly cut off her long fair hair, thereby indicating, according to Catholic tradition, her consecration to God. Her parents expressed their disapproval by no longer permitting her a room to herself, and by dismissing the maidservant. Catherine was thus deprived of hours spent in devotion which now had to be spent in work.

The girl went about her tasks joyfully, imagining she was in the holy house at Nazareth: her pious father represented Jesus Christ, her mother, the Blessed Virgin, and her brothers and sisters, the Disciples. The good Giacomo, happening to enter one day the room she shared with one of her sisters, saw his daughter kneeling in prayer, a white dove hovering above her head. To him, this was a sign from Heaven: thenceforth

Catherine was given freedom to lead her life as she wished. Her father gave her a small room below the kitchen which became her cell—it can be seen to this day—and here in solitude and darkness Catherine seriously undertook the severe disciplines with which she mortified the flesh.

Besides taking a minimum of bread and raw vegetables, she reduced her hours of sleep until she finally slept scarcely two hours in forty-eight. This, she confided to her confessor, was the "most difficult of all the ways of overcoming self".

Catherine was drawn strongly to the Dominicans and longed to become one of the Mantellate, as these women of the Dominican Order were known in Siena. They were a band of women of mature years, often widows, who lived at home and took no vows, but devoted their lives to good works. It is doubtful if Catherine would have been accepted, because of her youth: however, she was somewhat disfigured at the time, as a result of chicken-pox, and so the Prioress did not find in her a disturbing beauty, whilst at the same time she found the girl to be of a truly pious nature. Catherine was accepted, and to her supreme joy, clothed in the habit of the Mantellate on a Sunday morning in 1363 in the Capella delle Volte.

She remained in her cell, leaving it only to go to church, disciplining herself in the effort towards self-purification, the prerequisite of self-knowledge on the path to God-realization. In her *Dialogue*, the Voice of God says: "Wherefore I reply that this is the way, if thou wilt arrive at a perfect knowledge and enjoyment of Me, the Eternal Father, that thou wilt never go outside the knowledge of thyself. . . . In self-knowledge then, thou wilt humble thyself, seeing that in thyself thou dost not even exist; for thy very being, as thou wilt learn, is derived from Me, since I have loved both thee and others before thou wert in existence."

We frequently find in Catherine's letters the words "Let us enter the cell of self-knowledge", and they point to all that life in the cell meant to her. Within it, she gloried in direct communion with her Lord. Christ frequently appeared to her in her cell at dusk, often accompanied by good friends, for instance, St. John the Evangelist, Mary Magdalene, St. Dominic or one of the Apostles. We read of her listening in ecstatic rapture to the choirs of heavenly music and smelling the flowers of Paradise. Her love for Jesus Christ satisfied all of a woman's need for complete self-surrender, and her frail body was ultimately consumed by it.

Whilst chanting the Canticle, the Song of Solomon, with ecstatic devotion in her cell, Jesus appeared and bestowed upon her a kiss, which filled her with unutterable sweetness. She thereupon begged Him to teach her what she must do, that she might never be unmindful or unfaithful to Him.

Towards the end of the years spent in her cell, when nearing twenty years of age, Catherine learned slowly and painfully to read, an accomplishment not so widespread in her time. Her letters show a thorough knowledge of the Gospels and Epistles, but her favourite reading was the breviary.

The culmination of this period was the experience known as her "Mystical Marriage" with Christ, which took place on the last day of the pre-Lenten Carnival in 1366. Shut within her cell, whilst the crowds outside were heedlessly merry-making, Catherine fasted and prayed in order to make reparation for their sins.

The Lord appeared to her and said, "Because thou hast forsaken all the vanities of the world, and set thy love upon Me . . . behold, I here espouse thee to Me, thy Maker and Saviour . . ." This experience marked her transition from a purely personal mysticism to an active and altruistic way of life. The time had come when her divine Spouse, having conferred upon her the riches of His grace, now sent her out into the world. Each day she left her cell to nurse the sick and needy of her native city. Her gentle presence, selfless service and undoubted piety, healed not only the sick in body, but converted many sick of soul.

Gradually the force of her spiritual quality became known, and there gathered about her a circle of devotees, not only some devoted women of the Order, but friars, priests, and some of the wild scions of noble houses. Several of the latter, who had been turned from their wild ways by Catherine's vibrant spiritual power, remained in her *entourage* and later acted in the capacity of secretaries, taking down her numerous letters.

A strong tie of love bound Catherine to all her "dear children", as she called her spiritual sons and daughters. Although but a young woman herself, the ever-increasing band of followers looked upon her as their "sweet holy mother". Her little cell, where the candles always burned brightly, was the focal point to which crowds were attracted by the magnetism of her holiness, some in devotion, some in awe, others merely curious.

Raymond of Capua, her confessor and biographer, relates how, during her states of ecstasy, "her limbs became stiff, her eyes closed, and her body, raised in the air, often diffused a perfume of exquisite sweetness". This same Catherine, however, who experienced such raptures of communion with the Lord Jesus, could be found later at the head of a band of devoted men and women during the horror of the Black Death, which ravaged Europe and decimated its population. In the worst infected quarters of the city, in the hospitals, the streets, even at times burying the blackened corpses with her own hands, Catherine pursued her way, tranquil and serene, bringing solace and comfort to the sick and dying.

As a prelude to some observations on Catherine's activities in the political arena, it would be well to describe briefly the general state of affairs in her day.

Since 1305 the Popes had left the Eternal City and resided at Avignon on the banks of the Rhône. Internecine warfare ravaged the Papal States; the churches and monasteries of Rome itself were fast falling into ruins. Corruption, laxity and vice were rife among the clergy, who led lives of unparalleled luxury, battening on the poor.

Urban V was the first Pope to attempt the restoration of the papacy to the Holy City, and in spite of the protests of the French king and cardinals, left Avignon on April 30, 1367. He made a solemn entry into Rome on October 16 amid great rejoicing of the people, that at last Christ's Vicar on earth was in the Holy City. Urban left Italy, however, in 1370, and died in the same year. Another Frenchman ascended the papal throne as Gregory XI. To Catherine, the Pope was in very truth Christ's representative upon earth; his infallibility was unquestioned; and the Catholic Church was the mystical bride of Christ. It therefore grieved her sorely to see the Regent of Christ faithless to his sacred trust, and absent from the seat of authority.

Hence we find Catherine writing to the powerful papal legate in 1372, when she was twenty-five years of age: "I wish therefore and desire that like a good servant and son, redeemed by the blood of Christ Jesus, you follow in His steps with a manly heart and with willing care, and that you never turn aside from this way, neither for pleasure nor for pain, but persevere until the end." In this letter Catherine put her hand for the first time on the helm of the Church. That the unlettered daughter of a Sienese dyer should be able to use with impunity —nay, even so as to command the greatest respect—such phrases as "sweetest Babbo[1] mine" when addressing the Pope in her letters, is ample evidence of the spiritual authority that issued from her. The power of truth was so strong within the saint, she frequently allies herself with God, as when she writes to the King of France, "Do God's will and mine", or to the Pope, "Fulfil the will of God and the ardent longing of my soul".

Apart from the dissension among the various religious fraternities, there was war between the Papacy and the Tuscan republics. Catherine upbraided the rebels against papal authority, at the same time exhorting the Pope to begin a Crusade. In 1373 she gave him her whole-hearted support when he proclaimed a Holy War.

Her incursions into the political field, dominated by the Papacy in those days, brought much criticism upon Catherine. In the year 1374 she was summoned to the General Chapter of the Dominican Order in Florence to render an account of herself and her teachings. Raymond of Capua, who was at about this time appointed her spiritual director and confessor, presided over the enquiry. He was convinced of Catherine's extraordinary piety, and remained at her side for the rest of her short life, acknowledging her his spiritual superior in every way.

The corrupt and extortionate dealings of the papal officials had reached such a degree that the Florentines revolted, and by 1375 eighty cities had joined the League against the Pope. Catherine's heart bled for the injustices the Pope inflicted upon the citizens of Florence, yet true to her belief in the Pope's infallibility, rebellion against him would have been a mortal sin. If only the Holy Father would come to Italy! "Come as a brave man," she writes to the vacillating Gregory, "but take heed, as you value your life, not to come with armed men, but with a cross in your hand, like a meek lamb."

But the Pope had already sent mercenaries into Italy under the cardinal who was later to become Clement VII, and the

[1] 'Daddy' would be the English equivalent.

cruel massacre of Cesena ensued. We find Catherine writing to the Florentines urging submission, and to Gregory forbearance. The former eventually induced her to undertake a diplomatic mission to Avignon, to present their case before the Pope.

Catherine, accompanied by a band of faithful followers, including Raymond of Capua who acted as interpreter, arrived in Avignon in June, 1376. So eloquent was her pleading of the Florentine cause, the impact of her deep spirituality so potent, that the Holy Father left the matter entirely in her hands. According to Brother Raymond, he said: "In order to show you that I sincerely desire peace, I commit the entire negotiation into your hands; only be careful of the honour of the Church."

Catherine succeeded in persuading the weak and nervous Gregory to leave the pleasures and luxuries of his life at Avignon, and return to his rightful seat in Rome. After many vicissitudes and much wavering on his part, the Pope eventually arrived in Rome in January, 1377, thereby fulfilling Catherine's great wish.

We find her again in the rôle of peacemaker when, in 1378, Gregory sent her on a diplomatic mission to Florence. Catherine succeeded in reconciling the Florentines to papal authority, but was very nearly martyred in the process. Baring her throat before the armed mob, she bade the leader strike, saying: "I am Catherine; do to me whatever God will permit; but I charge you, in the name of the Almighty, to hurt none of these who are with me." At these words the mob dispersed in confusion.

Gregory died in 1378, and an Italian was elected Pope, taking the name Urban VI, under whom the Great Schism began. He was zealous in his efforts towards reform, but harsh in manner and violent in action: hence we find Catherine writing to him and begging him to "restrain a little those too quick movements with which nature inspires you". Her pleading was in vain: Urban was declared Antichrist by the opposing faction, and Robert of Geneva elected by his supporters as "Pope" Clement VII.

To Catherine, whose efforts in the outer world had been solely devoted to unifying the discordant factions in the body of Christendom, this was a most cruel blow. Urban summoned her to Rome where she arrived in November, 1378, with some forty of her disciples and friends. Her resolve to live only upon alms often brought her little band to the verge of starvation. She was immediately received in audience, and she urged Urban to summon to Rome all the holy hermits and recluses, whose lives, spent in prayer, formed a nucleus of all that was highest in Christendom. In the Church's hour of dire need they were to come and act as a bulwark against her enemies.

The response was so poor as to be utterly inadequate, and her disappointment at the failure of her scheme can be envisaged in the scornful lines she addresses to a solitary who does not wish to leave his cell. "Now, really the spiritual life is quite too lightly held if it is lost by change of place. Apparently God is an accepter of places, and is only found in a wood, and not elsewhere in time of need!"

The end of her brief earthly sojourn was approaching, and her frail body, weakened by continuous austerities and the consuming fervour of her soul, now had to endure acute mental anguish on account of the state to which the Church had been reduced.

Catherine was also a poet, possessed of a wealth of imagination, as we find in the ensuing extract from a letter to one of her spiritual daughters. "The soul is a tree, a tree of love. Dearest daughter, if then the gardener, free will, plants the tree where it should be planted, that is, in the valley of true obedience, and not on the mountain of pride, it will bear fragrant flowers of the virtues, and above all, the most beautiful of all flowers, the glory of the name of God. . . . And because the highest and eternal goodness sees that man does not live on flowers, but only on fruits (for we should die of the flowers, but we live on the fruit), He takes the flower for Himself, and gives to us the fruit."

The hour of evening glow had come for Catherine—she who had expressed in the actions of her life the sublime experience: "I am He who is; thou art she who is not." Towards the close of her life, she gave forth the *Divine Dialogue*, her great literary work. It is a summation of the direct teachings she received from God during her ecstasies and meditations, and was taken down by her several secretaries whilst she was in a condition of ecstatic trance. In the dialogue between Christ and her soul, Christ is represented as the Bridge between heaven and earth:

"How glorious", says the Voice of the Eternal, "is that soul which has indeed been able to pass from the stormy ocean to Me, the Sea Pacific, and in that Sea, which is Myself, to fill the pitcher of her heart." Where in the religious literature of the world shall we find passages vaster or more sublime in scope than this? It might equally well have been uttered by some Indian sage or Sufi mystic.

Catherine, who for many months had taken no food whatsoever, and subsisted solely on the Holy Sacrament, was now, in 1380, so weakened that she could not even retain water. Her whole being was on fire with divine love, a fire which within a few months was to consume her utterly. She wrote to Raymond, "This body keeps without any food, even without a drop of water, with such great and sweet bodily torments as I never endured at any time, so that my life hangs upon a thread". Her physical sufferings, together with her anguish over the condition of her beloved Church, would long before have overwhelmed a lesser soul.

Stretched upon a board, fenced about with four other boards as though already in her coffin, Catherine spent the last eight weeks of her brief life. She, their "sweet holy mother", was surrounded by her loving spiritual children. She blessed each one, and commended them to love one another. Her own aged mother was also at the bedside.

After receiving the last sacred rites, she whispered, in the words of her beloved Jesus, "Father, into Thy hands I commend my spirit", and passed away, radiant with peace.

Catherine of Siena, among the foremost of the Church's great mystics, scaled the Olympian heights of spirituality and yet faced the external world of her time, in all its cruelty, horror and violence, with a courage that never faltered, however formidable the task.

She exerted a great influence on her contemporaries: indeed, as we have endeavoured to illustrate in the early part of this sketch, she was called in consultation by the highest authority, Christ's Vicar upon earth, the Pope, and her guidance was sought by kings, nobles and many erudite clerics of her day. It is related of her that many hundreds of souls were converted to lives of piety and devotion, by simply having looked upon her face during her lifetime.

Although the world picture of today presents a vastly different canvas, we may well try to imitate the Saint of Siena in facing, with like courage and ethical purity, our own difficulties in the market-place of life.

Her message to the world is timeless. There are two realms: that of the world, sin and death; the other of love, self-denial and life. The door to the kingdom of death is self, the ego: the door to the kingdom of God is Jesus, the Word. He who abides in self, abides in that which perishes, and is lost: he who abides in Jesus is in the Eternal and is saved.

CHAPTER XXIV

TERESA OF AVILA

THE woman who was to be known to posterity as Saint Teresa was born in Avila, in the province of Old Castile, Spain, in 1515. Her upbringing, by reason of her noble birth, was sheltered, and in accordance with the strict Spanish custom prevailing in those days. Each family led a secluded life, receiving only relatives and intimates, and the women rarely left the seclusion of their homes, except to attend church. Teresa tells us but little of her early life. She records the fact that she lost her mother at twelve years of age, a loss which led her to seek consolation from the Mother of Christ; and that she was influenced by books of chivalry and the lives of the saints. These so fired her youthful imagination that she and a young brother decided to run away from home in order to seek martyrdom at the hands of the Moors; however, they got no further than the city walls!

At the age of sixteen, her father sent her to finish her education at an Augustinian convent. According to one of her contemporaries, she was gay, charming, fond of dress and ornaments, and liked to be well esteemed by others.

After a serious illness, she returned home and was sent to a married sister to recuperate. *En route* she stayed with an uncle, who asked her to read aloud from the *Lives of the Saints*. While reading she was struck by the emptiness and vanity of life: the fear of hell haunted her, and likewise the pains of purgatory. One must recollect that the Spain of those days was still smarting under the influence of the Inquisition: the rule was one of fear and violence, and the pains of hell loomed large.

It was now she decided upon the life of a religious, although, in her own words, it was "rather fear than love of God" which influenced her decision; the sufferings and pains of this life appearing much less than those of purgatory.

Her inner conflict lasted three months, after which she disclosed her intention to her father, who wished her to await his death before entering a convent. She would not promise this, however, for she had already made her decision; she once more ran away, and entered the Convent of the Incarnation. Teresa was then twenty-one years of age, and the following year she took vows.

All her life Teresa suffered from poor health, especially during the first years of her novitiate. She was sent to take the cure at a renowned spa, and once again visited her uncle *en route*. This visit was of profound importance, almost a turning-point in her life, for her uncle gave her a book on meditation, of which she knew nothing, although she already loved solitude and interior examination. This volume became her guide, philosopher and friend, for it was almost twenty years before she found a spiritual preceptor who understood her.

The treatment only serving to aggravate the illness, she was brought back to Avila. She then recalled the words of Job: "Since the Lord sends us His blessings, why should He not also chastise us?" Gravely ill, she was on the point of death, her tomb already prepared; yet she returned to life. The following words are attributed to her: "Why was I brought back? I saw hell. I have seen the monasteries I must found, that which I must do in the order and the souls I must save: I shall die a saint."

On her return to the convent, ill and unhappy, there followed a period of over twenty years when her allegiance was divided between God and the world. Describing those days, she wrote: "When I was in the midst of worldly pleasures, I was distressed by the remembrance of what I owed to God; when I was with God, I grew restless because of worldly affections."

It was in about 1555 that Teresa experienced a quickening of her spiritual life. There came a time when, in retrospect, she was able to see two distinct periods in her life: the ordinary life, and the life of God within her; and it was entirely due to her meditation that she attributed this profound change.

Teresa was not drawn by the cult of the Infant Jesus. As she developed and her earlier servile fear was transformed into a filial fear, divine love grew more strongly within her, and Jesus became the Chosen Ideal for her, as her divine Master and Friend whom she desired to possess utterly. She spared herself no effort towards the realization of her Ideal, and she who had erstwhile loved adornment and feminine vanities, renounced all possessions and even desired to beg her food. It is said that when Teresa left the Convent of the Incarnation to found that of St. Joseph, her sole possessions were a patched habit and a comb.

What does the saint demand of us in order to follow in her footsteps? Very little. Sacrifice each day a few moments to God; consecrate an hour or two to Him. Enter into solitude and silence. Have you never done so? There you will have everything to gain, and having once started the practice, you will never wish to abandon it whatever happens.

By meditation you will avoid the obsession with and agitation of the world. Discrimination will ensue, and a desire for liberation from the thraldom of the senses, and when interior purification is ultimately complete, Union will be achieved.

According to Teresa there are four principal stages of meditation, and in order to clarify her meaning, she uses the following simile.

Each one receives from God a piece of land, dry, barren and full of weeds. Our duty is to transform this into a garden. The garden does not belong to us, but must be tended for the Master, without thought of reward, solely for love of Him.

Our first task is to eradicate the weeds, and to cultivate and water the soil. We have to draw water bucket by bucket from the depths of our well. Here water stands for inner devotion. Complete withdrawal from the call of the world and the senses is enjoined, and the attention is to be focused within. Now one must examine oneself by sincere question and analysis, in order to arrive at self-understanding and knowledge.

This period of withdrawal requires great effort and Teresa admits that she found this discipline very difficult, for she always wanted to *see* the vision before her eyes: when the day finally did come it was rather that she *felt* the divine Presence within.

If devotion is lacking in the early stages, do not grieve unduly: try to create God's presence within by talking to Him, and be thankful that He has kindled even the desire to please and seek Him. If, after sustained effort, we find only repugnance, boredom and spiritual dryness, then is the critical period, for we are sorely tempted to give up the struggle. Teresa herself experienced for many years a certain aversion towards prayer and devotion, and used to await impatiently the striking of the clock which released her. This temptation must be overcome, being part of the purgative process in spiritual life. When, contrary to normal, the faculties are turned inwards violent reactions may occur. Teresa said of herself that during this period the Devil seemed to inspire her with much anger and bad temper.

At other times, doubts and fears overwhelm us; judgment becomes clouded. The first fervour gone, love is but lukewarm, and only dryness and barrenness is found within. Never let these moods be a deterrent: spiritual progress is accomplished without one's awareness, as the sailing-boat does not appear to move before only a light wind.

Our duty at this time is to analyse ourselves ever more sincerely, to discover in what respect we are still attached to the world, and each day to make a further sacrifice of our will. Now we must await the Lord's grace before going on to the next stage.

The water now flows more easily: the soul has achieved concentration, has attained higher planes, but is unable as yet to grasp and retain the Ideal, the object of her love. God begins to communicate directly with the soul, and makes her realize His proximity: a feeling of bliss ensues, and the soul remains still in her new-found peace. Some souls remain at this stage of peace and beatitude, unaware that higher states of consciousness exist. What is our task now? Whilst enjoying this foretaste of bliss yet to come, we have to prepare ourselves with humility for the work we have been chosen to perform. The divine love manifesting within will give us a humility unattainable by our own efforts, and a love for others devoid of all self-interest. The flowers in the garden are budding; it will not be long now ere they blossom.

In the third stage we no longer have to fetch water; we have tapped the source itself. The soul is plunged as it were in the blissful ocean of divine glory. This is not yet complete union with God, but the soul is already freed from all sense-bondage, and can be satisfied with nothing but God. At this stage, the soul abandons itself completely to the will of the Master: as Teresa tells us, she no longer belonged to herself, but to God alone.

The flowers of virtue now seemed to spring up in the garden of the soul with no effort on her part. The beloved Master Himself undertakes the office of gardener, and the soul can partake of its fruits, but must not yet distribute them to others.

Arrived at the last stage of meditation, the watering of the garden is no longer our care; the heavens themselves will distil their dews upon it. The soul is utterly quiescent and passive; there is not the slightest worldly attachment left. The process of inner purification is complete and we are close to perfection. Here the soul enjoys the ecstatic bliss of God-realization, and realizes, moreover, that in the state of divine union all beings are one, and that the One is veritably in all.

Thus to conclude Teresa's allegory, the moment of harvest is come, and the Master Himself distributes the fruits of His garden, the purified soul knowing that of itself it possesses nothing. Her teaching here is that we may promote the spiritual good of our neighbour without any direct action on our part. As she herself expresses it, the flowers will shed a sweet perfume, and others will be mysteriously drawn and attracted to the fragrance.

Teresa encountered many grievous trials. Her revelations and visions, which had been indiscriminately divulged by persons from whom, in her perplexity, she had sought guidance, had already drawn attention upon her in the town of Avila, and there was talk amongst the populace as to whether her visions were to be interpreted as from God or the Devil. Even her confessors hesitated to make a pronouncement, thus causing her much anguish of mind. Here again, during this period of trial, she perforce had to tread her own path to Calvary in the footsteps of her divine Lord. Only her inner consolations and the support of a few rare and enlightened souls upheld her.

Without abandoning the path of love, she must now tread the path of work. The Lord demanded of her that she observe the vows of silence and poverty, and fulfil her mission of saving souls.

Looking out upon her immediate surroundings, a reform of the prevailing conditions seemed essential. The nuns had vowed themselves to God and a life of prayer, but the rule was lax, convents were grossly overcrowded, and the exterior world with its distractions and temptations was breaking through to the cloister. Looking farther afield, great nations and masses of people seemed to be forswearing their allegiance to the Church, caught up in the rising tide of the Reformation, which brought in its train the dissolution of many monasteries.

The sovereign remedy for this state of affairs was clear to

Teresa—the reform of the religious orders. Her words at this time clearly show her own views in the matter: "The way of religious observance is so little used, that the friar and the nun who would really begin to follow their vocation thoroughly, have reason to fear the members of their community more than all the devils in hell."

Having received during her meditation the divine command to establish a convent wherein the primitive rule of the Carmelites should be followed in all its purity, she and a few of her intimates decided the time was ripe and made plans accordingly.

The project having been approved by St. Peter of Alcantara and the Bishop of Avila, the saint procured the necessary licence from the Provincial of the Carmelites, and with the financial assistance of a wealthy Spanish widow, the plans were set in action. A storm of protest at once broke out among her fellow nuns, the nobility, the local authorities and the general populace, the opposition to the scheme becoming so violent that the licence was withdrawn.

However, Teresa was secretly encouraged by a Dominican to pursue her enterprise; hence her sister and brother-in-law began to build the new convent at Avila in 1561, in such a manner that it was, to all intents and purposes, to be a new home for themselves and their family. During the erection of the building, the small son of the house, Gonzalez, the saint's young nephew, was crushed whilst playing on the site. Apparently lifeless, he was placed in her arms, whereupon she prayed earnestly to God and some few moments later, restored him whole and well to his mother.

After much hostility and many vicissitudes the Pope's brief for the erection of the new convent was received; the house was dedicated to St. Joseph, and Teresa and four novices took the vows of the Reformed Rule.

Mystic and visionary though she undoubtedly was, Teresa was also a highly practical woman. This quality was apparent in her selection of novices for the convents she subsequently founded. Her first requirement was intelligence, rather than a high degree of piety: one could train oneself to the latter, but hardly in the use of sound judgment. "An intelligent mind is simple and submissive: it sees its faults and allows itself to be guided. A mind narrow and deficient never sees its faults even when shown them. Even though our Lord should give a young girl devotion and teach her contemplation, if she has no sense, she never will come to have any, and instead of being of use to the community, she will be a burden." And, "May God preserve us from stupid nuns!"

We find her efficient in the smallest details of the daily routine. She would give advice on the most economical method of managing the laundry; she had a love of cleanliness unusual in her era: we even find her writing to her confessor about a cooking-stove which took her fancy, she herself being an excellent cook.

Her rule, though strict, was considerably tempered by her keen sense of humour; she often laughed her nuns out of the small self-indulgences to which they were prone. She liked to find that a young nun had three temptations—to laugh, to eat, and to sleep. "For", she said, "if she is tempted to laugh, she is of a cheerful disposition; if she is tempted to eat, she is healthy; and if she is tempted to sleep, she has no great sins on her mind". Hence she roundly scolded a prioress who had rendered herself unfit for her duties by her austerities.

She constantly reminded her nuns that "God walks even among the pots and pipkins. When obedience calls you to exterior employments (as for example into the kitchen amidst the pots and dishes), remember that our Lord goes along with you, to help you both in your interior and exterior duties."

During her fourth year at St. Joseph's, Teresa was bidden by the Father-General of her order to found other monasteries of the same primitive rule. The journeys she now embarked upon were long and arduous, particularly for a woman of her age and physical condition. The method of travel was by cart without springs, through scorching heat in summer and often raging floods and bitter cold in winter, over roads which often were no better than mountain tracks. The inns were usually verminous and in a condition revolting to one of her fastidious nature; the muleteers unreliable; and the few nuns accompanying her, together with a priest, terrified at their unwonted adventures.

Each foundation was fraught with difficulty and worry: at Toledo, for instance, Teresa found herself with only four ducats. "Teresa and this money are indeed nothing, but God, Teresa and these ducats suffice" were her words on this occasion.

Many of the foundations were extremely poor, subsisting solely on alms. But even those founded on revenues were the cause of great distress to her at times, for she was obliged to learn something of the intricacies of finance and, where it was a matter of endowment, the laws relating to inheritance.

Whilst at Medina, Teresa spoke to Father Anthony of Jesus, whom she had known as the Prior of the Carmes at Avila, telling him of her difficulty in finding any friars willing to follow the Reformed Rule. Greatly to her surprise, he offered himself, and was followed shortly after by John of the Cross. This latter, being a man of small stature and humble appearance, caused her in loving mirth to speak of "her friar and a half". Later John of the Cross became confessor to the nuns at the Convent of the Incarnation, whither Teresa was sent to take office as prioress.

This nomination by the Apostolic Visitor to her old convent, which had been badly mismanaged, meant to her a distasteful task, calling for extreme tact and profound skill in handling a large community of women. Many of her former fellow nuns had not forgiven her for her implied criticism of their house in founding others of a stricter *modus vivendi*, and at first refused to obey her. She told them she had not come to instruct but to learn from the least among them. "My mothers and sisters," she addressed them at her inauguration as prioress, "our Lord has sent me to this house by the voice of obedience, to fill an office of which I was far from thinking, and for which I am quite unfitted. . . . I come solely to serve you . . . I am a daughter of this house and your sister; let me know what I can do for each of you, for I shall be most willing to do what you ask, even were it to shed my blood for you. You have no reason then, to fear being under the government of one who is wholly yours by so many titles."

On the orders of her confessors, she wrote a summary of her life and teachings. In her writings anent visions, Teresa describes three different types of vision, and approximates them to the different stages of meditation:

Firstly, material visions, perceived by the external senses, and occurring in the purgative period, which corresponds to the first stage of meditation; secondly, mental visions, perceived by the internal sense-organs and characteristic of the period termed illuminative, which corresponds to the second and third stages of meditation; finally intellectual visions, which are formless, and correspond to the fourth state, the unitive period.

Teresa had few material visions, but as she progressed in her spiritual disciplines and pursued the path of meditation, she experienced a number of interior visions, that is, those perceived by the internal sense-organs. At first perhaps only a part of the form was revealed—the hands for example, then the face, and finally the entire figure. These visions were always bathed in a shining white light, which the saint compared to limpid water flowing as on a crystal wherein the sun was reflected. Yet by comparison the light of the sun was clouded, as the water of a lake becomes grey and overcast at the approach of a storm. Thus to Teresa, the inward light of her soul at these moments seemed the natural one, whilst the light of the sun appeared artificial.

On occasions, the complete form of Christ appeared before her as a living reality, full of incomparable splendour. This vision produced such a powerful effect upon the saint that she entered into a condition of ecstasy; yet if she attempted to analyse the details, the vision completely vanished.

In her attempt to formulate in words the experience of the intellectual vision she writes, "It is as if a person who had never learned anything, nor yet was able to read, nor had ever studied, were suddenly to find himself in possession of all the data accumulated by science". She knew beyond all shadow of doubt that her divine Lord was present. This is the unitive state, wherein the soul apperceives the divine Presence, without the intermediary of the senses, when she cries within herself, "Not I that live, but Christ that liveth in me".

Teresa also tells us of the voice she often heard during her meditation. The first words ever spoken to her thus were, according to her account, "I wish you to hold no further converse with men, but only with the angels". From this point onward, she tells us she had no further wish for the society of anyone who was not a lover of God. When one considers the general preoccupation in those days with fear of the Devil, one can well appreciate the anguish of spirit experienced by the saint as to the origin of the voice. Hearing, however, the comforting words of her blessed Lord, "Do not be afraid, my daughter, it is I. I shall never abandon thee", fear left her.

On one occasion Teresa heard the words, "Do not grieve:

I shall give thee a living book". At that particular time, the Inquisition was burning a great number of Spanish books, amongst which were certain volumes she enjoyed reading. At first she did not appreciate the significance of the words, but later recalled that "His divine Majesty has been the living book wherein I have seen the Truth".

Teresa also recorded her experiences of differing degrees of spiritual rapture. Body consciousness became more or less attenuated: in the higher states it seemed that the soul no longer animated the body, the pulse was almost suspended, the arms open, the hands stiffened. On the first occasion this state caused her great alarm; it needed courage to experience a condition of which she had not the least idea. Yet it was followed by what Teresa terms a veritable martyrdom of delights and sufferings which her ardent longing to see God enabled her to endure. Her divine Master also taught her not to fear the mortal anguish which often precedes the approach of a great spiritual rapture, for then the soul is tried as gold is worked and refined in the crucible.

Saint Teresa seems to have developed remarkable powers during the years of her spiritual unfoldment. She often predicted the course of events several years in advance, and could easily discern among her young nuns those who were genuinely practising renunciation, and those who merely gave it lip-service.

The quintessence of her teaching can be summarized in two words, love and humility. Humility had not come easily to this erstwhile haughty Spanish noblewoman; whilst love had grown with the growing realization of the divine Presence within, leading her to final union with the Beloved.

Towards the close of her life, and in spite of her failing health, she continued her activities, making arduous journeys to Toledo, Seville, Valencia and many other places, where she had earlier founded convents of her order.

She passed away on October 15, 1582, at the age of sixty-eight, and we can hear her murmuring the following words, "O my Lord and my Beloved, at last has come the moment I have so ardently longed for. I shall soon be delivered. . . . May Thy will be done".

CHAPTER XXV

LA MERE ANGELIQUE

THE story of Angélique Arnauld (1591–1661) and the convent of Port-Royal, a story of utmost dedication, ends with the defeat of Port-Royal and everything the Mère Angélique had created. It belongs to the sad chapters of European spiritual history, in which little of Christ's love and sense of forgiveness can be found, and which, consciously or unconsciously, gave His so-called followers a distorted idea of the essentials of His message.

All the Arnaulds possessed a certain fanatical zeal for what they believed to be their mission in life, and they knew how to rouse, through the power of their personalities, the same unconditional devotion for the end to which they were ready to dedicate their lives.

Though the forces opposing the Mère Angélique's high reformatory zeal were victorious and outwardly triumphed over her aims, her convent and friends, inwardly this defeat may not have been so final as her powerful enemies believed. For even in our day the name of Port-Royal still radiates the light of a great ideal, and some of its defenders like Blaise Pascal and Jean Racine are still, so long after their death, fighting for its cause through their works.

Port-Royal with its band of devoted nuns and solitaries is one of the many examples showing how often the sad lack of tolerance has deprived religion of its sincerest champions.

In the struggle for Port-Royal the chief protagonist was Angélique Arnauld, a strong-willed, undaunted, unbending, energetic woman of the deepest sincerity.

The paternal grandfather of Angélique, Arnauld de la Mothe, had been a Huguenot. But after the massacre of St. Bartholomew he had abjured Calvinism with several of his children, Angélique's father being one of them. There remained, however, some Huguenot aunts at La Rochelle.

The principal sin of Port-Royal was thus the Arnauld family, and above all the *Franc et Véritable Discours au Roi Henri IV* from the pen of M. Antoine Arnauld, Angélique's father. In this discourse he urged that the Jesuits, whom he had accused of having been the authors of every assassination in Europe for a period of forty years, should not be allowed to return to France. The Arnaulds were undoubtedly the origin of all the later persecutions of Port-Royal, of the Mère Angélique and all her followers, and also of Jansen and his friend Jean Du Vergier de Hauranne, Abbé de Saint-Cyran.

Jansen, or, as he was generally called, Jansenius, was born in 1585 and died as Bishop of Ypres in 1638. While he was alive his orthodoxy had never been questioned. On the contrary, being a Spanish subject, he was twice sent to Madrid by his colleagues of the University of Louvain in order to support its cause against the Jesuits. He would never have been considered a heretic had he not left a voluminous manuscript to be printed by his executors after his death, the *Augustinus*.

Angélique's enemies made use of Jansen's doctrine of grace as it was said to be found in his book, as well as of the life and utterances of his friend Saint-Cyran and some members of her own family, stigmatizing them as dangerous crypto-Calvinists, people that were dangerous to the Church, the Pope and the King of France.

We should, however, be very careful not to confound Port-Royal and the Mère Angélique's reform with Jansenism, as her enemies tried to do. Saint-Cyran was entirely unknown to her at the time of her reform, and she came in touch with him, and through him with Jansenist conceptions, more than twenty years later when the convent was virtually established. There were periods in the relentless struggle when it seemed as if Port-Royal would be allowed to continue its life of self-purification and prayer, but this was not to be.

Angélique died long before the very last act of the tragedy, but she would have accepted the final downfall of everything she had created as she had accepted every joy and every hardship, as coming from God and being the fulfilment of His wishes. She had never doubted the Divine wisdom even in the darkest hours of seeming frustration and human hopelessness. To her, all trials were a sign of God's grace. So resignation, unquestioning resignation, to God's will, was the principal law for everybody who followed the religious life. Without it no man and no woman could be called religious in her eyes, or ever become a true monk or a true nun. Without it, no one could keep his vows in a deep essential sense.

Grace was everything, and grace could not be had through purely personal striving, through acquiring any merely personal merit by one's own actions. It was not a reward due to us if we strictly followed the commandments. So even the utter destruction of all Angélique had held dear would have been acceptable to her. There could not be any rebellion in the heart of a truly religious person against God's highest decrees, neither could they ever be cheaply evaded for the sake of public opinion or some personal affection or attachment. Rebellion would have meant disobedience to God's will. Port-Royal only tried to maintain the old truths as they had been proclaimed by St. Augustine and recognized by the Church against Molina's theories of free will, which unconditionally subordinated the efficacy of grace to human merit.

Angélique was far more than a mere reformer. She influenced a wide circle of men and women through her life, besides the cloistered simple nuns of her convent, in spite of the almost repellent harshness of her creed. She not only proclaimed the necessity of extreme self-denial and self-searching to others, but herself practised the strictest personal discipline.

And yet, strangely enough, a lie formed the prelude to the reform of Port-Royal and to her own religious life. For in order to obtain the necessary papal bulls for the eight-year-old girl, she was made eight years older. M. Antoine Arnauld did not foresee, when he took his little daughter to the Abbey of Maubuisson, where she was to undergo her novitiate, that one day the doors of Port-Royal would be firmly closed against him, and the rule of St. Bernard enforced even against Angélique's own family and nearest relations.

Six years later, in 1608, when she had already become abbess at Port-Royal, Angélique happened to listen to a sermon preached by a debauched Capuchin friar. She suddenly resolved to reform her abbey; and she effected it notwithstanding the desperate outcries of her relatives and the open or veiled opposition of her early directors. After the famous *journée du guichet*, forming one of the most dramatic incidents of her dramatic career, Port-Royal soon became as well known as the Carmelites, and St. François de Sales's Order of the Visitation.

The *journée du guichet* happened on September 25, 1609, when the Arnaulds paid a visit to Port-Royal where they thought themselves to be the supreme rulers. The command given to an indignant father to respect the rule of the cloister was the first sign of Angélique's extreme unflinching attitude where the religious life was concerned, and the conscientious fulfilment of the monastic vows.

She had been made a nun against her wish, which is clearly shown by a conversation she had had years earlier, when she said to her grandfather, M. Marion, that she was unlucky to be the second daughter, for if she had been the eldest, she would have been the one to be married. But having been made a nun against her wish, and by the very parents who now tried to oppose her resolution, she wanted to live the monastic life sincerely and make her sisters follow its rules in all their details with unconditional self-surrender. To her, the religious life without absolute fulfilment of one's religious vows was nothing but hollowness and hypocrisy, and hypocrisy was one of the most hateful and unforgivable sins a religious person could commit.

The effort of the young and inexperienced abbess, whom everything seemed to call to an easy and pleasant life, to lead Port-Royal back to the original rules is very strange and almost looks like the hand of Providence, for all round her there reigned dissipation and the moral laxity of her time. To this reform Angélique brought all the ardour of her young passionate soul that knew no middle path and was always ready to go to extremes. And it is a curious fact that this very exaggeration drew many to the religious life by creating in them a lasting enthusiasm for self-sacrifice and the stern asceticism of absolute self-denial.

Long after Angélique's death such a cynic as Voltaire was still impressed by the deep sincerity and faith of the Port-Royal community she had reformed, of that little band of silent nuns and learned solitaries who had let themselves rather be wiped out than sacrifice their deepest convictions and become traitors to that which, to them, was Truth itself.

Angélique's first endeavour was to reintroduce the strict observance of the monastic rules of chastity, poverty, humility, obedience and seclusion, which are required by the Cistercian Order. To her, those who were sincerely trying to lead the religious life and not merely seeking their own comfort while paying outward lip-service to an ideal they had no wish to make their own, had to free themselves from every personal tie or relationship and from all desire, in whatever form it might appear. They had to relinquish everything and give themselves unconditionally to God. They had to be silent and prayerful. For the true monk and the true nun had to become living temples or shrines for that which was holiest. Even the emotional satisfactions offered by the religious life, its sweetness, ecstasies and visions, to which women so easily succumb and which so very easily become a sensual delight to them, had no place in her scheme. She was very little interested in the mere cloaks and vestments of religion that could so pleasantly be worn by the religious hypocrite and used as veils to hide his worldliness: everything that belonged to externals, the empty outward shell of a religious life, unless the principal rules and conditions were whole-heartedly and joyfully adhered to, held no attraction for her.

Another important incident in her life was Angélique's meeting with St. François de Sales at Maubuisson, where she had been asked to go in order to introduce her reform and replace the Abbess Angélique d'Estrées, whose scandalous conduct could no longer be tolerated after the death of Henri IV who had always given her his powerful protection. The five years she stayed at the abbey where she herself had been a novice and taken the veil, with all their dramatic vicissitudes and dangers, were a time that required the greatest courage and real heroism.

At Maubuisson we see Angélique's unflinching character, her absolute dedication to her task regardless of dangers and disappointments, her contempt for an easy life, her self-surrender to what she believed to be her duty and an expression of the highest Will—qualities which made her so admirable, but now and then seem to be a little inhuman, a little too hard and exacting to allow her ever to become fully balanced and calm.

St. François de Sales arrived at Maubuisson on April 5, 1619, in order to confirm one of Angélique's novices. As Angélique had been cherishing the desire to meet him and even to join the Order of the Visitation under Jeanne de Chantal, this visit made her very happy. They saw each other several times, and St. François de Sales also went to see her sister Agnès at Port-Royal. But he did not allow Angélique to carry out her wish of joining the Visitation and becoming a simple novice under Jeanne de Chantal, giving up her post at Port-Royal with all its unpleasant responsibilities and struggles.

After their last personal meeting in September, 1619, she never saw him again, but he continued writing to her glowing letters full of affection and sound advice, which are still the despair of pious editors of his correspondence, who cannot enlist him on their side in the condemnation of Port-Royal, and of all the Arnaulds and their friends. These letters and St. François de Sales's whole attitude towards the Mère Angélique express one of those deep lasting relationships between a man and a woman that are so hard to understand for the worldly mind in their intensity and purity, and that have frequently been so fruitful in the spiritual development of those who shared them. It would be almost impossible to think of St. Clare without St. Francis of Assisi, of St. Teresa of Avila without St. John of the Cross, of Ste. Jeanne de Chantal without St. François de Sales—and in the case of the Mère Angélique, too, St. François de Sales's influence helped her unfoldment and took away much of her exaggerated rigidity and one-sidedness, much of her hard, impatient, even fanatical clinging to what she considered to be the right and only standard of a truly religious life, and her perhaps too uncompromising judgment of her own shortcomings as well as those of others.

Three years later St. François de Sales died. In his beautiful letters he warned her many times against her own impetuous nature and also against exacting too much from herself and the community over which she ruled. His whole attitude and conception of the religious life differed considerably from hers, just as their temperaments differed, for his God was not a terrible God of so relentless a severity that it almost bordered on tyranny, nor a God who had to be feared and respected with a trembling heart.

St. François de Sales had always desired that Jeanne de Chantal and the Order of the Visitation should become closely linked with Port-Royal and the Mère Angélique. After his death in 1622, Jeanne de Chantal remained Angélique's best friend for the following twenty years. The last letter she wrote to her in 1641, shortly before her death at Moulins, was to recommend once more the close union of Port-Royal and the Visitation. It is all the more strange and almost an irony of fate that in later years the spiritual daughters of St.

François de Sales and Jeanne de Chantal were so fanaticized and blinded by the Jesuits that they became the merciless and cruel jailers of the Port-Royal nuns.

In 1625 Angélique gave up the convent of Port-Royal des Champs and moved to Paris, to the Faubourg St. Jacques, partly because of the unhealthy conditions at Port-Royal and partly because she wanted to free herself and her community from the influence of their superiors, the ignorant and worldly-minded monks of Citeaux, and put herself under the Archbishop of Paris.

At Paris she came in close touch with the Bishop of Langres, Sebastien Zamet. He was, at that time, full of admiration for her reforms and cherished a plan to found a new order for the perpetual adoration of the Blessed Sacrament. As Angélique had already introduced this practice at Port-Royal, this formed a very strong bond of sympathy between them. Sebastien Zamet was so enthusiastic and seemed to possess such a deep spirituality that Angélique was charmed and entirely carried off her feet by his eager impulsiveness, not realizing the essential shallowness of his nature, his narrow-mindedness and lack of stability.

In 1630 her old desire to resign her office was fulfilled, and the king granted Port-Royal the privilege of electing its abbess triennially. Unfortunately the new abbess, Geneviève Le Tardif, one of Angélique's Maubuisson novices, was completely under Zamet's influence, and Angélique, as a simple nun, had to stand by and watch her tear down everything she had built up with such labour during the long and difficult years of her reform. Geneviève thought that their poverty, resignation and unquestioning docility had made the nuns utterly imbecile and therefore decided to make them study and learn how to write, at the same time introducing sensational penances and austerities, which Angélique detested just as much as laxity and an easy, pleasant, comfortable life for the religious. She knew that such practices only served to foster a strong sensual emotionalism and, in many cases, a certain sense of self-glorification in those who gave themselves to them.

When in 1633 the Order of the Adoration of the Blessed Sacrament was founded, Sebastien Zamet no longer wished Angélique to occupy the post of mother-superior. The Archbishop of Paris, however, insisted on her appointment, but the convent of the Adoration very soon ceased to exist, and Angélique returned to Port-Royal in 1636, taking the nuns with her.

Yet it was Zamet who gave Jean Du Vergier de Hauranne, Abbé de Saint-Cyran, to Port-Royal, an event which was to have momentous and bitter consequences for the whole community. It was this connection with Saint-Cyran that made Port-Royal so widely known, and it was this more than anything else that brought about its final ruin. Saint-Cyran had been a great friend of Jansen, Cardinal de Bérulle and St. Vincent de Paul. He had been highly esteemed by Richelieu, who had tried hard to gain him for himself, but who had been irritated by his spirit of independence, in which he might have felt a threat to his own power. Saint-Cyran was by teaching and by practice the most intransigent advocate of that religion of fear which was so closely interwoven with Angélique's own ideas, and for him, too, being a true Augustinian in this sense, grace could never be a question of individual merit, but was a gift freely given by God, which He did not owe anybody, not even His most devoted servants. Angélique believed she had found a new St. François de Sales, and the entire Port-Royal community, including the solitaries, soon began to cherish such a deep veneration for their new director that Sebastien Zamet appears to have become jealous, and broke off all relations with Port-Royal, taking the side of their enemies. Saint-Cyran himself was denounced to Richelieu and imprisoned at Vincennes because of his obstinate refusal to annul the marriage of Gaston d'Orléans, and also because of his ideas and teaching on attrition, which widely differed from those of the Cardinal.

From prison Saint-Cyran continued to direct the nuns of Port-Royal, and when he left Vincennes, after Richelieu's death, his first visit was to them. He died shortly afterwards. There is no doubt that he was the greatest tamer of souls of the seventeenth century. To Port-Royal he had become like a father. Few men and women have been so identical in temperament and convictions as he and the Mère Angélique: both were stern and rigorous; both were strong personalities who made the light of others appear dim and nebulous; both knew how to inspire their fellow men with their own ideals and make them follow their example; both were unbending in whatever they believed to be right.

Between 1642 and 1649 Angélique was elected abbess of Port-Royal four times in succession. They were years of comparative quiet. In 1648 she returned with some of the nuns after an absence of twenty-two years to Port-Royal des Champs, where she was welcomed by the solitaries who had gathered there.

During the war of the Fronde Angélique opened the doors of the convent, giving shelter to all who sought refuge. Never do we see her so self-denying, so full of deep pity for the suffering, so ready to sacrifice everything the convent possessed for the sake of the homeless and those in danger. Never does she show so much of common sense and balance, so much of her extraordinary power of organization.

With the same unswerving resoluteness with which she met the cruelties of war she faced persecution. In 1653 she and her nuns had to sign the first formulary condemning the five Propositions that were said to be found in the *Augustinus*. But even this did not bring them any peace.

For a short time, however, the persecutions and slanders seemed to come to an end by an event that was accounted a miracle by the whole Port-Royal community and by the outside world. A relative of the Mère Angélique, a priest, had acquired a thorn that was said to come from the Crown of Thorns, and had sent it to Port-Royal. At that time there happened to be a little ten-year-old girl staying at the convent who had a malignant growth which had been declared incurable. But the sister in charge touched it with the crystal case containing the relic and it disappeared, leaving not even the slightest scar. The doctors certified that the cure surpassed all the ordinary powers of medicine. The Archbishop of Paris pronounced it a miracle. Blaise Pascal also mentions it in enthusiastic words in one of his famous letters. To many, even at Court, it seemed impossible that God had shown such grace to a band of heretics professing and propagating dangerous and blasphemous doctrines. But this period of respite was not to last long. A new formulary was drawn up a little later, which all were to sign without any reservation, the Pope having definitely declared that the five Propositions were to be found in Jansen's book.

The Port-Royal nuns, however, refused to sign without putting some precautionary lines at its head, for its signing meant a condemnation of Saint-Cyran as well as of Jansen.

Many even refused their signatures altogether. Jacqueline Pascal, Blaise Pascal's sister, who had joined the Port-Royal community years earlier, died of a broken heart.

The solitaries were dispersed, the schools closed. On April 23, 1660, the Paris nuns were ordered to send away all their *pensionnaires*. La Mère Angélique hastened to Paris to give support to the sisterhood there. She was then seventy years old. Her parting words to her brother d'Andilly are recorded. They spoke together as she was about to get into the carriage outside the convent gates.

"Farewell, brother;" she said, "whatever comes, be of good courage".

"Do not fear for me, sister;" he replied, "I have plenty of courage".

"Ah, brother, brother, let us be humble;" she answered, "we must remember that though humility without firmness may be cowardly, yet courage without humility is presumption".

On May 4 the nuns were commanded to send away all the novices and postulants, and were forbidden to receive new ones. This was the finale of Angélique's life of self-denial and high spiritual aspiration, and the end of her reform. Everything she had lived for and dreamed of was destroyed, ruthlessly trampled in the mire—and that by the Church she revered and adored. To Angélique, not tyranny, not malice had brought their griefs upon them, but the hand of God. "Let us not be astonished and cast down, my sisters, but let us humble ourselves"—that was her constant exhortation. "God does all things with a wisdom and benevolence that we can see for ourselves. We needed all that has happened to make us humble. It would have been a danger to us to remain any longer in such riches. Not another community in France was so overwhelmed with spiritual blessings. We were talked about everywhere. Believe me, we needed to be humbled by God; if He had not brought us low, we might have fallen. Men do not see the reasons for their actions, but God, who makes use of them for His own purposes, sees all clearly."

She died in August, 1661, without wavering in her faith. She had always been afraid of death, but she passed away with greater calmness than her friend Jeanne de Chantal. To her it was "the hour of man", but she was convinced that "the hour of God" would come.

With her death died the true Port-Royal. For we must never forget that the true Port-Royal, its very soul and spirit, was the Mère Angélique. It was her example, her energy, her faith, her sincerity, her influence that attracted the best men and women of France in her time and made them seek a higher reality than the licentious pleasure-seeking life they saw all round. It was Angélique's personality and unswerving courage that worked through her nuns and solitaries. She fully deserves to be placed in a line with the other great women reformers of the West, nay even of the whole world, though she has never been canonized nor even been recognized as a true daughter of her Church, for whose sake she had tried to bring about a purification of the whole religious life of her country.

Even in our day her example can still be a living flame, though the sternness and inflexibility, one might almost say the harshness of her conception of God, may not be acceptable to many.

Outwardly her Port-Royal died with her, but in a spiritual sense it is still alive and will remain so wherever sincerity, courage and truthfulness are revered. Lives such as hers are holy in their consecration and shed the light of holiness on all those who come in touch with them.

CHAPTER XXVI

MOTHER CABRINI

ON June 21, 1953, a chapel was dedicated in Rome in honour of the "Mother of the Emigrants", Saint Frances Xavier Cabrini. This chapel was in the Church of the Holy Redeemer, built by Mother Cabrini early in the present century —less than fifty years before this notable event. Like everything she did, the church was erected in obedience to the suggestion of the Holy Father. Obedience, prayer and work were the key-notes of her life and accomplishment. And though from childhood she desired to become a missionary to the Chinese people, it was again in obedience to the Supreme Pontiff that she set out for the United States where much of her work was to be done.

Maria Francesca Cabrini was born at Sant' Angelo di Lodi (Lombardy), Italy, on July 15, 1850. She was the last child in a family of thirteen. Her parents were known to be pious people. Because of her mother's age, Francesca was brought up by her sister Rose, a dry, sharp-spoken and domineering young teacher who had a small private school. This stern upbringing seems to have been good preparation for Francesca's future career as a nun. Although it helped to mould her character, the future Mother Cabrini learned that this type of severity was not the best means for the purpose. And thus she was always noted for her kind disposition.

As a child Francesca was rather frail and sickly, and throughout her life she suffered from delicate health. During her childhood she evidenced an intense interest in the religious life. Her dolls were dressed as nuns and she would preside over them as the lady abbess. It was at this early age that she revealed to her sister Rose the desire to become a missionary. This desire would be given expression when she visited her uncle, who was a local priest in a neighbouring town. Here she would play with paper boats along the swift waters of a canal that divided the town. Violets were placed in the boats and Francesca would imagine that she was sending them around the world as missionaries. For a child of seven, this method of play marked her as unusual; but the experience she was soon to have would mark her as extraordinary. On July 1, 1857, at her confirmation, she passed into ecstatic union with God. This experience —an early sign of her sainthood—was explained years later by Mother Cabrini: "The moment I was being anointed with the sacred chrism I felt what I shall never be able to express. . . . I seemed no longer on earth. My heart was replete with a most pure joy. I cannot say what I felt, but I know it was the Holy Ghost."

At this early period her self-control and devotion to God developed a concentration which enabled her to sit meditating quietly during an earthquake while her parents searched for her in alarm. This may be attributed to her regular practice of meditation. To this spiritual discipline was added another. At the age of eleven, Francesca was permitted to take a vow of chastity by the curate of the parish who was her first spiritual director. However, it was not until she reached nineteen that ecclesiastical permission was received to make it permanent. Many years later the curate wrote that he had always considered her a saint. Francesca's second spiritual director was the pastor of the local church. She passed into his care when she reached fifteen. This proved to be a most fortunate occurrence since it was his pithy instructions which were to be the preparation for Francesca's future life. Whenever the child presented her problems to the pastor, he would reply, "Go tell that to Jesus". This enabled her to develop a close and intimate relationship with God—a development of the highest importance for one who was never to have any regular spiritual direction.

At thirteen Francesca was sent to a private school conducted by the Daughters of the Sacred Heart at Arluno, a neighbouring town. She remained there for five years and obtained her teacher's certificate at eighteen. Her studies were completed at the Lodi normal school where she passed the examinations *cum laude*. At this time she made two attempts to enter religious communities, but was rejected because of her delicate health. Upon returning home Francesca did charitable works and, at the request of the parish priest, taught the catechism to neglected children. In 1872 a smallpox epidemic broke out in Sant' Angelo. With her sister Rose, Francesca cared for victims of the disease but caught the infection herself. After her recovery she took a position as teacher in the public school at Vidardo, an adjacent town. During this period many nights were devoted to prayer vigils. In addition she undertook external ascetic practices which brought her already frail health near to breaking-point. This she was later to regard as a mistake. Her mature conclusion was to stress a theme which played a dominant role in her own life: as the founder of a religious order she emphasized that the perfect observance of the Rule provided the most complete mortification. In this regard she wrote to her nuns, "Be obedient and you will be saints. . . . One act of obedience is worth more than a whole year's fasting through one's own initiative".

In 1874 Francesca accepted the position of directress at an orphan school in the small town of Codogno. Founded in 1857 as the House of Providence, the school received the patronage of an erratic, wealthy woman who contributed her money to it and served as headmistress. Upon the persuasion of the Bishop of Lodi this woman, Antonia Tondini, became a nun. The Bishop hoped that this might produce a change in the woman's character as well as in her management of the orphanage. But little improvement resulted. Into this atmosphere of a school mismanaged by an unbalanced directress Francesca entered for a trial period. Here she stayed for six years and here, on October 15, 1874, she took the habit of a nun. Though the eccentric headmistress prevented any real improvement of the school, the number of orphans grew and several young women entered the novitiate. These girls gathered about Francesca Cabrini who fired them with her spiritual zeal and desire for missionary work. Already Francesca's future career was developing; it was soon to receive an added impetus. Toward the end of 1880 difficulties with Antonia Tondini had grown so that the Bishop of Lodi decided to dissolve the House of Providence. This left Francesca and her companions homeless. The Bishop knew that it was this little inner group that kept the House of Providence going; also he knew that Francesca's ideal was to be a missionary. Therefore it was not illogical for him to request Francesca to found an order of missionary nuns. And so Francesca's real work began. On November 14, 1880, Francesca Cabrini and her companions moved into an abandoned Franciscan monastery in Codogno. This day is regarded as the birth of her Institute which was later to be called the Missionary Sisters of the Sacred Heart. A statue of the Sacred Heart was placed above the building,

Mass was said, and Mother Cabrini began her activities which were, in time, to reach many parts of the world.

As the foundress of a missionary order, Mother Cabrini assumed the title *Saverio*, the Italianized version of Xavier, as her name in the religious life. She would not permit herself to be called "Mother Foundress" but simply Mother Cabrini. She explained, "Our Foundress is the Mother of Grace; our Master, the Heart of Jesus; St. Francois de Sales is our Manager; and St. Francis Xavier, our Provider".

During this time Mother Cabrini continued to mould herself by spending much time in contemplation. But the members of her Institute were not neglected. They were now being trained for their future work. And their Mother General was a born teacher. Firm but kind, Mother Cabrini through private interviews and spiritual conferences taught her young nuns to depend on a power greater than themselves. Her guide-book was the *Spiritual Exercises* of St. Ignatius. These spiritual directions she gave to her nuns and followed herself.

Two years after the founding of the Institute, Mother Cabrini accompanied four Sisters and their twenty-five-year-old superior to Grumello, a town near Cremona. Here they opened a small day-school where, among other subjects, cooking, needlework, and religion were taught. This was the first step in a missionary activity that was to establish many foundations throughout three continents. In 1888 schools had been established in Milan, Boronetto, Livagra, Rome, and other places.

Toward the latter part of the nineteenth century, Italian emigration to the United States was growing rapidly. News of the abominable conditions among the poor Italians in New York, Chicago, and other cities reached Rome. Little had been done to alleviate this acute problem. Pope Leo XIII felt that an order of Italian nuns in America would be able to give substantial aid to these poor and suffering immigrants. About this time Archbishop Corrigan of New York requested Mother Cabrini to establish a foundation in New York City for this purpose. In an audience with the Holy Father, Mother Cabrini asked him to decide whether she should accept this invitation. His reply was in the affirmative and she was given the papal blessing to undertake this work.

On March 31, 1889, Mother Cabrini and a group of her nuns reached New York. Here she was to have an orphanage and other facilities for establishing her foundation. But through some error, Archbishop Corrigan did not expect them. And worse, he did not feel that they should undertake the work. When he suggested that Mother Cabrini return to Italy, she replied, "Here the Holy Father has sent me and here I will stay".

Intrepid, courageous and fired by her spiritual ideal, Mother Cabrini overcame her difficulties with the Archbishop and established the orphanage. However, funds were lacking, and so money was obtained through the solicitation of subscription lists and by direct begging in the Italian quarter. The need was immediate and the Sisters often went about with large baskets in their arms, for contributions of food were equally acceptable. The homeless children had to be cared for, housed and fed; but their religious heritage had to be maintained as well. Also the religious training of the other children living in the Italian quarter could not be overlooked. To meet this need Sisters were assigned to work at St. Joachim's Church in New York's "Little Italy". Here they looked after the children during Mass and taught them the catechism in the afternoon. Shortly afterward, classes in Christian doctrine were set up for young women and older girls. In this way St. Joachim's began to develop into an Italian centre.

Although constantly in delicate health, Mother Cabrini was an indefatigable worker. Almost the only rest she had was while traversing the Atlantic between the United States and other countries. Yet even then she was merely taking a respite to prepare for her next work. These voyages, thirty-seven in all, were also opportunities for the exchange of nuns: American postulants were taken to Codogno and Italian Sisters would accompany their Mother General to America. She would often say to her nuns: "We are good for nothing, but in God we can do all things. Do not seek rest on this earth, but be ready to die on the battlefield in company with Jesus. . . . The more you fight, the greater will be your reward, a crown that in Eternity no one can usurp." Whether it was crossing the Andes mountains where she almost lost her life, being expelled from Nicaragua because of the political dissension, working in the midst of corrupt politicians and racketeers in New Orleans, facing fierce hatred for the Italians in that city where eleven Italian men were lynched because of a supposed murder,

Mother Cabrini carried on with faith in her God and obedience to the work which was set before her. She told her Sisters, "Nothing is ever to daunt you. You are to press on, not of yourselves, but under obedience. I have already learned that whenever I failed in any undertaking it was because I trusted too much in my own power. None of us will fail if we leave everything in the hands of God. Under Him the question of possible and impossible ceases to have any meaning." Again she reassured them, "To become perfect all you have to do is to obey perfectly. When you renounce your personal inclinations you accept a mortification countersigned with the Cross of Christ."

Inspired by their Mother General's personality and spiritual ardour, the Missionary Sisters faced the most difficult odds with faith in her counsel: "Difficulties are children's toys. Imagination is what makes them big." And so the Institute in New Orleans was kept going for ten years on the door-to-door begging of that branch of the order. The Columbus Hospital in New York which, over the years, has cared for thousands of patients, was started on two hundred and fifty dollars. Less than three weeks after their arrival in Denver, Colorado, the Missionary Sisters had established a new house; and on the opening day of the school, two hundred children arrived. But that was not all. The fathers of these children were not neglected: Mother Cabrini and her nuns went down into the mines, day after day, to help the miners who worked under miserable conditions. Chicago and Philadelphia had hospitals established. An orphanage and chapel were founded in Seattle. A tuberculosis sanatorium was opened in Los Angeles. Italians in poor houses and prisons were visited. On and on the work continued. By the time of her death on December 22, 1917, Mother Cabrini had established sixty-seven foundations. In 1931 her order had grown to eighty foundations, two of these being established in China, the country in which she had always wanted to work. By 1954 one hundred foundations had been established throughout the world. Mother Cabrini's life is marked by three cardinal virtues; simplicity, humility, and obedience. Throughout her constant whirl of activity, she was always reported to have had a calm and peaceful countenance with a quiet and subdued voice. This constant recollectedness in the midst of all her worldly cares revealed an "habitual union with God" which was visible for all to see. However, so little is known of her relations with her God that this is considered one of the most unusual characteristics of this Catholic saint. She left no writings except part of a diary and some letters. Her library consisted of *The Imitation of Christ*, the *Exercises* of St. Ignatius, the works of Father Pinamonte, Alphonsus Rodriguez, a Jesuit writer, and St. Alphonsus Liguori. Since she belonged to no particular school of spirituality, and since she did not wish to confuse her Sisters with involved doctrines, Mother Cabrini's Institute was kept to simple devotional practices. There were many prayers in common beside the practice of private meditation. Although the Missionary Sisters were known for their hard work, six hours a day were given to prayer and contemplation. Mother Cabrini contended that no external activities should interfere with the aspirations of the soul.

A serenity and peace that came from her detached outlook enabled Mother Cabrini to remain recollected in God while attending to the many details of her expanding work. From time to time she retired to the cloister only to return to her activities reinvigorated and ready to cope with their many details and problems. It was her growing desire to retire permanently and give herself entirely to prayer and contemplation. But this was a wish never to be fulfilled. In a talk with one of her nuns she said, "If I followed my secret desires I would go to West Park[1] and there, far from all distractions, do many beautiful things for the Institute. But because I see that the Lord does not wish this of me for the time being, I forget solitude and attend to the affairs of the order. In this way I carry out God's will, even on the street, in the train, aboard ship—everywhere I feel as though I were meditating in my cell." Mother Cabrini's one aim to bring all human beings to the knowledge, love and service of their God was to occupy her entire life. Her constant thought is expressed at the end of a diary-letter: "Prayer, confidence and total abandonment to God will always be our arms. We are good for nothing. . . . But I can do all things in Him who strengtheneth me."

From the early days Mother Cabrini kept her interior life a guarded secret. However, she was unable to veil completely her mystical experiences. On occasion during chapel a Sister

[1] A convent of the Missionary Sisters of the Sacred Heart in Upper New York State.

would find her in an ecstatic state beyond the range of ordinary sense-consciousness. Other mystical experiences and miracles were reported by her colleagues. Upon her arrival in London, Mother Cabrini had a vision of the Virgin. Describing this experience she said, "I then saw our Blessed Lady, wearing a beautiful diadem, with the Child Jesus on her knees stretching out His arms in the act of protecting us". Prevented from having a regular spiritual director because of her constant travel, Mother Cabrini was able to develop a close communion with and reliance on her Creator. She wrote in a letter: "The soul learns that there is no necessity to look for her Beloved outside her own being, and that she can find Him within herself, as on His own throne and in His tabernacle". Here was a mystic whose way was through devotion and work. Spirituality to her was "robust, vigorous, strong, masculine". And these words of hers resounded through her life and the lives of the members of her Institute. False piety, complaints and despondency were to be ruled out. When the rosary was not in use, it was to be put away.

Mother Cabrini's tremendous capacity for work was the direct result of her inner life. She wrote in a little notebook of resolutions, "I would become weak and languid and risk losing myself if I were to occupy myself only with exterior things, however good and holy these may be; or if I were to be without sleep or prayer . . . in the heart of my beloved Jesus. Give me, O Jesus, an abundance of this mystical sleep." Though her human accomplishment was enormous, there remained a constant detachment, for her heart was elsewhere. She wrote, "The holy passion of Jesus pursues me so much that I cannot resist. . . . Come what may, I shall close my eyes and not lift my head from the Heart of Jesus". In a letter she told her nuns, "My book will be the crucifix, and I will always keep it before my eyes to learn how to love and to suffer. . . . The Missionary Sister who does not wish to suffer should give up the name. Whoever assumes the title of the Sacred Heart must always suffer by looking at the thorns that intertwine around the heart of Jesus. . . . How beautiful it is to suffer for Jesus, with Jesus, and out of pure love to consume oneself by suffering for Jesus."

This woman, who left a legacy of social, religious, educational, health and cultural developments in many lands was, in her inner being, the simple devotee and handmaid of the Lord. In her notebook she wrote directly to Christ. "From the moment I became acquainted with You I was so enchanted by Your beauty that I followed You. The more I love You, it seems the less I love You, because I want to love You more. I can bear it no longer. Expand, expand my heart! . . . O Jesus, Jesus Love, help always Your poor miserable one, Your miserable little bride, and carry her always in Your arms. . . . I love You, I love You so very, very much."

On December 22, 1917, Francesca Xavier Cabrini died in Chicago in Columbus Hospital, one of the many she founded during her lifetime. Soon after her death the Study of the Cause of Beatification was begun. The Process, or legal inquiry into the sanctity of a Servant of God by the Church at Rome, began two years later. This action was the direct result of the Pope's intervention when he waived the rule requiring the passing of fifty years before the opening of the Process. This was an extraordinary event without precedent in modern times. After a thorough investigation, which included the presentation of two official and authenticated miracles, Mother Cabrini was declared Blessed on November 13, 1938. She was the first citizen of the United States officially pronounced Blessed in Heaven. Eight years later the decree of her canonization was signed.

At the beatification ceremony, the pontifical High Mass was sung in the Vatican Basilica by Cardinal Mundelein who had celebrated Mother Cabrini's funeral Mass in Chicago twenty-one years before. This was the first time in Church history that a cardinal celebrated both the funeral services and beatification ceremonies for the same person. In his radio address at the beatification the cardinal said, "When we contemplate this frail little woman, in the short space of two score years, recruiting an army of four thousand women under the banner of the Sacred Heart of Jesus, dedicated to a life of poverty and self-sacrifice, fired by the enthusiasm of the crusaders of old, burning with the love of their fellow men, crossing the seas, penetrating into unknown lands, teaching peoples and their children by word and example to become good Christians and law-abiding citizens, befriending the poor, instructing the ignorant, watching the sick, all without hope of reward or recompense here below—tell me, does not all this fulfil the concept of Catholic Action, practised by a modern saint?"

Saint Frances Xavier Cabrini brought a power into her life which guided her every action, transformed those who joined to work with her, blessed thousands of people during her lifetime, and continued to bless increasing numbers year after year. Her bequest to humanity is one paean of prayer expressed in the God-centred action of her daily life.

PART IV

WOMEN SAINTS OF JUDAISM AND SUFISM

CHAPTER XXVII

HENRIETTA SZOLD

HENRIETTA SZOLD, founder and designer of hospital and welfare services in Palestine, and organizer and administrator of Youth Aliyah, the organization which rescued thousands of orphan children from Nazi inhumanity, fulfils through her life-work the Jewish conception of sainthood. She loved God and her fellow creatures more than herself and dedicated her faculties and abilities to improve their lot.

She was born in Baltimore, Maryland, U.S.A., in 1860, the eldest daughter of Benjamin Szold, Rabbi of that city, and his wife Sophia. It was from them that she imbibed the love of God and the service of her fellow-men—the mainspring and motif of all her thoughts and actions. Benjamin Szold hailed from Hungary and had arrived with his young wife in America the year before Henrietta's birth. Having no son, Rabbi Szold gave his eldest daughter the education and training which were normally reserved in those days for the boys of the household. Leaving High School, where she excelled, she taught and wrote—a Rabbi's meagre emoluments being insufficient to maintain five daughters. For the period of fourteen years during which she taught in High School, she engaged also in many other pursuits.

While in her teens she accompanied her father upon a tour of Europe and this made a lasting impression on her. Prague, with its ancient memories of the Jewish past—glorious and tragic—and the remains of a German ghetto, left an indelible imprint on her mind and gave her "a sense of belonging to her people". The tour engendered in her a certain impatience of the faults of her community in Baltimore. She condemned their irreligiousness and their eagerness to copy the customs of their neighbours.

Soon after her return to America a wave of immigration began. The May Laws of 1882 compelled thousands of Jews to flee from Russia. Many emigrated to friendly neighbouring lands: some went farther afield to America. And of these a not insignificant number found their way to Baltimore where their strange manners and language made them none too welcome.

The Rabbi and his daughter listened with sympathy to each man's troubles and helped him to become integrated into the new society and environment. Henrietta took the first step to help them become "Americanized". She took a room above a shop and opened a night school. When, four years later, her "Russian School" was taken over by the Baltimore Education Authority it had grown to five thousand pupils.

Her experiences with these despised Russian fugitives impelled her to re-value Jewish history. It was not only the Czarist government which sought to degrade the Jews: persecution and intolerance were prevalent everywhere in smaller or larger measure. If only they had their homeland, their ancient dignity would be restored. Thus even before Dr. Theodore Herzl, Henrietta was pioneering for the return of Israel to its own soil. "I became converted to Zionism", she said later, "at the very moment that I realized that it alone supplied my bruised, torn and bloody nation, my distracted nation, with an ideal—an ideal inflicted by others—an ideal that can be embraced by all, no matter what their attitude may be to other Jewish questions".

At the age of 33 she left teaching and took up the post of literary secretary in Philadelphia to the Jewish Publication Society of America, a post she held for twenty-three years. In order to equip herself for her important work she studied at the Jewish Theological Seminary of America—an institution which had never admitted a woman over its threshold. "A lady studying Talmud" was a strange thing. Many students found her a sympathetic listener and counsellor. She wrote articles for the *Jewish Encyclopedia* and many other learned journals. She was honoured by an invitation to deliver two lectures before the World Parliament of Religions held at Chicago in 1893.

Her working hours a day varied between fourteen and sixteen, year in and year out, until she became ill and was ordered to rest. Her recovery was slow and the Publication Society, in appreciation of her services, defrayed the cost of an ocean trip which included months of travel in Europe and Palestine. She had long yearned to pay a visit to her ancestral home: now it was made possible; her feet would stand within its borders. It was here—little did she know it at the time—that her life's greatest work was to be accomplished and a new page to be written in the history of the unfolding and rebirth of Israel.

Palestine, when Henrietta visited it in 1909, was but a backwash of civilization. It formed part of the Ottoman Empire and was ruled by the despotic Sultan. His officials were corrupt and neglectful, and received their revenues from heavy taxes and bribes. The land was barren and sterile. Its inhabitants were poverty-stricken and bereft of hope. The first Jewish colonists struggled not only with a stubborn and cruel soil but with plague and disease. The plight of the children especially tore at the heart-strings of Henrietta. Walking one day through the sandy paths of Tiberias—once the seat of Roman governors—she and her mother caught their first glimpse of the ragged, emaciated children, whose dark, hollow eyes were covered with disease. Congenital blindness and blindness from syphilis were rife. Sanitary conditions were appalling: infant mortality extremely high.

Henrietta, then forty-nine, determined to inaugurate a campaign to establish health and social welfare services for the whole of Palestine, for Jews and Arabs alike. "If it can be done in one school," she said, "it can be accomplished everywhere".

The task, she knew, was no easy one. When she returned to New York, her health restored, she threw herself unstintingly into her new work, to which she now dedicated the rest of her life.

At this time there was a group of women Zionists in New York who had banded themselves into a Society under the name of Queen Esther. Its object was to assist Zionist efforts, though its primary function was that of a literary society. It was to this group that Henrietta divulged her mission. Her account of what she had seen was so moving as to win their immediate support. Other groups affiliated themselves to this group, which now took the name Hadassah—the word in Hebrew for 'myrtle' and an alternative Biblical name for Esther. Her work of fund-gathering was no easy one for a woman of fifty. It took her to all parts of America. At meetings she addressed the few as she did the many. Her manner was "prim and academic"—like some college professor. She was not an eloquent speaker but an impressive one, and she illustrated her appeals with lantern slides.

Numerous passionate pleas reached her from Palestine for

help, and eventually she was able to send some trained nurses in 1913. Miss Szold herself remained in America to raise the funds to carry out and intensify the work.

In 1916 her mother died after months of suffering, during which time Henrietta tended her and recited prayers with her till the end. Henrietta herself was nearly sixty and the advancing years were taking their toll. Her doctors ordered her to follow a less arduous life. Her heart was becoming tired and her health deteriorating. But Henrietta determined to pursue her plans and purpose though she promised to slacken her pace. She set out for Palestine in the same year and was seen off by a few friends who agreed that she looked forward to the third period of her wonderful career just as a young woman might do. She intended to stay for two years, but remained till her death twenty-seven years later. During those years—the period of and between the two World Wars—she created and supervised the development of the social health service of Palestine, and was responsible for bringing thousands of poor, abandoned and orphaned children to that land from many countries of oppression, and for their rehabilitation and education.

The First World War had brought untold misery to the inhabitants of Palestine. At this critical stage Henrietta Szold arrived in Palestine. Her immediate task was to provide nourishment and medical care for the victims of poverty and illness. The medical unit she had set up had already saved Palestine from an epidemic during the War, and had sustained numerous children and their mothers. But it was now entirely inadequate to meet the tremendous demands which were made on it.

Funds came from America in a thin trickle and were totally inadequate to meet the constant new demands on her. By 1920 she had some four hundred doctors and nurses working for her—and a large deficit. The Palestine girls whom Henrietta enlisted for nursing were unaccustomed to professional ethics as were the American nurses, and, dissatisfied with conditions, would often walk out in a body and leave patients without attention. Henrietta was patient with them and gradually developed them into a disciplined body. Her task was not easy as there were no nursing textbooks in Hebrew.

Immigrants were arriving in Jaffa at the rate of three

hundred a week, and within a few weeks many of them were laid low by malaria. Miss Szold knew that with a settled income it would be possible to overcome the ravages of the disease by proper planning and precautions, yet she did not allow her sense of frustration to obtrude upon her tasks. She travelled the country—though there were no proper roads—in a waggon or on the back of a donkey. In one of her letters she wrote: "These pioneers—a war-bred generation—are living a primitive life and are grappling with elementary, basic problems of living. I have a strong desire to join them. Of course I can't break stones as they do, but I may be able to organize them so that their living conditions are improved". Organization and improvement of conditions were her natural bent: wherever she went she wanted to improve conditions. She had great respect for the pioneers who were rebuilding their ancient homeland. "My hope lives with the Chalutzim," she said, "a fresh stream that may carry away on its swift current all the deposits of decay".

The coffers of her Unit were still empty and she was deeply in debt. There were no funds to pay the tradesmen or the salaries of her staff. But Miss Szold determined to carry on. Her anxieties were partly relieved by the receipt of twenty thousand dollars from Nathan Strauss, but this was only a fraction of the funds required. Her doctors and workers rallied round her and did not press for their salaries so that she could use the money to pay the tradespeople and secure fresh medicines.

It was only at this stage, as the work became more stable and less exacting, that Henrietta permitted herself to take an interest in other aspects of the growth of modern Palestine. She now travelled between America and Palestine in advancing the welfare of her hospital services, and took an interest in education which, like medicine, was in the pioneering stage. When she entered this field of activity, she had to face numerous difficulties.

She succeeded in bringing unity, balancing the budget, and introducing modern standards into the school system. She was respected on all sides, and admired for her sincerity and selflessness. She introduced the school-meal system, which ensured that the pupils had at least one good meal a day. In 1929 she opened a Health Centre in Jerusalem, and a modern hospital in Tel-Aviv. Thus she was engaged in both tasks, health and education, at the same time doing both successfully.

Henrietta Szold was resolved also to reclaim the land. "Humanitarian though she was, concerned with the primary needs of human beings . . . she never lost sight of the idea that work in Palestine was not philanthropy but the upbuilding of a country—a habitation of the spirit." She became a member of the National Assembly and fitted herself for this new work.

At the age of seventy-five, in 1934, when most people have yielded to advancing age and have retired to a semi-active form of life, Henrietta Szold felt the call to undertake yet another form of meritorious activity. It was the time of the Nazi excesses, the beginning of the sadistic attack on the Jews of Germany by Hitler, which culminated in the destruction of six million men, women and children. An organization was set up to send the children to Palestine. In 1934, some five thousand were received in their homeland. Henrietta Szold undertook the task of becoming their "mother". "These will be my children", she exclaimed.

The first group arrived at Haifa in February, 1934. Her presence gave them confidence and helped them to overcome their separation from their parents and accustomed surroundings. She planned to send them into homes where the conditions were similar to those in the homes they had left. The work grew apace, and more and more children were arriving.

Nazi excesses were now known throughout the world and help came to her from all sides to continue and enlarge her merciful errand. She saw the utter desolation of the Jewish community and their pitiful plight, and determined to devote all the powers with which a beneficent God had endowed her, to the rescue of at least the innocent children.

During the years that followed, over sixty thousand children from all parts of the world were received, educated, rehabilitated, taught useful trades or professions, and finally integrated into the community as useful citizens. Of course, this could not have been accomplished single-handed. She had gathered round her a body of men and women and imbued them with the zeal so necessary for the delicate task. "She gave them new faith in the Divine and in mankind."

Until the last year of her life Henrietta Szold continued to meet her children and conduct them to their new homes. By night she sat at their cots, as any mother might do. She listened patiently to their complaints and taught them new songs. She established Children's Villages, and helped the young people to spin, weave and dye wool from the flocks. She became a legend—the mother of sixty thousand children!

She had the satisfaction of seeing the opening on Mount Scopus in 1939, of the Hadassah University Medical Centre, one of the largest in the world for healing and research; and the opening of the first Nurses' School for some 350 nurses, which bore her name. Some fifty welfare stations for pre-natal and infant care alone had been established. She lived to see some of her own nurses—brought into the world and trained by her—serving in the Second World War, bringing relief and healing to the victims of man's inhumanity to man. God had been good to her to have given her the opportunity to serve His children. "I am a happy person", were her last words.

Rabindranath Tagore wrote: "He who wants to do good knocks at the door: he who loves finds it open".

Henrietta Szold loved doing good. She gave sixty years of her life selflessly and unstintingly to saving men, women and children. She fought prejudice, ignorance, inhumanity, disease and persecution—not least, the prejudice against her sex—and won. She was one of those—

> Who, doomed to go in company with Pain,
> And Fear, and Bloodshed, miserable train!
> Turns his necessity to glorious gain;
> In face of these doth exercise a power
> Which is our human nature's highest dower;...

She reached the age of eighty-four and went to her Maker on February 13th, 1945, loved and honoured, to receive the reward of her labours well done.

Judaism does not canonize its noble sons and daughters; if it did Henrietta Szold would surely have earned the title of a Jewish woman saint. Death came to her, but not the end. From the unseen world she yet speaks. Her memory is a blessing and an inspiration: her work goes on.

CHAPTER XXVIII

RĀBI'A

A Short Life-sketch of Rābi'a

RĀBI'A belonged to the tribe of 'Adī, and hence was known as Rābi'a al-'Adawiyya. She was also called Rābi'a al-Baṣriyya as she was born in Basra (Iraq) in A.D. 717. Her parents were very poor, but supremely religious-minded. They already had three daughters, and so she was named Rābi'a, meaning "the fourth". She was left an orphan at a very tender age and was also separated from her sisters due to a famine that occurred in Basra soon after. Poor and helpless, wandering alone through the streets, she was captured one day by a wicked person and sold as a slave for a trifling sum. Her master was a cruel man, and made her work very hard. But this unbroken series of mishaps and hardships, right from her very birth, failed to cow or damp Rābi'a's supreme courage and deep faith, her indomitable spirit and pure heart, her indefatigable energy and unfaltering determination. Even under the heavy and cruel shackles of slavery, she never lost heart even for a moment, never despaired of a brighter future, never gave up her striving for a Life Divine and Life Perfect, in an eternal union with God Himself. That was why she used to fast the whole day while carrying out her continuous round of hard daily duties, and pray to God uninterruptedly during the whole of the night. One night when she was thus wrapped in deep contemplation of God, and lamenting her inability to think of and serve God day and night without break, as she was subject to another, her master woke up from sleep and, to his surprise, saw a lamp above her head, suspended without a chain and illuminating the whole house. Greatly perturbed at this strange sight, he set her free next morning. Then Rābi'a retired to a desert to live the life of a recluse. After some time she returned to Basra, built a retreat for herself and spent a life of asceticism and devotion there.

When, soon afterwards, Rābi'a's fame as a great mystic spread far and wide, she received many lucrative offers of marriage from rich and celebrated men of those days. But she rejected all of them and chose a life of celibacy and sanctity, dedicated to the worship and service of God alone. When a very rich man, Muhammad Sulayman, the Governor of Basra, offered her a princely dowry, Rābi'a turned him down with scorn with the words, "You should not distract me from God for a single moment. God can give me all you offer, even double it". She even rejected the offer of Abd Zayd, a celebrated theologian and preacher, the founder of one of the first monastic orders near Basra, with equal scorn and vehemence.

Thus, freed from all earthly trammels, Rābi'a started a life of constant meditation and preaching, and was soon recognized as one of the most renowned of early Ṣūfī saints. She had a large number of disciples who flocked to her house day and night to listen to her teaching, to seek for her advice in spiritual matters, to participate in her prayers. Legends connect her with many famous persons of those days, and although their authenticity cannot be vouched for in all cases, yet there is no doubt that many saints and scholars of those days were benefited much by the teachings of Rābi'a, and unhesitatingly acknowledged her, though a woman, as their spiritual preceptor and guide. But true to her vocation as a humble servant of God, Rābi'a herself never posed as a preacher or leader of men. On the contrary, very humbly and modestly she only tried to help others and show them the way to salvation so far as she could, and never set herself up as an intermediary between God and man, interceding on his behalf. When once a man pleaded with Rābi'a to pray for him, she promptly replied: "Who am I? Obey your Lord and pray to Him, for He will answer the suppliant when he prays".

As a devout Ṣūfī, Rābi'a not only preached asceticism, but herself practised it with utmost scruple and unrelenting severity. That is why her holy life stands to us, even today, as one of the most inspiring examples of a life of supreme purity, unselfishness and self-sacrifice. Just as she voluntarily chose a life of celibacy, so she also voluntarily embraced a life of utter poverty and dire austerity. Although she was a penniless slave in the early years of her life, yet later on when she won fame as a great saint, she came to have many rich and influential friends to render her financial assistance. But she persistently refused to take any help of any kind from any one whatsoever. When her friends remonstrated with her for this, she said in a most touching manner: "Verily, I should be ashamed to ask for worldly things from Him to whom the world belongs; so, how should I ask for them from those to whom it does not belong?"

Rābi'a herself learnt this discipline of austerity and asceticism through sweat and tears. Her famous biographer 'Aṭṭar relates the following beautiful story regarding her: Once Rābi'a had spent a whole week in praying, day and night, without food, without sleep at all. Then she felt extremely hungry, and was given a cup of food by some one. But a cat upset the cup. Then she wanted to drink some water, but the water-jug, too, fell from her hands and was smashed to pieces. Unable to bear the pangs of hunger any longer, she began to lament and complain to God for his cruelty, whereupon a divine voice reminded her that desire for God and desire for worldly objects could never dwell together in one heart. Bitterly ashamed and repentant, thereafter Rābi'a learnt to check all worldly desires and rise above all animal instincts under all circumstances, and succeeded in gaining such a complete control over the lower, physical side of her nature that even bodily injuries and pains could not affect her at all. Once she was struck on the head and bled profusely as a result, but was quite oblivious of any pain. When her friends expressed surprise at this, she said easily: "God has made me occupied with something other than the tangible things of the world".

Rābi'a died in A.D. 801 and was buried in Basra. Her last hours were worthy of her long, dedicated life of constant prayer and communion with God. Calm and unafraid, she surrendered herself completely to her Beloved, and was welcomed by Him to Life Eternal with, so say her biographers, the ringing words: "Return to thy Lord, satisfied with Him, giving satisfaction to Him". To her, thus, death was but "a bridge whereby the lover is joined to the Beloved".

Only a sketchy account, mostly based on legends, of this great and good life is available to us now. But still, from this unsatisfactory account no less, we get the glimpse of a unique personality, sublime in its lofty grandeur, yet utterly lovable in its simple sweetness and unostentatiousness. In her early life she got no opportunities for ordinary education at all in a school; and in her later life also, no scope for any spiritual training from a *shaykh* or spiritual preceptor. Still, who can stop the onrush of the soul towards God, if God draws it to

Himself? Such was the case with Rābi'a—one of the greatest women saints the world has ever seen. Unschooled and unassisted, she opened up her heart to God alone to receive His Light from Him direct. That is why, in the midst of the slave-like drudgery in the master's home, in the midst of the lonely severity of a burning desert, in the midst of the austere poverty and squalor of a great and busy city, Rābi'a, the chosen daughter of God Himself, trained herself for a higher spiritual life, leading to the realization of God Himself. Rābi'a's life, indeed, is an inspiring example to all ordinary women who also can aspire to a height of spiritual perfection through their own unaided efforts, provided they have the heart to do it.

Rābi'a's Teachings

As already mentioned, Rābi'a was one of the most prominent of early Ṣūfī saints, who died between the middle and end of the second century A.H. (A.D. 767–815), like Ibrahim ibn Adham, Abu Ali Shaquiq Daud of Tayy and Faday'l 'Iyad.

Early Ṣūfīsm is not at all a philosophical or speculative system, but rather an ethical one. That is, in it we do not find metaphysical speculations or discussions regarding the nature of God, soul, salvation, union with God and so on; but only some practical directions as to how God can be attained. Thus, early Ṣūfīsm is only "a practical religion and rule of life", as beautifully brought out by Junayd in his famous dictum: "We derived Ṣūfīsm from fasting and taking leave of the world and breaking familiar ties and renouncing what men deem good —not from disputation".

Thus, the two main characteristics of early Ṣūfīsm are asceticism and quietism. Asceticism, as the word implies, is an ethical theory which aims at a love of severe self-mortification and penance. The early ascetics over-emphasized the Quranic teachings about sin, Day of Judgment, hell and God as a relentless, severe Judge and Dispenser of Justice. Hence, over-awed at the fear of retributive punishment and burning hell, they completely renounced worldly life, and lived a life of utmost austerity and physical chastisement. The Ṣūfīs, besides being strict ascetics, were also something more. For, first, their asceticism was not a selfish one, that is, not one undertaken for selfish gain, such as the attainment of Heaven and avoidance of hell, but only for the supreme end, that is, the attainment of a complete union with God. Secondly, with the Ṣūfīs the stress was always more on the inner motive than on the outer conduct. That is, to them poverty and austerity meant not only the absence of worldly possessions, but also that of worldly desires—"not only the empty hand, but also the empty heart". Thirdly, the Ṣūfīs were not only puritanic hermits, but also devout mystics. Herein lies the quietism of the Ṣūfīs. Quietism, as the term implies, is the ethical theory which recommends the absolutely calm and quiet contemplation of God, as well as such a resignation to His Will, as the only means to spiritual perfection. The Ṣūfīs, too, enjoin an uninterrupted meditation on God as the only means to a direct vision of Him. Hence the Ṣūfīs were not mere ascetics (Zahid) and hermits (Faqir), but also mystics. "Ṣūfīsm", as Suhrawardi pithily says: "is neither poverty (Faqir) nor asceticism (Zuhd), but a term which comprehends the ideas of both, together with something besides. Without these superadded qualities, a man is not a Ṣūfī, though he may be an ascetic (Zahid) or a hermit (Faqir)".

Rābi'a, too, as one of the most celebrated of early Ṣūfīs, aimed at providing mainly a practical path to the Goal, which she conceived as union with God—rather than indulging in speculations regarding the nature of God, soul and union between the two. God, to her, was an incontrovertible Truth, needing no proof; equally indisputable, according to her, was the soul's absolute necessity for a direct communion and union with Him. Hence, instead of wasting her time in vain speculations regarding such undoubted truths, Rābi'a engaged herself mainly in chalking out an ethical path, consisting of a number of graduated stages, through which alone can the supreme Goal of life, namely the beatific vision of God and complete union with Him, be attained.

The path consists of the following main stages:—Repentance, patience, gratitude, hope and fear, voluntary poverty, asceticism, complete dependence on God and finally, love, including passionate longing for the Beloved, intimacy with Him, and satisfaction. A similar path has been recommended by other Ṣūfīs no less.

(i) *Repentance* is taken by all as the very first stage in the moral path, the mystic path which alone can lead to the salvation of the soul from earthly trammels, and unite it with God Himself. For the very first requisite of a moral life and of a spiritual development is the consciousness and admission of one's own sins and shortcomings, and sincere grief for these; for then alone can one make amends and start and strive for a more perfect, purer and fuller existence. All the Ṣūfīs, for this reason, emphasize the essential necessity of repentance in the moral path. We may, here, briefly refer to the view of the celebrated Ṣūfī Dhul Nun-al-Misri who has given us an elaborate classification of the main kinds of repentance in Ṣūfīsm. First, we have to distinguish between the repentance of common men, repentance of the elect (the Ṣūfīs), and repentance of the saints; an ordinary man repents for his actual deeds only; a Ṣūfī repents not only for sins of commission—actual impious acts—but also for his sins of omission—pious acts left undone; a saint repents for his own imperfection. Secondly, repentance may be a repentance of fear due to conceiving God as the Terrible, consequent on the revelation of His supreme might and majesty; and repentance of shame consequent on the vision of His infinite beauty and tenderness. The first makes a man sober only; the second makes him intoxicated. Hence, from the Ṣūfī standpoint, the second is a much higher kind of repentance.

In Rābi'a's teachings also, we find the whole emphasis laid on this higher and purer form of repentance. Although intensely conscious of her own faults and failings and constantly weeping and lamenting for these, Rābi'a had no selfish motives in her at all. That is, she never for a moment thought of asking God's pardon for her sins so that she might thereby escape the just retributions thereof. On the contrary, sin, according to her, is intensely hurtful and hateful, not because it involves punishment hereafter in hell, but only because it brings about a separation between the soul and God. In fact, as Rābi'a not only teaches but also demonstrates by her own life, such a separation is itself the greatest punishment to which a devotee can ever be subject.

Rābi'a also teaches that repentance itself is a gift from God Himself, for no one can attain this stage of repentance by his own unaided efforts. Hence in many places she says beautifully, "If I seek repentance myself, I shall have need of repentance again", "Our asking forgiveness of God, itself needs forgiveness", and so on. Al-Qushayri relates that when a man asked Rābi'a, "If I repent, will God accept my repentance?" Rābi'a replied at once: "No, but if He turns towards you, you will turn towards Him".

Thus, Rābi'a, the perfect daughter of God, depended on His Grace at every moment, in all matters whatsoever.

(ii) *Patience*, the calm and uncomplaining acceptance of what God has been graciously pleased to grant us, is the next highest stage. A saint, rightly says the famous Ṣūfī Bayazid-al-Bistami, is "that one who is patient under the command and prohibition of God". Another prominent Ṣūfī, Kalabadhi, also points out that in a lower stage, patience implies bearing all hardships with fortitude, but expecting consolation from God. But in a higher stage, it never even involves such a selfish expectation.

Rābi'a teaches this higher kind of patience, and as before also demonstrates it in her own life. We have seen how from early childhood Rābi'a bore, without a murmur, a series of mishaps like bereavements, disease, slavery and poverty. To doubt God's wisdom and mercy, according to her, is the height of folly and unbelief. "If I will a thing" she says with deep devotion and firm conviction, "and my Lord does not will it, I shall be guilty of unbelief".

(iii) *Gratitude* is a still higher stage in the mystic path, and complementary to patience, for, while patience is rather negative in nature, involving as it does, a calm resignation to God's Will, gratitude is more positive, implying a grateful acceptance of what God, in His infinite mercy and wisdom, has thought fit to bestow on us. A higher kind of gratitude means not only a gratefulness for prosperity, but also for adversity. As a true Ṣūfī, Rābi'a also constantly taught and practised this noble quality of gratitude, accepting sufferings and afflictions as thankfully as joys and favours.

Like other stages in the path, "gratitude", too, as Al-Qushayri points out, "is a gift from God Himself". The celebrated Ṣūfī Hallaj also holds that although a saint should cultivate an attitude of utter humility and gratitude, he should at the same time know his inability to be fully and adequately grateful to God for what He has done for us. Hence, the highest kind of gratitude is to realize the utter futility of human gratitude. "O God!" touchingly says Hallaj, "Thou knowest that I am not able to thank Thee according to all Thy bounties. Wherefore, I pray Thee, thank Thyself for me".

The same kind of supreme gratitude is found in Rābi'a's life and teachings right from the beginning.

(iv) *Hope and Fear* are also important stages, according to the Ṣūfīs, in the mystic path. Here "hope" means the eternal hope of the devotee for union with God. "Fear" means the equally eternal fear of the devotee of separation from God. Thus, hope and fear are two complementary states that supply constant inspiration to the mystic to strive for the Goal. Very aptly have these two been described by the Ṣūfīs as the two wings of a bird, flying upward.

Rābi'a was perhaps the most prominent of the early Ṣūfīs who developed these concepts of hope and fear in a new way, and thereby she formulated her famous doctrine of disinterested love. Both hope and fear may involve selfish motives, hope of reward or Heaven, and fear of punishment or hell. But Rābi'a divested hope and fear of all selfish elements whatsoever, and raised them to the sphere of purely selfless love and devotion. To a true Ṣūfī, Paradise is not a place of sensuous, or even spiritual, joys, but only a place where the vision of and union with God is attained; in the same manner, hell is not a place of torture and punishment, but a state of separation from God. Hence a Ṣūfī says, with Bayazid-al-Bistami: "Paradise is of no worth to those who love". In this connection Rābi'a's famous saying, quoted amongst others by the celebrated al-Ghazali, has become a classic: "First the neighbour, then the house". This means that the neighbour or God is more important than the house or Paradise.

(v) *Voluntary Poverty* is one of the fundamental tenets of Ṣūfīsm. It means a complete cleansing of the heart of all selfish desires, and turning it towards God alone. We have seen how Rābi'a not only preached, but herself practised, this great and difficult vow of poverty.

(vi) *Asceticism* too, is a main prop of Ṣūfīsm, and interconnected with the stage of poverty. Asceticism means the perfect control of the lower, physical self by the higher, spiritual one. Here also, the preachings and doings of Rābi'a give a new, exhilarating turn to Ṣūfīsm. Rābi'a teaches, in her usual simple and straightforward way, that such a self-control means really one-pointed concentration of the mind on God and God alone, with nothing to distract it from Him. As an ascetic, in the truest sense of the word, Rābi'a feared even to possess the reputation of a saint, lest it should give her satisfaction in something other than the Lord; and always refrained from displaying her knowledge and power.

(vii) *Dependence on God* is the result of the above stages in the path. It is the supreme stage of absolute self-resignation to the Lord, complete dedication of one's whole being to the Being of all beings. This attitude of the Ṣūfīs is reflected very poignantly in the beautiful prayer of the great Ṣūfī Hallaj: "Thy Will be done, my Lord and Master. Thy Will be done, O my Purpose and Meaning! O Essence of my being, O Goal of my desire, O my Speech and my Hints and Gestures, O All of my all, O my Hearing and my Sight, O my Whole and my Particles". Exactly the same was Rābi'a's teaching in this regard.

(viii) *Love* is the last stage in the mystic path—the final way to the beatific vision of the Beloved and union with Him. Love, Rābi'a teaches, must possess two main characteristics: first, it must be all-absorbing; secondly, it must be equally disinterested. A saint must think of God and God alone, none else. God is, indeed, a jealous Beloved who brooks no rival. The true nature of such a sublime, all-absorbing love, is beautifully brought out by the following anecdote regarding Rābi'a: One day she was asked, "Do you love God?" She unhesitatingly said "Yes". Again she was asked "Do you hate Satan?" Equally unhesitatingly, she replied "No, my love for God leaves no room for hating Satan. My love for God has so possessed me that no place remains for loving or hating anyone save Him".

The absolutely disinterested nature of her love has already been referred to.

Rābi'a's Writings

The very high esteem in which Rābi'a was held by Islamic saints and scholars is clear from the large number of quotations of her sayings, as found in different treatises, biographical or philosophical, of later periods. In fact, almost all the great Ṣūfī writers refer to her teachings and quote her sayings. Amongst these authorities, mention may be made of Abu Nasr al-Sarraj, Abu Talib, Kalabadhi, Abu al-Qushayri, al-Ghazali, al-Suhrawardy, and Hujuiri. Although we do not know of any separate work by Rābi'a, all these numerous quotations give us a clear idea regarding her very simple and sincere style. As a specimen, we may refer to her famous verses on the two types of love, as quoted by Abu Talib:

I have loved Thee with two loves,
  a selfish love and a love that is worthy.
As for the love which is selfish, I occupy
  myself therein with remembrance of Thee to the
  exclusion of all others.
As for that which is worthy of Thee, therein
  Thou raisest the veil that I may see Thee.
Yet is there no praise to me in this or that.
  But the praise is to Thee, whether in that or this.

As a specimen of her prose, we may take the following beautiful prayer, recorded by her well-known biographer 'Aṭṭar: "O my Lord, if I worship Thee for fear of hell, burn me in hell; and if I worship Thee for hope of Paradise, exclude me thence; but if I worship Thee for Thine own sake, withhold not from me Thine eternal Beauty."

All her prose and poetry, as known to us, breathes forth the same sublime glory, the same depth of feeling and freshness of vision. It is her own great Beloved indeed that speaks through her; and that is why all her sayings go straight to our hearts and stir up the innermost depth of our being.

An Estimate and an Appreciation

Far-reaching indeed was the influence of Rābi'a on contemporary and later thought. True to the predominant features of Sūfism in its early stages of evolution, Rābi'a's doctrine was mainly practical. But besides asceticism and quietism, we find in Rābi'a an intense feeling of ecstasy, and also a mixture of speculation and devotion that marks the beginning of a new phase in the history of Ṣūfism. In her sayings we have glimpses of not only a deeply devoted heart, but also a deeply thoughtful mind, which, though fully convinced of the incontrovertible Truth, yet thought fit, occasionally, to give vent to its inner beliefs in outer proofs. This happy union of thought and feeling, theory and practice, is her lasting contribution to Ṣūfism as a whole.

But by far her most valuable gift to her own generation, as well as to posterity, is her own unique personality—her life of spotless purity, sweet simplicity, sublime unselfishness and deep devotion. The most commendable feature of her character was that she herself was the most shining example of her own precepts.

We may appropriately conclude with the elevating tribute to this great saint and savant by her biographer Fariduddin 'Aṭṭar, a scholar of repute: "That one set apart in the seclusion of holiness; that woman veiled with the veil of religious sincerity; that one on fire with love and longing; that one enamoured of the desire to approach her Lord and be consumed in His Glory; that woman who lost herself in union with the Divine; that one accepted by men as a second spotless Mary; —Rābi'a al-'Adawiyya, may God have mercy upon her."

ADDENDUM: THOUGHTS ON WOMEN

By Swami Vivekananda

(Excerpts from his lectures)

The best thermometer to the progress of a nation is its treatment of women. In ancient Greece there was absolutely no difference in the state of man and women. The ideal of perfect equality existed.

The great Aryans, Buddha among the rest, have always put women in an equal position with man. For them, sex in religion did not exist. In the Vedas and Upanishads, women taught the highest truths and received the same veneration as men.

There is no chance for the welfare of the world unless the condition of women is improved. It is not possible for a bird to fly on only one wing. Hence in the Ramakrishna Incarnation the acceptance of a woman as the guru, his practicing in the woman's garb and frame of mind, and too his preaching the motherhood of women as representations of the Divine Mother.

At the present time God should be worshipped as "Mother," the Infinite Energy. This will lead to purity and tremendous energy will come here in America. Here no temples weigh us down, no one suffers as they do in poorer countries. Woman has suffered for aeons, and that has given her infinite patience and infinite perseverence. She holds on to an idea. It is this which makes her the support of even superstitious religions and of the priests in every land, and it is this that will free her . . .

To all women every man save her husband should be as her son. To all men every woman save his own wife should be as his mother. We should not think that we are men and women, but only that we are human beings, born to cherish and help one another.

INDEX

Āchāryā, 5
Āchāryānī, 5
Aditi, 3
Aghormaṇi Devī, her spiritual initiation, 125; her devotion to Baby Kṛishṇa, 125; her spiritual experiences, 126; sees divinity in Śrī Rāmakṛishṇa, 126; death, 127
Akka Mahādevī, as *vachana* writer, 30; her birth and parentage, 31; a prince's love for, 31; her ecstatic devotion to Chenna Mallikārjuna (Śiva), 31 ff.; the three conditions of her marriage, 33; violations of the conditions, 34–35; Harihara on, 36; her spiritual disciplines and experiences, 35–36; her meeting with Basaveśwara, 38; at Śrīśaila, 39; ecstasy of her poems, 38–40
Ambapālī, Buddha accepts her alms, 152; her gifts to the Saṅgha, 152; her services to the poor, 152
Āṇḍāḷ, her birth and foster-father, 23–24; meaning of her name, 23; her mad love for God, 25; her poems, 28; Sri Devendranath Sen's tribute to, 29
Angélique Arnauld, her reformatory zeal, 229; her disciplined life and influence, 231; made a nun against her wish, but was true to the monastic ideal, 232; Voltaire on her faith and sincerity, 232; her work at Maubuisson, 233; St. François de Sales' influence on her, 234; her meeting with Saint-Cyran, 236; as Abbess of Port Royal, 237; her persecution, 237; her fiery faith, 238; death, 238
Apālā, 3, 88
Āryā Chandanā, 157
Avvaiyār, a contemporary of Tiruvaḷḷuvar, 9; born a few centuries before Christ, 9; her prayer to God and dedication to learning, 10; her life of celibacy, 10; her wisdom, 11; her works, 12; some of her ethical teachings, 12–14

Bahiṇābāī, birth and parentage, 64; her betrothal, 64; her devotion, 65; her acceptance of Tukārām as *guru*, 66; her doting on her cow, 69; her passing away, 71; her previous lives, 71
Baiyābāī, *alias* Bayābāī Rāmadāsī, 63; her Urdu poetry, 63
Barnett, Dr. Lionel, 42
Bhāratī, 4
Brahmavādinīs, 2
Brigit of Kildare, legends about her, 187; born as a slave, 187; her excessive generosity, 188; her efforts for peace, 189; becomes nun, 189; as foundress of convent settlements in Ireland, 189; as wise friend and guide of the people, 190–191
Buddhism, social and spiritual equality in, 139–140

Cabrini, *see* Mother Cabrini.
Catherine of Siena, her birth and parentage, 209; her vision of Jesus in her childhood, 209; spurns marriage, 210; her severe self-disciplines, 211; her life in her cell at home, 211; her mystical marriage with Christ, 212; her nursing the sick and the needy, 212; her political activities, 213–216; her literary work, 216; sickness and death, 217; her influence on her contemporaries, 217
Chaitanya, 42
Chaṇḍī Dās, 42
Chaṅkrottu Amma, her birth, 81; her supreme devotion to Vishṇu, 81; her observance of Ekādaśī fast, 81
Chhātrīśālās, 2
Chokhamela, 58, 61, 62
Christine, Sister, her work for Indian women, 8
Convents (Christian), foundresses of, 171–172

Gaṇinī Vīramatī, 158
Gārgī Vāchaknavī, 2
Gaurībāī, birth and parentage, 73; becomes a child widow, 74; her attainment of superconscious state, 76; her spiritual greatness, 77; her pilgrimage, 78; her devotional songs in Gujarātī and Hindī, 78
Gaurīmaṇi Devī, her early education, 133; refusal to marry, 133; her renunciation and pilgrimage, 134; her meeting with Śrī Rāmakṛishṇa, 134; her educational work for Indian women and girls, 135; as *guru*, 135; her passing away, 135
Ghoshā, 3, 88

Note— e in 'Peṇṇu' in the name 'Naṅga Peṇṇu' on the previous page is a short vowel in Malayāḷam, which belongs to the Dravidian group. All the other e's in the Indian words in this Index are from Sanskrit and are long.

OTHER VEDANTA PRESS BOOKS

I. Meditation

In the Hours of Meditation Frank Alexander. Peaceful reflections for meditation, by a Western disciple of Swami Vivekananda. 113 pages, paperback $1.50

Meditation Monks of the Ramakrishna Order. A practical guide to the theory and practice of meditation as taught by senior monks who lived in the West for many years. Subjects covered include japam, the ways to control the mind, the mantra, and the kundalini. 161 pages, paperback $3.50

Meditation According to Yoga-Vedanta Swami Siddheswarananda. From talks given to students on meditation and its practice. The author discusses the role of japa in the awakening of the kundalini, the object of meditation, and the value of the "great silence." 190 pages, paperback $2.25.

The Mind and its Control Swami Budhananda. An explanation of what the mind is, and the easiest ways to control it, using the teachings of Vedanta and Yoga. 112 pages, paperback $1.00

Toward the Goal Supreme Swami Virajananda. Direct and pertinent instructions on meditation in particular and on spiritual life generally. Gives practical answers to the doubts which overwhelm spiritual aspirants. This is a personal contact with a teacher who has actually experienced what he teaches. 155 pages, paperback $2.95

II. Yoga

General

Common Sense about Yoga Swami Pavitrananda. The science of Yoga from a basic rational standpoint. Dispells some of the continuing misconceptions about Yoga. 80 pages, paperback $1.00

Yoga and Mysticism Swami Prabhavananda. Four lectures: "Peace and Holiness," "Yoga–True and False," "Mysticism–True and False," "Know Thyself." The author differenciates between drug induced psychic experiences and authentic mystical experiences. 53 pages, paperback $1.25

Bhakti Yoga

Bhakti Yoga is widely regarded as the easiest and most natural approach to God. It is a practice that begins, continues, and ends in love.

Bhakti Yoga Swami Vivekananda. A handbook on the philosophy and practice. 113 pages, paperback $1.25

Religion of Love Swami Vivekananda. Covers different points and approaches on bhakti yoga compared to the previous title. A good follow-up text. 114 pages, paperback $1.50

Narada's Way of Divine Love: The Bhakti Sutras Swami Prabhavananda, translator. Introduction by Christopher Isherwood. Narada's Bhakti Sutras are well known in India as a scripture on love as a means of God-realization. 176 pages, hardback $5.25

Raja Yoga

Raja Yoga is the psychological or mystical way to union with God through control of the mind by concentration and meditation. A prime source for the philosophy, practice and powers of this yoga is the Yoga Aphorisms of Patanjali. Each of the following two translations has a different emphasis.

How to Know God: The Yoga Aphorisms of Patanjali Swami Prabhavananda and Christopher Isherwood, translators. The extensive commentary emphasizes aspects of Raja Yoga that are of particular value to the Westerner. Over 178,000 copies in print. 224 pages, hardback $3.95

Raja Yoga Swami Vivekananda, translator. A detailed commentary on Patanjali's complete text, with original lectures by Swami Vivekananda on Raja Yoga. 280 pages, paperback $2.50

Jnana Yoga

Jnana Yoga is the path of intellectual discrimination, the way of finding God through analysis of the real nature of phenomena. This is a difficult path, calling for tremendous powers of will and clarity of mind. But it has attracted and made saints of many who would otherwise have not embraced religion in any form.

Jnana Yoga Swami Vivekananda. Lectures on such topics as "Maya and Illusion," "God in Everything," and "The Freedom of the Soul." 399 pages, paperback $2.50

Karma Yoga

Karma Yoga is the path to God through selfless work. It is a path best suited to vigorous temperaments which feel the call to duty and service in the world of human affairs. It leads such people through the dangers of over-eagerness and undue anxiety and shows them how to find "the inaction that is in action," the calm in the midst of turmoil.